1. 1991

THE
NUMISMATIST'S LAKESIDE
COMPANION

THE
NUMISMATIST'S LAKESIDE
COMPANION

VOLUME THREE
EDITED BY Q. DAVID BOWERS

PUBLISHED BY BOWERS AND MERENA GALLERIES, INC.

ISBN 0-943161-25-8

Published by:
Bowers and Merena Galleries, Inc.
Box 1224, Wolfeboro, NH 03894

All rights concerning this book are reserved by the copyright owner. Written permission is required for the reproduction of any information in this book, except for brief excerpts used in a review in a newspaper or magazine.

The cover design is by Elli Ford of Jungle Graphics, Center Sandwich, New Hampshire.

© 1990 by Bowers and Merena Galleries, Inc.

Table of Contents

Introduction	page 9

The Enjoyment Factor
from Kingswood Galleries Amherst Sale, *May 1990* 11

A Biography of Byron Reed
from Rare Coin Review No. 60, *Spring 1986* 19

Metamorphosis: Coin Collector to Coin Dealer
from Rare Coin Review No. 60, *Spring 1986* 27

B. Max Mehl on the Subject of Commemoratives
from Rare Coin Review No. 58, *Winter 1985/86* 31

The Coin Adventures of Uncle Scrooge
from Rare Coin Review No. 58, *Winter 1985/86* 41

The "State of the Art" in Numismatics
from Rare Coin Review No. 58, *Winter 1985/86* 45

The "I Like It" Investment Theory
from Rare Coin Review No. 58, *Winter 1985/86* 51

The Secret of an Old Estate
from Rare Coin Review No. 68, *Spring 1988* 55

A Trip to Colorado
from Rare Coin Review No. 62, *Autumn 1986* 57

Let's Talk About Auction Sales
from Rare Coin Review No. 61, *Summer 1986* 65

Sunny Jim and the 1912-S Nickel
from Rare Coin Review No. 61, *Summer 1986* 87

Some Barber Silver Rarities
from Rare Coin Review No. 61, Summer 1986 95
Money and Wealth
from Rare Coin Review No. 47, April 1983 101
Auction Catalogues as Collectors' Items
from Rare Coin Review No. 47, April 1983 109
Profit and Pleasure in Coin Collecting
from Rare Coin Review No. 55, September 1985 113
**Robert Gilmor, Jr. and the Cradle Age
of American Numismatics**
from Rare Coin Review No. 58, Winter 1985/86 121
The Pleasures of Book Collecting
from Rare Coin Review No. 68, Spring 1988................................... 137
The Great 1942/1 Dime Search
from Rare Coin Review No. 68, Spring 1988................................... 147
Early Days in Vermont
from Rare Coin Review No. 68, Spring 1988................................... 153
Research Methods
from Rare Coin Review No. 67, Winter 1987/88 157
Joseph J. Mickley
from Rare Coin Review No. 67, Winter 1987/88 171
Design of the Buffalo Nickel
from Rare Coin Review No. 67, Winter 1987/88 179
Re-evaluating a Famous American Token
from Rare Coin Review No. 67, Winter 1987/88 183
The 1873-CC No Arrows Quarter and Dime
from Rare Coin Review No. 66, Autumn 1987 193
The Early Silver Coins of the United States
from Rare Coin Review No. 65, Summer 1987 199
Random Notes from United States Mint Reports
from Rare Coin Review No. 65, Summer 1987 203
The 1964 Peace Dollar Episode
from Rare Coin Review No. 65, Summer 1987 207
Frank Gasparro Reminisces
from Rare Coin Review No. 65, Summer 1987 213

Introduction

By Q. David Bowers

Welcome to *The Numismatist's Lakeside Companion,* the third volume in our "companion" series which began with *The Numismatist's Bedside Companion* in 1987, followed quickly by *The Numismatist's Fireside Companion* in 1988, after which the pressure of business, other publishing projects, etc., intervened—until now.

Like its predecessors, the present book contains a diverse selection of numismatic articles which originally appeared in the *Rare Coin Review* and our other periodicals.

Originally the "companion" series was envisioned as a collection of stories for bedside reading, something to publish a few copies of and then let go out of print. However, in their own right these books have become surprisingly popular—of course I am delighted—and have even been reprinted! While bid and ask prices, market quotations, investment news, etc. may or not represent the heartbeat and pulse of the hobby (or industry)—depending on whom you ask—there is no doubt that coins still remain basically interesting to own and collect. To set the theme in this regard I have selected as the lead article "The Enjoyment Factor," which recently appeared in the Kingswood catalogue of The Amherst Sale. After that pont the reading becomes eclectic—you are apt to find just about anything!

Now that we have "Lakeside," and we have already had "Bedside" and "Fireside" what will our next "companion" book be titled? We will be thinking about this and will let you know in due course. In the meantime, I invite you to curl up with this book lakeside or seaside in your favorite dock chair or on the sand—or if you live in the middle of the Mojave Desert, then to go to the nearest oasis (if there are any) and do your best. In any event, I hope you enjoy reading these stories as much as I and the other authors have enjoyed writing them!

—Q. David Bowers
July 1, 1990

The Enjoyment Factor

| By Q. David Bowers   1990 |

Why collect coins? The answers to this question are many. Dr. George F. Heath, who founded the American Numismatic Association in 1891, was fond of referring to the hobby as the goddess Numisma, an enlightened lady who led her followers to many pleasures.

Today in 1990 the question, "Why collect coins?" is apt to be answered by, "I want to make a profit" or "They are a good investment." And, these answers are just fine, for there is no doubt that in today's world of uncertain economic conditions, ever-increasing expenses, and the high cost of living, every dollar of profit that can be added to one's net worth will find a good use. I recently read a prediction that in 20 years the average cost to attend a good four-year university is expected to be $175,000—hardly a sum to be taken lightly.

In the 1890s when Dr. Heath was editing and publishing *The Numismatist* monthly for the American Numismatic Association, investment was not a consideration, at least not a major one, in the hobby. To be sure, Heath and other contributors to the magazine interjected a few investment comments now and then, such as the suggestion that 1893 Isabella commemorative quarter dollars were undervalued and that 1893 Columbian half dollars were overpriced, but by and large the editorial thrust of *The Numismatist* was in other directions.

Heath was a medical doctor by profession, but he still had time to serve several terms as mayor of his home town, Monroe, Michigan, and to read extensively and travel widely. To Heath life itself was a grand adventure, and coins furnished the passport to untold enjoyment. Coins are the footprints of history, it has been said, and no one agreed more than Dr. Heath. To him and most of his contemporaries, a 1793 large cent was not an object simply to be bought and sold, but was a tangible link to the early days when the newly-established Philadelphia Mint was struggling for its very existence (more on this subject in a following paragraph). A 1652 Pine Tree shilling was an object, history in tangible form, that was on the scene and an important part of everyday life in colonial Massachusetts. Who knows, perhaps Judge Sewall had this very coin in his pocket when he presided over the infamous Salem witch trials. Could George Washington have owned that 1796 half dollar? That ancient coin may have been part of a Roman soldier's pay.

The good goddess Numisma offered her followers a rich life. From a medical viewpoint, Dr. Heath knew that those who had absorbing hobbies felt better, had fewer problems, and led more contented lives. This theme was not unique to Heath's writings; it was expressed in the pages of The Numismatist by many others over a long span of years. To gain the advantages that spilled from Numisma's cornucopia it was necessary to learn about coins, to study their surfaces and inscriptions, to read about the historical eras in which specific coins were produced.

In 1982 I had the pleasure of cataloguing and offering for sale the celebrated collection of 1794 cents formed over a long period of years by John W. Adams, a gentleman who was and is one of America's leading figures in the field of investment securities, a partner in Adams, Harkness & Hill. He contributed this sentiment to the catalogue describing his coins:

"The charisma of the cents of 1794 is based on many factors—the nobility of the basic design, the distinctive features of the different dies, and the aesthetic properties of the copper itself, to name just a few. However, as time passes and the edifice of tradition builds up, a still more compelling dimension of the hobby has arisen. Cherished as they were by various owners, the coins have woven a fabric of caring people, each of whom has seen in these humble tokens of commerce a symbol of something vastly more important. It is difficult to articulate the meaning of the symbol; indeed its significance may have been quite different for each who has shared it. However, the kinship of spirit is a common thread which is understook by all who participate. To own a coin owned by Maris or Hays, Clapp or Sheldon, Hines or Newcomb is to own a piece of history. The owner is at once a recipient of the tradition of the past and a trustee of the treasures of the future."

The Enjoyment Factor

In 1794 the Philadelphia Mint was young, having been set up in 1792 and having produced its first coins for general circulation, half cents and cents, in 1793.

Dr. William H. Sheldon, in his 1949 book, *Early American Cents*, told of conditions at the Philadelphia Mint in 1793 and of the circumstances surrounding the production of cents. I quoted Sheldon in the Adams Collection catalogue:

"There is no precise record of just what went on at the Mint during the first year [1793]. However, the general conditions under which work was carried on, and some of the difficulties peculiar to the undertaking are known. All employees worked 11 hours a day, 66 hours a week, beginning at six in the morning during the summer and at seven during the winter. Average pay for the coin press operators was $1.29 per day. All power was furnished by horses and human muscle. The rolling machinery [for the manufacture of strips from which the planchets were struck] fell short of expectations. For a decade or more there was a chronic and often acute shortage of copper as well as a great variability in the assay and consequently in the color and hardness of that metal. We have only begun the list of hardships and difficulties. The struggle to manufacture copper planchets was apparently heroic."

When I see a 1793, 1794, or other early cent, especially a well-worn one, I see a chapter in American history, the Philadelphia Mint in its early days, a copper disc used as payment for a glass of ale in a country tavern along a dusty road in Massachusetts, a penny in a child's hand in an early-day candy store in Baltimore, or any one of many other daydreams.

The sentiments of Dr. George F. Heath in the 1890s and those of John W. Adams in 1982 are similar: coins can be a tangible link with the past and, above everything else, they are *interesting*.

Today in 1990 coins are as interesting as ever. However, in the eagerness to acquire coins as an investment, many buyers overlook this aspect. What are the most popular series today? Any survey would certainly rank these areas at or near the top of the list: commemoratives, Morgan silver dollars, U.S. gold coins, and U.S. coins by design types.

Morgan silver dollars are one of the most actively traded of all American series. They offer numerous advantages to the buyer, not the least of which is the fact that a sparkling, lustrous Mint State specimen of a common issue such as 1881-S, 1883-O, or 1884-O can be purchased for less than $50. Even a superb gem MS-65 example costs only a few hundred dollars. For, say, $5,000 it is possible to put together a running start on a collection of Morgan dollars minted during the early part of the series, 1878-1904, and to own a holding of several dozen different varieties, including examples struck at all four mints which made dollars in the early days: Philadelphia, Carson City, New Orleans, and San Francisco.

Books have been written about Morgan dollars, but virtually without exception, their emphasis has been on such aspects as market value, investment potential, and the number of specimens known in a specific grade category. I have yet to read a book dedicated to the history of Morgan dollars and the pleasures to be found in collecting them (although a grateful nod must be given to Leroy C. Van Allen and A. George Mallis, who devoted a section of their book, *Comprehensive Catalogue and Encyclopedia of U.S. Morgan and Peace Dollars*, to the historical background of the series).

And yet the history of the Morgan dollar series is absolutely fascinating. To begin with, there was no compelling reason to mint Morgan dollars, or any other silver dollars, in 1878. Dollars of the Liberty Seated type had been struck from 1840 onward, and by 1873 there were enough on hand that production was suspended. At the same time Nevada's Comstock Lode, which had been discovered in 1859, had been exploited to the point at which the price of silver bullion became depressed on world markets; once-booming Virginia City, which sat squarely atop the silver deposits, faced closure of its saloons, gambling parlors, and other businesses, as miners were thrown out of work; and a pall was spreading not only over Nevada, but over other Western states as well.

Clearly, something had to be done, and politicians came to the rescue. The Bland-Allison Act was pushed through Congress, and by early 1878 Uncle Sam was directed to buy millions of ounces of silver each month, in order to prop up the sagging price. What to do with this silver? Coin it into dollars; dollars that were not needed in the channels of commerce.

George T. Morgan, a young engraver who had come to America in 1876, was given the task of creating a new design. Apparently Chief Engraver William Barber had more important things to do at the Mint, as did his heir-apparent, his son Charles. The work passed to Morgan, who, instead of creating a new design, simply modified motifs he had created in 1877 for use on a pattern half dollar. The obverse was modeled by Anna Williams, a Philadelphia schoolteacher who sat for Morgan as he sketched her facial features.

As there was an urgency early in 1878 to create as many silver dollars as possible in the shortest amount of time, Morgan's motif was

The Enjoyment Factor

hurriedly adapted to dollar size and rushed into production. Problems developed with the striking of the design, and during the next year several modifications were made.

One of the more curious changes did not involve production problems, but had to do with ornithology. Some enlightened observer, presumably a watcher of eagles in real life, commented that it was illogical that Morgan's bird should have eight tail feathers, for eagles had one central feather that was longer than the others and, hence, the total number of feathers should be an odd number, not an even one. A directive was issued to the Mint Engraving Department: change the feather count from eight to seven. Many dies had already been made with eight tail feathers, and, indeed, some 750,000 coins had been struck. However, at least a half dozen dies were on hand that had not yet been used. A new master die with seven feathers was quickly made, and the unused eight-feathers dies were overpunched with the seven-feathers master. Coins from the corrected dies were put into circulation. Later, collectors examining 1878 dollars under magnification noticed that certain pieces showed seven tail feathers, as did all Morgan dollars made after early 1878, but that on these certain pieces there were some extra feather tips protruding from beneath the feather ends—what collectors now call the "7 over 8 tail feathers" variety.

Month after month, year after year, the Philadelphia, Carson City, New Orleans, and San Francisco mints turned out an endless silvery cascade of dollars. The Treasury Department, which handled coin distribution, didn't know what to do with them, so they were put in cloth bags of 1,000 coins, sealed, and stored. The Philadelphia Mint had countless tons of unwanted dollars in a special storage facility, a large building-within-a-building right on the premises, the New Orleans Mint had its vaults full of dollars, and elsewhere Morgan dollars were piling up at an alarming rate.

From time to time the Treasury Department considered problems such as that involving a large group of dollars that had become damp, causing the bags to rot, or the times when political administrations changed, and the supply of dollars had to be inventoried. By the end of 1904, hundreds of millions of unwanted, unneeded Morgan dollars were stockpiled. The Pittman Act, passed in 1918, provided the solution, and under this piece of legislation some 270,232,722 Morgan dollars, which the government had paid to have coined and had paid to store for many years, went to the melting pot and were reduced to bullion. Of course, how the American taxpayers benefited from all of this was never considered!

Beginning in the 1940s, collecting Morgan silver dollars became quite popular with numismatists. Mint production records were analyzed, but it quickly became apparent that some varieties with relatively low mintages were easy to find, and other varieties with very high mintages were rarities. The situation didn't make a great deal of sense, until it was realized that when the wholesale melting occurred under the 1918 Pittman Act, no record was kept of what specific dates and mintmark varieties were destroyed.

In particular, the 1895 Philadelphia Mint dollar emerged as a rarity. Mint records stated that 12,880 were made, divided into 12,000 business strikes or "Uncirculated" pieces made for commerce, and 880 Proofs sold at a premium to collectors. Search as they may, no collectors or dealers ever saw an Uncirculated coin. The only pieces to come on the market were Proofs. Today it seems clear that the 12,000 business strikes, representing 1,000 dollars in 12 cloth bags, went to the melting vat in 1918.

While the 1895 dollar was considered to be rare, *the* rarity was the 1903 dollar made at the New Orleans Mint. Although 4,450,000 had been struck, and although worn specimens were seen with regularity, few numismatists had ever seen a Mint State coin. The prevailing theory was that in 1903 a quantity of 1903-O dollars had been released into circulation and had subsequently become worn, but because few collectors were interested in dollars at the time, no more than a few hundred had been saved in Mint State grade. In 1941, when B. Max Mehl catalogued the William Forrester Dunham Collection, a landmark offering of United States coins, including Proof gold and many great rarities, he featured the Mint State 1903-O as one of the prime pieces in that holding. Had an analysis been made of collections at the time, it probably would have revealed that fewer than 10 Mint State 1903-O dollars were known!

By 1962 the 16th edition of *A Guide Book of U.S. Coins* listed an Uncirculated 1903-O dollar for the princely sum of $1,500, the same price quoted for a Proof 1895. By contrast, an Uncirculated 1879-CC was listed for $95, an Uncirculated 1889-CC for $275, and an 1893-S in the same grade was figured at $1,200. An Uncirculated MCMVII High Relief $20 was listed at $525 and Proof Liberty Head $20 pieces were posted as low as $1,000 each in the same book. (By way of comparison, in MS-63 grade the current (1990) edition of the *Guide Book* gives these prices:

The Enjoyment Factor

1903-O $1 $350, 1895 Proof $1 $20,000, 1879-CC $1 $2,400, 1889-CC $1 $12,000, 1893-S $1 $27,500, MCMVII $20 $11,000, [MS-60, the highest grade listed], and typical Proof Liberty Head $20 $18,000.)

Obviously, something happened to the 1903-O, the darling of the 1962 *Guide Book* at $1,500, but now listed for only $350. The answer is provided by the great Treasury release of autumn 1962. Although the government melted hundreds of millions of silver dollars in 1918, it still had hundreds of millions left. These remained in storage, until in 1962 in the course of normal business a number of bags were released into banks as part of the traditional Christmastime demand for dollars as gifts. Lo and behold, thousands of 1903-O rarities came to light!

The rest is history. A mad scramble ensued, and in a matter of months the Treasury vaults were emptied of dollars, except for three million or so which, at the tail-end of the release, the Treasury decided to hold back. These dollars, including many Carson City issues (particularly the 1882-CC, 1883-CC, and 1884-CC), were subsequently sold at a premium by a governmental agency, the General Services Administration.

Many observers felt that the vast flood of dollars which came on the market in the 1962-1963 period would spell the end of collecting Morgan dollars, for they became so common. Exactly the opposite happened! While the supply of dollars in the hands of collectors probably increased a hundredfold or more, the number of collectors probably increased a thousandfold! With the exception of just three varieties—1898-O, 1903-O, and 1904-O—*all* Morgan dollars are worth *substantially* more now in 1990 than they were before the Treasury release of 1962-1963.

The point of all this discussion about Morgan dollars? It is this: Morgan dollars are among the most historical, most fascinating coins ever issued by the United States of America. For every story I have told—and I have told just of the 1878 7 over 8 tail feathers and the 1903-O—dozens of other anecdotes and tales could be related. To me, a Morgan dollar is something more than a coin with a price of $50, or $500, or $5,000. It is a tangible link with American history, a reminder of another era, an incredibly *romantic* item!

Like butterflies and many other good things in life, such stories are free. The enjoyment factor is an added extra which automatically comes with every 1881-S, or 1886, or 1903-O Morgan dollar, with every 1920 Maine or 1938 New Rochelle commemorative half dollar, with every 1893 or 1908 $20 gold piece, and with every other coin.

The present Amherst sale conducted by Kingswood Galleries offers many worthwhile coins, nearly all of which, I expect, will be viewed with enthusiasm by prospective bidders. When all is said and done, the pieces will be widely dispersed to many new collections, investment portfolios, and owners, pleasure not only in the financial or investment sense of acquiring a store of value, but as messengers from the past, from the early days of the Mint in the 1790s, from the Comstock Lode in the 1870s, from the expositions, celebrations, and fairs which saw the issuance of commemoratives in the present century.

May each coin you buy bring with to you its own story, its own pleasure factor.

A Biography of Byron Reed

| By William D. Beckett   1986 |

The following is from a paper read by William D. Beckett before the Nebraska State Historical Society, Lincoln, Nebraska, January 12, 1892. A transcript of this was kindly furnished to use by David H. Cohen, a reader who has made other contributions to us.

The Byron Reed coin collection is owned and displayed by the City of Omaha today.

Every man's life, meaning thereby what he has said and done on this earth, may, without metaphysical refining, be said to have both a biographical and a historical aspect. As it began and ended with the individual, it is a subject for biography; as it has influenced the collective life of humanity, it is a subject for history.

Now of the biographical significance of a man's life, though much may be thought, imagined, or believed, but little can be said. He lived and loved and hoped and died. What remains for him after death is not a subject for biography, but for speculation or prophecy.

Therefore it is that the language fo those who speak about the dead as individuals is always the same. There is but one thought, and long ago that thought was spoken in words whose fitness compels all later speech to repetition. "He is like the flower of the field that grows up in the morning and in the evening is cut down and withers away; his frame is dust; his life is but a breath in the nostrils; nay, even less substantial than that—it is a figment; an unreal thing such as poets and lunatics imagine and brought forth in words; it is a tale that is told."

So men do not form biographical societies. They would perpetuate nothing but memories; their proceedings would be uninspiring; their records would be brief and monotonous, like the book of Chronicles or the generations of the patriarchs from Adam to Noah written in one chapter, "All the days of his life were so many, and he died."

But in its historical bearings a man's life is an enduring force and expands to proportions so vast that no human eye can see its limit. Like the pebble that is thrown into the ocean, it rests quietly upon the ocean's bed, but the circles it has started go on widening and crossing and combining with other circles to rock the ocean and sway its currents through all eternity.

In the first place, every man is a sojourning workman upon earth, and his work, that is, the material and social changes he makes there, must modify all life that comes after him. In the second place, and more influential than the thing he has done, is the spirit that moved him to it and his manner of doing it. Thus, not the humblest carpenter is a mere builder of houses wherein people can temporarily live; he is also a teacher of the art of housebuilding and in the use of tools, and the master builder's great work may not be any visible structure, but only his idea of a house, which never is built, yet which is potent in architecture when his houses of brick and iron have crumbled into dust.

By the individual man this terrestrial globe is unimpressible, like that magic well which filled up between the strokes of the pick; but as a part of collective humanity he becomes, as it were, immortal, and works in the might of the generations. The seas are filled up, the mountains are leveled, the whole face of nature is transformed. This chaotic, unintelligible world is wrought into form, is classified, divided, and subdivided till the original is no longer known. Not the earth and the sky, but religions, philosophies, science, creeds, and systems constitute the creation into which men are now born; not death's but humanity's creation, and filled with its trophies, statues, tombs, and stories, its victories, its triumphs, and its glories.

On the sixth day of June, 1891, Byron Reed, a member of this society and a citizen of this state since the year 1855, died at his residence in the city of Omaha. His death was not unexpected, for, though he was not an old man, ill health had made him feeble, and his hold on life had for some time been a frail one. Among Mr. Reed's papers was found a sketch of his life written by himself in the last few weeks preceding his death. Becasue what one says about himself doubly describes him, and also because this sketch is an accurate and concise summary of Mr. Reed's life, it is here set forth *verbatim:*

A Biography of Byron Reed

"Byron Reed was born at Darien, Genesee County, N.Y. March 12, 1829. He attended the Alexander Classical School, but left before graduating by reason of his family, with several other families of the same town, moving to the far west, the then territory of Wisconsin. They settled on the virgin prairie in Walworth County, naming the new settlement "Darien," after the old home. Mr. Reed first entered business life as an operator. The electric telegraph was invented in 1844, and in less than five years the large eastern cities were connected and the wires extended as far west as Cleveland. From 1849 to the beginning of 1855 Mr. Reed worked on the Cleveland and Pittsburg line, most of the time at Warren, O., midway between the two cities. He was one of the first to adopt the system of receiving by sound, a system which is now universal, although at first received with doubt and hesitation. Even after the first year's trial it was condemned and ordered abandoned by most of the lines then in operation. When the act of Congress organizing the territory of Nebraska was passed, in 1854, Mr. Reed gave notice to the superintendent of his company that he wished to leave the next month. He was prevailed upon to stay, however, until the next year, when he left for Nebraska, arriving at Omaha, November 10, 1855. A few weeks later he went down to Kansas, and passed the winter at Leavenworth, Kansas City, Lawrence, and other places, during which time he acted as correspondent for the New York *Tribune*. The territory of Kansas at this time was the theatre of the 'border ruffian war,' celebrated in history as one of the preliminaries to the great rebellion. The *Tribune* published the most complete and truthful accounts of this eventful period in letters from Mr. Reed, Mr. Phillips, and others. When the papers containing these letters found their way back to Leavenworth City and other pro-slavery strongholds, they caused much excitement and rage among the slaveholders and leaders of their party. The writers found it necessary to exercise great caution in concealing their identity. More than once Mr. Reed heard the remark made that if the correspondent of the New York *Tribune* could be discovered his life would not be worth an hour's time, but not the slightest suspicion at that time was entertained that Mr. Reed was himself that correspondent, or one of them. He was soon discovered, however, through the theft of some of his letters, and his arrest ordered forthwith. He escaped by a narrow chance, leaving the city in the middle of the night. Mr. Phillips, another correspondent, was also discovered, but being a resident of the city (Leavenworth), and a very prominent man, they did not like to attack him without some further pretense. The further pretense was found and Mr. Phillips was attacked and killed about four months afterward. (See Greeley's *American Conflict,* volume 1, page 245). One object of Mr. Reed's visit to Kansas was to make a choice between that territory and Nebraska for his future home. His experience of about four months in Kansas effectively settled that question in favor of Nebraska. He returned to Omaha, opened an office in the old state house building, and established the real estate and conveyancing business which he has conducted up to the present time with a measure of success equaled by no other business enterprise in the state, starting without capital and without pretenses. The Byron Reed Company is now a corporation with a paid up capital of $200,000, and probably does a business as large as the best of our national banks.

"Mr. Reed was elected to the office of city clerk of Omaha in 1860, at a time when no emoluments were connected with the office. He served as such for six terms in succession, being succeeded by William L. May in 1867. In 1863 he was elected county clerk for the term of two years, having served the previous term as deputy. During the two years from 1861 to 1863 he recorded all the instruments and documents that were filed, in his own handwriting, quite a contrast with the amount of business in that office at the present time. He was councilman, representing the Fourth ward in 1871, and president of the city council in 1872.

"Mr. Reed gave to the public fifteen acres of land on Prospect Hill, to be used as a cemetery. This is one of the most beautiful locations in the city limits, and the land is now of great value. It is usual, in gifts of this kind, for the donor to provide that when the land has served the purpose for which it was given, it shall revert to the donor or his heirs. In this case the deed of gift provides that in case the cemetery be discontinued or removed the land shall go to the city of Omaha in trust for the use and benefit of the public, to be used as a public park, or for the erection of public buildings, or for any other use wherein the public will receive the benefit. The deed also contains the condition that no portion of the land shall ever be alienated or leased for a valuable consideration. When the cemetery was established Mr. Reed undertook the management of it. It was indispensable that someone do it, and everybody else refused. The result was that Prospect Hill cemetery soon became the finest and best appointed cemetery in the West, and at a cost to its patrons of only about half as much as in other cities of the same class as Omaha. The Forest Lawn Cemetery Association was formed through the efforts of Mr. Reed and the late John H. Brackin, with the understanding that Prospect Hill should be turned over to the new association as soon as it was organized. This was done in 1885."

A Biography of Byron Reed

Here this sketch ends—not finished, but broken off. From the date therein last mentioned Mr. Reed lived quietly, spending most of his time in his office and his library. In February, 1891, he was appointed by President Harrison one of the commission to make the annual test of the coinage at the Philadelphia Mint. This was his last public service but one.

By his will he gave to the city of Omaha a parcel of land as the site for a public library, and also his collection of coins, medals, manuscripts, autographs, and literary relics, together with his own private library. The gift is in every respect a generous one, and in itself is a public service such as few men are able to render in a lifetime.

It only remains to make a brief and necessarily imperfect estimate of his character. Mr. Reed's life must have been based upon a faith. No such life as his could have been founded upon sentiment or impulse, or upon any doctrine of chances. To accumulate a fortune of millions by the slow process of accretion, to bear up against the grind and worry, the vexations, disappointments, losses, and lawsuits, as surely proves a faith as does religious or political martyrdom. And to understand a person's faith, to know what he thinks that good thing to be, which a man should do all the days of his life, is to have the key to most that is valuable in him. Now, in spite of many personal traits which caused Byron Reed to be regarded as a peculiar man, which indeed, to a great extent, isolated him from his fellow men, I believe that his ruling motive was to obtain the approval of his fellow men. Not of this or that particular man or set of men, for no one seemed more indifferent as to whether it was some poor tenant or an ex-president of the United States that spoke to him, but of that whole body of men whom he looked upon as the select men of the world. It is said, that one's reading more than anything else shows what his ideals are. Mr. Reed was a historian. His ideal seemed to be what may be called the historic character; whether it were Cromwell and his band, arraigning a king for treason, or Daniel Boone holding a council with the Indians, or John Smith making the first entry under a new homestead law, the man and the event had for his mind a peculiar charm. They were marked with the historical sign. His coins and ancient manuscripts were, in my opinion, chiefly regarded by him for their historical associations. There was the story of the nations stamped in metal—in the faces of the kings, in symbolical feasts and triumphal processions. There were the original records from which history is made, the edicts of the emperors, paper bulls, state trials, and contemporaneous accounts of political and military conflict.

As corroborative of this view, it may be said that Mr. Reed was, in most things, a conservative. He believed that the social structure up to this time is substantially built, and that what is needed is not a departure from ancient forms, but a closer adherence to them. In short, he was one whom the ideals and achievements of the race sufficed. He wanted no new doctrine, he desired no new inspiration. To live worthily and obtain a goodname among the men of this time was his highest ambition. In his method and manner of working, Byron Reed was an example which it were profitable for any man to study. Accuracy, thoroughness, patient application of means to ends; in these he put his trust. All his dealings were marked by exactness and attention to detail. No point was overlooked, no contingency was left unprovided for. He believed that the laws of business were as certain as those of mechanics; that plan and purpose would bring financial gains as surely as they turn wheat into flour. Even in the court room and before juries, where all is proverbially uncertain, he thought there were conditions of success; that, on the whole, it was well for him who had the most witnesses and the best lawyer. In all his long record as a conveyancer, as notary public, and as county clerk, it is doubtful if a single error has ever been discovered. So high was his reputation in this regard that abstractors were accustomed to accept his notarial certificates as conclusive of the regularity of the instrument. All matters of importance he put in writing, besides much that seemed of no importance; at what date he took possession of a lot, what was aid to the officer who served a writ of ejectment. On account of his accuracy he was considered one of the best witnesses in the trial of a lawsuit in Douglas County. Other things being equal, it could be argued with absolute confidence that the opposing witness must be mistaken. It is believed that during his life Mr. Reed represented more foreign capital invested in Nebraska than any other man in the state. He held more unlimited powers of attorney than any other six men in Douglas County, and the facts show that those who joined with him in business enterprise made gains when he made them. There are many persons in Douglas County whose fortunes are to be counted from the date of their association with Byron Reed.

    This is the day of reformers and social doctrinaires—persons who hold the present lot of man to be barren of all that is good or noble—not worth the attention of high-minded people. So they profess no interest in it, but
    Dip into the future far as human eye can see;
    Paint the vision of the world and all the wonder that will be.

A Biography of Byron Reed

It is not for us to scorn the work of Utopia builders or despise these tellers of dreams. They are the signs of a living humanity, for that is the sleep of death in which there are no dreams. But let it be remembered that the only hope of the future is in the faithful workers of the present. This social structure will not go higher except by diligent use of the tools which are in the hands of each of us. Truly, there is much philosophy in the world, but not many philosophers. The life of Byron Reed was a life of work well done. The world is less inharmonious and more in order for his having been in it. And what truer test of the value of a life is there than that? Has it been a force to clear humanity's path and help bear its burdens? Has it, so far as it went, made the rough places plain and the crooked places straight? If so, then was it good.

Metamorphosis: Coin Collector to Coin Dealer

By Kenneth L. Hallenbeck 1986

I had secretly hoped to become a coin dealer for a number of years. I wanted to get in on the big bucks and all that good stuff. Well, May 17, 1983 I got my chance and opened the Ken Hallenbeck Coin Gallery in Colorado Springs, after leaving employment at the American Numismatic Association. I had worked for the ANA for just over five years handling complaints, building management, security, donations, the museum, and, for a very short time, ANACS. It was wonderful working at ANA headquarters. The ANA is the hub of much numismatic activity and is a very special place to work with very special and dedicated people. I miss the camaraderie a lot.

My wife, June, was very supportive in the concept of opening the coin gallery, and we had many discussions about what we wanted to do and accomplish. As good fortune would have it, at the very time we were talking and planning our coin store, Dave Bowers wrote a series of articles in *Coin World* on "How to be a Successful Coin Dealer." Later reprinted in booklet form, these articles were extremely valuable to us. We got a few good ideas from them and the rest reinforced what we had already been thinking. It was as if Dave was writing the articles just for Ken and June Hallenbeck. I even wrote Dave thanking him for the articles. His timing was perfect. If you are thinking of going into the coin business, by all means obtain Dave's booklet and follow its suggestions as closely as you can. We did, and it is working. Our business wasn't the instant success we had naively hoped for, but it has shown steady growth and we may now be turning a small profit.

It has often been said that you can't be a dealer and a coin collector as well. You shouldn't compete with your customers. Well, don't you believe it. I'm still a very active collector of counterstamped coins, love tokens, almost anything pertaining to the early mining days of Cripple Creek and Victor, Colorado and, yes, even plastic credit cards. Yes, that's right, plastic credit cards. There aren't many of us silly enough to collect them, but they are a form of money, and inexpensive to collect (if you don't over-use them!). Actually, many of my friends know I collect them and save their expired cards for me. My goal is to get a MasterCard and Visa card from each of the 50 states and various U.S. possessions. Collecting "off-beat" material doesn't compete with very many of my customers, and there is actually a bond between the few of my customers who do collect these things. They know I openly collect these items, yet they get some pretty good duplicates. And we do some great trading. It is still fun to collect and hope I never lose the desire to do so. One difference between most coin dealers and myself is that I collected actively for over 40 years before becoming a dealer. It is very satisfying to find a nice coin, medal, token, or piece of paper money that a customer really wants. There are some things I would prefer to keep, yet I let them go to a customer.

Being a coin dealer has been and is a lot of fun. It is a lot of work as well. But make no bones about it, there is satisfaction in making a profit, especially a good profit. There are various kinds of coin dealers such as shop dealers, show dealers, suitcase or briefcase dealers, mail order dealers, auctioneers, etc. and many variations and combinations of the foregoing. Some dealers prefer "strictly wholesale" and don't care to deal with the public. I personally enjoy dealing with the public. And like the Frank Sinatra song says, "I did it my way," or perhaps Dave Bowers' and my way.

I'd like to believe I'm a fairly friendly person. I have been involved with many numismatic organizations over the years. I'm currently president of the Colorado Springs Coin Club, first vice-president of the Colorado-Wyoming Numismatic Association and on the Board of Governors of the American Numismatic Association. In the past I've spent lots of time with the Old Fort Coin Club in Fort Wayne, Indiana and the Indiana State Numismatic Association. The American Numismatic Association catches a lot of heat. It is *the* national coin collector organization, so any mistakes or controversial decisions made are subject to magnification. Yet, having served with these and other organizations numismatically, there are many similarities: people and their likes and dislikes, their personalities. Things go in cycles with times of unrest and discord

Metamorphosis: Coin Collector to Coin Dealer

in organizations as well as calm and compatibility.

The ANA Board had two pretty good years of relative calm and compatibility under the presidency of Dave Bowers, in regard to board members' personalities, but poor Dave sure caught a lot of heat in regards to the problems with the Authentication and Grading Service (ANACS). This will no doubt continue to be controversial for many years to come. As chairman of the ANACS committee, I'm trying to work quietly behind the scenes to improve consistency and make careful changes for the good of the organization (ANA) and numismatics in general. We want to improve ANACS and avoid the sensationalism of the recent past.

It is a real privilege and responsibility to serve on the ANA Board. There are some fine people on the Board. We do some careless things occasionally and they get a lot of publicity. We also do a lot of good things. There is much satisfaction in participating and contributing to the advancement of numismatics through the ANA Board activities. It is downright exciting thinking about some of the ideas which have been put forth and which the ANA may be able to implement. I have high hopes for the future actions of the current ANA Board and truly believe we may be entering into what future generations may ultimately call "The Golden Age of Numismatics." Logic for this thinking comes from the realization that much original research is being done currently in many areas and with current and future projections for publications plus some of the projects being contemplated. I'm looking toward the future with much anticipation.

There's some bad in numismatics—there's bound to be. However, we need to look beyond the bad to the great good that exists in this wonderful field. Knowledge in this field or any field cannot be substituted for. By reading and studying, you can not only protect yourself, but multiply your enjoyment many fold. This applies whether you are an investor or collector. So why not do both? There are many paths to travel in numismatics, and they can be as individual as you want them to be.

As a collector and now a dealer-collector I've had the opportunity to explore many areas of numismatics. There's much opportunity for enjoyment and profit. Why not consider looking at your own numismatic position with the long term future in mind? It can change your life for the better.

Ed. Note: Ken Hallenbeck was elected president of the American Numismatic Association in 1989 for the 1989-1991 term. Congratulations Ken!

B. Max Mehl on The Subject of Commemoratives

| By Q. David Bowers | 1985 |

The following comments are excerpted from a booklet, "The Commemorative Coins of United States," by B. Max Mehl, published in 1937, just as the commemorative boom was beginning to fade. Mehl, the well-known Fort Worth, Texas dealer, spiced the text with his own comments, a number of which are extracted here. Keep in mind that the published text is much larger, and we are printing just a few samples from it.

The comments published may and may not be wrong. We all have the privilege of expressing our own opinions. Although it is my opinion, as well as that of a goodly number of collectors, that the privileges of the issuers of these commemorative coins have been, in some instances, abused, and that collectors to a certain extent have been in some cases unfairly treated, the fact still remains that these coins, or a least a majority of them, are of historical interest and to a great extent represent and are of much numismatic and historical value.

Regardless of what may have been said for or against the commemorative issues, it is an undeniable fact that since these issues have made their appearance rapidly, the increase in number of collectors has correspondingly kept pace in increase in numbers. Whether or not we approve of some of the designs of some of the methods used in the distribution of coins, we find that with very few exceptions purchases of the commemorative coins have proved a good investment as well as a source of pleasure.

1915 PANAMA-PACIFIC HALF DOLLAR: Due to the fact that a great number of these coins were purchased by the non-collectors at the

Exposition they are now very scarce, particularly in mint condition, and are considered one of the scarcest of the entire issue of half dollars.

1918 LINCOLN-ILLINOIS HALF DOLLAR: Approximately 30,000 specimens were in a bank in Springfield [Illinois] and handled by the Chamber of Commerce of that city. That particular bank "took a holiday" during the Bank Holiday of 1933, and the remainder of these coins, the exact number of which is uncertain, were purchased by several dealers at less than the original price of $1 each, so that the market was considerably flooded with them, but it seemed that the surplus has now been well absorbed. It is one of the most attractive coins of the entire series of commemorative half dollars.

1920 MAINE CENTENNIAL: While the issue of the Maine half dollar was rather "liberal," they were well distributed so that now they are fairly scarce.

1920, 1921 PILGRIM HALF DOLLARS: Of the 1920 coins a total number of 200,212 coins were struck, and offered at $1 each. Apparently the sale was very successful as none were returned to the mint and all were either sold or distributed.

Apparently the committee in charge thought they could do as well with another issue, and in 1921 they proceeded to strike 100,053 more of the coins, but they soon found that some things can be done successfully only once, and the committee returned 80,000 of the coins to be remelted, leaving only 20,053 sold at $1 and remaining in so-called circulation.

Naturally this makes the 1921 a very scarce commemorative half dollar, and incidentally this was the beginning of the hot idea of trying to "get" the collector at least twice.

1922 GRANT MEMORIAL HALF DOLLARS: Two varieties of these half dollars, as well as two varieties of gold dollars, were struck to commemorate the 100th anniversary of the birth of General Grant. Grant was undoubtedly a great man, but I hardly think he rates an issue of four coins.

1923 MONROE: Soon after their issue the market was flooded with them and quantities were obtained at less than their issue price of $1, but apparently they are now well distributed, and they are not easily obtainable in choice condition.

1925 LEXINGTON-CONCORD: Although the number issued would indicate that the coin is not scarce, apparently it was well distributed, and with the increasing number of collectors the value of these half dollars is constantly advancing in price. To my mind it is really one of the most historically interesting coins of the entire commemorative series.

1925 FORT VANCOUVER: As is readily realized, with an issue of less than 15,000 back in 1925, these coins today are classed among the rarest of the series and the coin is destined to become a real rarity.

1926 SESQUICENTENNIAL: While this coin is not a beauty from the artistic point of view, it does have the distinction of being the first United States coin bearing the portrait of the then-living president, President Coolidge. The other portrait, of course, is that of George Washington. Personally, I think it is one of the poorest designed and struck coins of the entire series. A total of 1,000,528 were struck of which number 141,120 were sold at $1 each and the balance of 859,408 were remelted. The number of coins sold of this issue is indicative of rather poor salesmanship. Philadelphia, with a population of over 2 million people, and the so-called World's Fair (which was almost finished just before it closed), should and could have disposed of a greater number of coins.

OREGON TRAIL: This issue marks the beginning of the deluge of varieties, mintmarks, etc. of the commemorative issues. In 1926, according to Mint reports, at the Philadelphia Mint, 98,030 specimens were struck. At the San Francisco Mint 100,000 of the coins were struck.

The number actually distributed or sold at $1 each is not known, for in 1927 I was invited to make an offer on quite a large quantity of the coins still on hand, but I do not recall whether the coins were then struck or whether they were available to be struck. That was before the day of small issues, and I was not smart enough "to invent the idea." However, the idea was invented by someone else, and in 1928 another issue of these half dollars appeared.

1934 MARYLAND: The number authorized and struck was 25,000, the greater proportion which was sold at $1 each with the assurance that none would be offered for less. However, some 5,000 of the coins were left unsold and later offered in large quantities at 75c each, and I understand that the remainder were sold at even a lower price than that. However, with the advent of so many collectors, the coins were soon absorbed and now are fairly scarce.

1934 TEXAS CENTENNIAL: Of course, those of us who know a little about Texas history know that the Texas independence was won at the Battle of San Jacinto on March 2, 1836, and not the 1834 [for the coins were issued in 1934 to commemorate the "centennial"]. But the idea of commemorative coins was advanced by the Texas Division of the American Legion. The idea was to raise funds from the sale of these coins to build a memorial building. The bill authorized 1,500,000. In 1934, according to mint reports, 250,000 coins were coined.

The Texas issue is also one of "high finance," and I am not entirely free from guilt that so many different issues of these coins were issued. The committee called on me and I gave them my idea as to how to sell more of the coins.

The design of the coin looks great when drawn on paper in huge size, but when reduced to actual coin size it is not too hot.

DANIEL BOONE: This coin also is interesting because it has created more comment than any other commemorative half dollar due to unintentional "rarity manufacture." The 2,000 issued in 1935 with the "1934" reverse, Denver and San Francisco mints, created quite a furor in numismatic circles. Apparently, the distributor did not know or realize the difference in rarity between a 2,000 issue and a 5,000 issue. Naturally, he was tremendously swamped with orders greatly over subscribing the 2,000 issue. Whether or not very many of them were distributed to original subscribers, I do not know, but I do know that as much as $100 per pair was paid for them and that later the distributor offered and supplied the sets in lots of 10 sets at greatly reduced prices. Also understand that single sets were offered later to collectors at about 20 times the original advertised prices.

ARKANSAS CENTENNIAL: Another coin which "beat the gun." Arkansas was admitted to the Union in 1836, and this coin commemorates that important event—to Arkansas. However, the first issue was coined in 1935. I don't think the coin would win any beauty prize.

1935 HUDSON: Hudson is a town of about 14,000 population, and why it should rate a coin to commemorate its 100th anniversary is beyond me. However, whoever was responsible for the coin did a good job, both in its design and its sale. The reverse represents Neptune on a whale, this being the first intimation of whales being prevalent in the Hudson River!

1936 RHODE ISLAND: They were advertised to be issued at $1 each, but as far as I know, precious few collectors obtained them at that price. However, a dealer in Providence seemed to have had quite a large quantity of them and they were obtainable at an advance in price.

1936 BRIDGEPORT OR BARNUM: Considering the status of commemorative coins we think that Barnum's likeness [on the obverse of the coin], in view of his famous remark, certainly most appropriate. As regards the obverse, it is best described by a comment made by one of the suckers, pardon me, I mean purchasers, as published in a recent issue of a publication:

B. Max Mehl on the Subject of Commemoratives

"The eagle (?) on the new Bridgeport half dollar is the biggest joke as a specimen of our noble bird that ever appeared on a coin. Not a feather appears on its tin-roof surface, and several beholders said that it resembled an airplane. Turn it around and you have a fine shark with two dorsal fins, an open mouth and a tongue. The shark appears to be laughing. I wonder at whom? And how apropos that P.T. Barnum's portrait adorns the other side. He was right in his famous remarks years ago."

1936 CLEVELAND: The design of the coin is well executed and the coin is well struck. It is a worthy addition to the long list of commemoratives.

1936 LYNCHBURG: Press reports state that Senator Carter Glass vigorously protested having its portrait on the Lynchburg half dollar to commemorate the sesquicentennial of his home city. As a last resort he is said to have called at the Philadelphia Mint recently to ask 'if it were permissable for the profile of a live man to appear on coins." Told that there was no law against it, Senator Glass shook his head and said: "I had hoped there would be an avenue of escape." His fellow townsmen arranged for the coin.

1936 YORK COUNTY: The design reminds one more of a medal than a coin, and in my humble opinion would hardly win a beauty prize.

1936 LONG ISLAND: The obverse bears conjoined portraits of two rather tough-looking gentlemen, but so far I have been unable to ascertain just who they are or who they are supposed to represent. The reverse is suppose to be a sailing vessel and was apparently modeled from one of the usual toy ship models. However, since it is a legal coin authorized by the United States Congress, we accept it with more or less grace as a member of the fast growing family of commemorative halves.

1936 CINCINNATI: The reverse is suppose to represent the Goddess of Music holding what is supposed to be a lyre, but apparently this lyre must have been bought at a five- and 10-cent store—it seems to be only a toy.

1936 ELGIN: An experienced gentleman was appointed as sales manager or distributor, and I understand he is making a good job of it. However, I still believe that $1.50 each for an issue of 25,000 coins is a little high as an issue price.

1936 ALBANY: The coin is rather beautiful, in fact one of the most attractive in the entire series. A total of 25,000 specimens were minted at the Philadelphia Mint and offered at $2 each. A great to-do was made by the commission about their sale and about the limitations that were to be placed on their distribution. But, apparently collectors did not fall all over themselves to buy the coins at $2 each, and some months after their issue, the coins were still being offered by the commission at the regular issue price.

1938 NEW ROCHELLE: [This issue was authorized by Congress but had not yet been issued in 1937; issuance came in 1938.] Having visited New Rochelle on two or three occasions I don't quite comprehend why this town rates a commemorative coin to celebrate its 200th anniversary. The only claim to fame that this town may have is that its only about "45 minutes from Broadway." But, apparently it must have, and it does have, some active collectors who apparently knew the art of string-pulling and got the bill for the coin through Congress.

1916-1917 McKINLEY MEMORIAL GOLD DOLLARS: Issue of these gold dollars was prompted by some personal friends of the President. The original plan was to strike 100,000 of the gold dollars to sell them at $3 each and use the proceeds to erect a memorial building at the birth place of McKinley at Niles, Ohio. However, like all similar plans promulgated by those who are experienced in numismatics, the sale of the coins met with meager success.

In 1916 20,026 of the coins were struck of which approximately 15,000 were sold. In 1917 another issue of 10,000 were minted, of which only about 5,000 were sold. By that time the committee in charge apparently realized that the number of collectors in the country could not and would not absorb an issue of 100,000 coins at $3 each. The committee had some 10,000 coins left on hand. These were disposed of at a greatly reduced price to the "Texas dealer" [Mehl himself], who in turn distributed them extensively among collectors of the country at a reduced price from the original issue price of $3 each.

1893 ISABELLA QUARTER: The number struck was 40,023 of which number 14,809 were returned to the Mint for remelting, and the balance of 25,214 were supposed to have been sold at $1 each. However, a great percentage of this number was purchased by a prominent member of the Board of Lady Managers and were afterwards released as the demand required. I well remember that these coins were obtained from the late Mr. Stevens of Chicago at 50c and 60c each in lots of 100 or more until about 10 or 12 years ago. However, with the increased interest in commemorative coins the value of this, the only commemorative quarter dollar, increased rapidly where today it retails for $3 each and is destined to become more valuable and higher in price from time to time.

B. Max Mehl on the Subject of Commemoratives

MEHL'S AUTOBIOGRAPHY: The following paragraphs were written by B. Max Mehl and appeared at the back of his 1937 commemorative coin booklet. Then, Mehl was at the height of his career, a life in numismatics which would continue until his death in 1957. Mehl tells his own story.

Some 36 years ago, a then much younger man than I am today (although I still try to kid myself that old age is still in the far and distant—I hope—future), I discovered that my then meager earnings as a clerk in a store went into my equally meager coin collection, which I must have started during my cradle days, as I do not recall of my childhood ever not being interested in coins. I heard of and read about the great rarities, which I did not even hope to ever see much less to own.

I thought that by dealing in coins it may be possible for me, if not to add to my earnings, to at least add to my numismatic joy.

An initial small advertisement brought fair results. I worked at the store during the day, and at "numismatics" during the evenings and late into the night. Within two years I made sufficient progress and felt safe to take a chance and "resign" my clerkship and venture out as a full-fledged "numismatist."

In 1903 my first coin circular appeared: In 1904 my first fixed price catalogue made its appearance, and in 1906, my first auction sale made its debut. I was the cataloguer, typist, secretary, mail clerk, etc. My establishment consisted of a second-hand desk at home. It was then that I observed that the numismatic business was still being conducted in ruts made 30 or 40 years before. I noticed that no effort was being made by anyone to popularize coin collecting and to create new collectors. The idea occurred to me to try advertising in general publications. My first "large" advertisement appeared in *Colliers,*—a five-liner—at the huge cost, at least to me then, of $12.50. The results were gratifying.

In the same year, 1906, I felt sufficiently warranted and financially able to move out of my "home office" into small rental desk space in a downtown office. A year later, in 1907, I experienced the thrill of moving into a real office; of course, only a single room, but nevertheless an office. I could even afford the luxury of an assistant then. And in August of the same year, I made my most eventful, delightful, and most successful venture of my life. I formed my life-long partnership with a sweet and beautiful young lady, Miss Ethel Rosen, who during these 30 years as Mrs. B. Max, made life sweeter and more beautiful for me. And her fine, sympathetic understanding, sweet companionship, and wise counsel is responsible more than anything else for what success we have attained.

Our "home establishment" consists of a pair of beautiful daughters, two not so beautiful but fine son-in-laws, and one glorious grandson.

I continued to expand my advertising in general publications so that in a few years I felt justified and able to plunge and pay $1,000.00 for a single advertisement—a quarter page in *Colliers*.

When the year 1912 rolled around I had already held some rather important sales, such as Professor Rooks, Cowell, Griffith, and others. And by that time my business had prospered to the extent that it required an entire half floor of office space in a downtown office building and a staff of 10 assistants.

By 1916 I had accumulated sufficient reserve to be able to make a "down payment" and to build my own building, which I now own without a single dollar of indebtedness against it. And by 1924 I was spending some $50,000.00 a year for general publicity advertising. And since then I have averaged approximately $100,000.00 per year for publicity and radio advertising, and handling an average of more than one million pieces of mail per year. I have paid as much as $20,000.00 for a single advertisement. And those who know admit that this great publicity is responsible for the present great increase in interest in numismatics by the general public. In the meantime, to be exact, in 1921 and 1922, I held some of the most famous sales, such as the Manning, the great Ten Eyck and many others.

From then on it is more or less "modern history," having had the pleasure and good fortune of handling a goodly number, probably the greater majority of all fine collections offered in this country, such as the H.O. Mann, Fred Joy, Dr. French, Judge Slack, Rees, Dr. Wilharm, Stoddard, and a great many others, including the greatest of all collections of American coins ever to be sold, the great Newcomer Collection, valued at a quarter of a million dollars.

I now occupy practically my entire building, devoted to numismatics exclusively; employ an average of 50 people, and have created a mailing list of active coin collectors of upward of 10 thousand names. My staff, I believe, is larger than the combined staffs of all other numismatic dealers in the country.

In 1931 I found it necessary and desirable to enlarge and remodel my offices, where today they are pronounced by those who have visited them, as the finest, most complete and well appointed numismatic offices to be found anywhere in the world, and where a most cordial welcome awaits you.

B. Max Mehl on the Subject of Commemoratives

The policies I inaugurated in the conducting of my business at the very beginning are in force today. Every transaction is handled by me only on the fair basis of satisfaction guaranteed or money refunded. Whether your transaction amounts to one dollar or $100,000.00 it receives the same careful and friendly consideration. The small purchaser or seller is treated just as courteously and just as fairly as the larger buyer or seller.

If you desire to sell your collection, you have at your disposal my services which have at their command a capital of more than $250,000.00 and resources of half a million dollars. And if you desire to place your collection for sale at auction you may have a liberal amount of cash advanced without interest. In other words, I endeavor to conduct every department of numismatics in a business-like, friendly and courteous manner. What I desire and value most is the creating not just of collectors, but the creating of good friends. When a transaction is made, it is never considered closed. I want and certainly try to merit the continued friendship and good will of everyone I come in contact with.

With the above resume I "rest my case." I shall be delighted to hear from you whenever you may require ANY KIND of numismatic service. My 36 years of proven success, square dealings, and ample financial responsibility is at your service and command.

The Coin Adventures of Uncle Scrooge

| By Q. David Bowers | 1985 |

Reader Tom Skulan, who deals in old-time comic books, recently sent us a file of comics detailing the numismatic adventures of Walt Disney's Uncle Scrooge, more formally known as Scrooge McDuck.

In an early cartoon sequence, Donald Duck visits Uncle Scrooge, who is seated at a sturdy desk and who tells Donald, "I'm just polishing some dimes that got moldy from long disuse!" Donald scans the dimes arrayed on the desk, points to one, and Uncle Scrooge identifies it as the first dime he ever owned.

A sorceress enters Uncle Scrooge's office and offers to pay him a dollar for his dime. Sensing a profit, he sells it, soon realizing that he had parted with a sentimental memento.

Ducklings Huey, Dewey, and Louie were dispatched to track down the sorceress. An international chase ensued, and finally the prized dime was retrieved just as the sorceress was lowering it in a pot into a pool of molten lava.

No, the comic strip contained no numismatic identification of the 10-cent piece.

A subsequent issue, No. 43 (originally published in 1959), has a cover depicting Scrooge McDuck taking an eye test, with coins instead of letters on the eye chart. The lead article in the inside is titled "For Old Dime's Sake" and concerns the sorceress who is still after his first dime. The crafty sorceress feels that owning the dime will bring her the same good luck that caused Scrooge McDuck to amass his vast fortune. Through a series of misadventures the dime is lost again, a scramble ensues, and, as might be expected, it is retrieved, to be given an honored resting place on velvet under a glass dome.

The prized dime surfaces again a few issues later, is lost at sea, and is once again recovered.

The same coin reappears in another issue featuring on the cover mason jars full of coins as well as a slip of paper telling how coins should be preserved. In a cartoon panel Uncle Scrooge proudly shows Donald Duck a vast area of money, noting: "It has made me the richest duck in the world! Owner of three cubic acres of money, uncountable oil wells, gold mines, railroads, factories, and fish houses!" To this, Donald suggested that Uncle Scrooge has probably never taken the time to enjoy the finer things in life, like a "tall, cool, fizzy soda."

Some of the best numismatic references are found in issue No. 5, printed in 1954. In one sequence, Uncle Scrooge gave Donald Duck a nickel as payment for collecting a debt for him. Nephews Huey, Dewey and Louie immediately recognized that it was a rare "Balonian nickel" from a country no longer in existence. "That coin must be rare!" one says. A coin guide is consulted and, sure enough, the nickel is worth $5!

Donald tells Uncle Scrooge, and Scrooge buries his tearful head on his desk, lamenting again and again his error of giving away such a precious piece. Then he states he is going to make it up. He takes a recently-received 1916 quarter and states: "I'm going to make it into the rarest coin in the world!"

Advertisements are sent to every newspaper in the country, stating "Scrooge McDuck will pay double for 1916 25 cent pieces!" Radio and television carried the message further. Stacks of mail accumulated, so that finally Scrooge, buried in a pile of quarters, proclaimed: "According to the government figures, I now have every 1916 quarter that was ever minted!"

Selecting one piece from the hoard, he puts it into a safe, stating that "soon it will be the only 1916 quarter in the world!" The others are loaded aboard a jet transport plane, taken out to the middle of the Atlantic Ocean, and dumped into the sea.

Subsequently, he goes into a shop, which bears the sign "MO THE COIN BUYER," to learn that his single remaining quarter is worth a million times face value. Scrooge McDuck proceeds happily along the street, repeatedly tossing the coin into the air, congratulating himself on his extra wealth. Oops! The coin falls to the pavement, rolls down the street, goes in the window of a pie factory, and ends up as part of a pie on a conveyor belt. Pies are thrown back and forth in the factory, just

The Coin Adventures of Uncle Scrooge

like in an old-time movie, and finally the quarter is discovered, but before it can be retrieved a pigeon grabs it and flies skyward. The quarter is dropped by the pigeon, then run over by a steamroller so that it becomes the size of a dinner plate and is ruined.

The rest of the duck family is dispatched to the middle of the Atlantic Ocean in an effort to retrieve one of the sunken examples. One was found, given back to Scrooge McDuck, who announced that he was now happy once again. To prevent a recurrence of the earlier loss, Donald encourages Uncle Scrooge to sell the quarter as soon as possible.

Going into a coin shop, Scrooge announces, "I've come to sell my 1916 quarter—the only one in the world!" Whereupon the shop owner replies that "The price is still 10 skyrillion dollars!"

Scrooge McDuck suggests that the coin shop owner buy it, where upon he is told that there is only one person in the world with enough money to buy that coin—"an eccentric old jillionaire named Scrooge McDuck!"

Scrooge McDuck comics are copyrighted by Walt Disney productions.

The "State of the Art" In Numismatics

By Q. David Bowers   1985

While doing research for the book *Abe Kosoff: Dean of Numismatics,* I came across that dealer's description for Lot 1948, 1924-S double eagle, in the Adolphe Menjou Collection catalogue, 1950. As you may know, Menjou was a movie actor who achieved prominence during the era. The catalogue description follows:

"1924-S the rarest of all double eagles. There are perhaps fewer than five specimens extant. The recent Dr. Green sale offered a specimen which we sold to him. It showed evidence of having been handled. The cataloguer indicated that it was the first specimen to be offered at auction, and he certainly was close but not quite accurate. In 1947 at the Buffalo convention [of the American Numismatic Association] we sold an Uncirculated specimen from the C. David Pierce Collection. It was in neither the Bell nor the Atwater sales. I consider this brilliant Uncirculated Gem to be the best of all I have seen, including the Berenstein, Green, and Pierce pieces. It is a prize which will certainly give pride of ownership to its buyer and should prove to be an excellent investment. The Pierce coin brought $2,250!"

In bidding competition, the Adolphe Menjou 1924-S double eagle subsequently fetched $2,000.

In 1950, the year of the previously-quoted sale, the 1924-S was indeed recognized as a major rarity in the double eagle series. Very few were known to exist, but that does not mean that just a very few existed. There is a distinction, a difference which can be described as "state of the art," as they might say in the computer or electronics trade.

Back then, it was *believed* that just a few pieces survived from the original mintage. However, later it turned out that hidden in Swiss bank vaults were many millions of American double eagles. When the United States government called in gold coins beginning in 1933, and subsequently melted them, coins which had been sent overseas earlier to settle international transactions were not repatriated. If anything, the Swiss bankers and others held onto their American double eagles more tightly than before! It certainly was the last thing in their minds to change these hard gold coins in for American paper dollars.

When numismatically knowledgeable bankers began to sort through their coins, many 1924-S double eagles turned up. By a decade after the Menjou Collection Sale the 1924-S had descended in status to just a rarity, not an extreme rarity but an "ordinary" rarity, so to speak.

When David W. Akers wrote his *United States Gold Coins, An Analysis of Auction Records, Double Eagles* book in 1982 he traced 98 appearances at auction of the 1924-S double eagle, citing records from 1950 onward. Many of these 98 appearances involved listings of the same coin in different sales. It is logical to assume that further pieces changed hands in private transactions, so if one assumes that David Akers' 98 auction appearances represent, say, 50 to 75 different coins, and then add an equal number of coins changing hands by private transactions, one has a population of somewhere between 100 and 200 examples—a figure which probably is in the ballpark.

In the accompanying text, David Akers notes that prior to the early 1950s, the 1924-S was generally considered to be the rarest of all of the Saint-Gaudens double eagles. It was considered to be rarer than the 1927-D. He noted:

"In particular, the 1924-S was widely thought to be far rarer than the 1927-D, and only the 1926-D was talked about in the same reverent tones. The 1922-S, 1925-D, 1926-S, and 1927-S were also considered to be great rarities at that time. Surprisingly, in the 1940s, the 1920-S, 1931 and 1932, now highly regarded dates, were not put in the same rarity class as any of the foregoing issues. Most of the great sales of the 1940s were missing the 1924-S, and the first appearance of one of these at auction occurred at the 1947 Buffalo American Numismatic Association sale where the C. David Pierce specimen brought a phenomenal $2,250.."

In 1982, David Akers ranked the 1924-S double eagle as the 14th rarest of the 55 different varieties among Saint-Gaudens issues. "It is not as rare as either the 1925-S or 1926-D but it is rarer than the 1924-D and 1926-S," he observed.

The "State of the Art" in Numismatics

In the 1950 sale of the Adolphe Menjou Collection the opposite situation occurred with the 1854-O double eagle and the 1856-O. In 1950 Abe Kosoff, the cataloguer, recognized them as being scarce, but their true rarity had not been appreciated. Years later they were to be among the most valuable of all issues in the double eagle series. In the Menjou sale, Lot 1955, an 1854-O, fetched $177.50 and was described as "Very Fine with nice lustre; very rare and seldom offered," while Lot 1957, an 1856-O, was described as: "Very Fine and very rare. Several splendid collections, including the World's Greatest Collection, did not have this date; has records to $300." The piece sold for $280.

There you have it: in 1950 the 1924-S was considered to be a prime rarity and to be very expensive, whereas the 1854-O and 1856-O, while considered rare, were relatively inexpensive; indeed, they were worth about a tenth the price of the 1924-S.

Contrast that with the present-day "state of the art." The 1854-O in 1982 was estimated to exist to the extent of just 20 to 25 specimens, according to David Akers. The present writer concurs. By that time it had become better known, for David Akers wrote: "The 1854-O is one of the famous dates in the double eagle series and it is also one of the rarest."

Concerning the 1856-O, David Akers placed the number in existence at 15 to 18, noting "this date is one of the classic rarities of the double eagle series and is certainly one of the most famous and popular."

In 1982 the present writer catalogued The United States Gold Coin Collection, the gold coins formed over a long period of years by Louis Eliasberg, the well-known Baltimore collector, who had died several years earlier. Mr. Eliasberg did something that no one before or since has accomplished: he acquired one of each date and mintmark issue of United States coin known at the time! Thus, his gold coin collection was complete in this regard. When all was said and done, and the hammer had fallen on the last lot, $12,400,000 worth of coins had changed hands!

The 1854-O double eagle, catalogued as AU-50, fetched $44,000, while the 1856-O, catalogued as EF-45 to AU-50, brought $49,500. The 1924-S, its status by then recognized, was no longer the major rarity of yore and brought $2,750—for an MS-60 coin.

In the 1986 edition of *A Guide Book of United States Coins* the 1854-O catalogues $33,000 in EF-40 grade and $50,000 in AU-50 preservation, while the 1856-O catalogues $35,000 and $57,000 in those grades, and an MS-60 1924-S is listed at $2,000.

In the 35 years since 1950, things have changed, the 1924-S is realized now to be more plentiful then it was back then, and the 1854-O and 1856-O double eagles are recognized as scarcer issues.

The "state of the art" has changed for many numismatic issues. Concerning prices and rarity, many pieces in various series are now considered to be scarcer than was believed years ago, but there are exceptions. The 1903-O silver dollar in Uncirculated grade was an extreme rarity prior to 1962, when over a million were released by the Treasury Department—pieces that had been stored since the time of issue. If you were to have surveyed leading collectors and dealers in early 1962, most of them would have agreed that fewer than a dozen Uncirculated 1903-O dollars were known. Today the 1903-O is relatively common, although there are so many collectors in the field of Morgan dollars that the price has edged upward, from a low of about $17 realized after the Treasury release.

Thirty-five years ago, few people paid attention to *condition rarities.* That is, while attention was paid to the rarity of an item as a date or mintmark or as a die variety, the separate rarity of a piece in a given grade was not considered to be as important. Thus, a collector desiring, for example, an 1849-O Liberty Seated quarter would know that the piece was scarce, possibly even rare, but he might not have realized that an Uncirculated coin was an *extreme* rarity. The same goes for numerous other issues in the American series. Today, we are all more aware of things, as there has been more numismatic research done since 1950 than in the entire century before then! Still, there are numerous uncharted areas.

Sometimes the "state of the art" changes so far as acceptance or denial of varieties is concerned. If you purchased an 1851 Proof silver dollar 35 years ago you would have bought a Proof—that's it. It was not until later that it was disclosed that two varieties exist, *originals* with the date slanting upward (and the type made in the business strike format) and *restrikes,* with centered date, struck only in Proof. Thus, some people who acquired 1851 Liberty Seated silver dollars prior to 1950 later found that they had restrikes in some instances and originals in other instances.

Somewhat related is the situation concerning the 1869/8 "overdate" Indian cent. For many years *A Guide Book of United States Coins* listed this variety as a separate issue. Virtually anyone assigned to own a complete collection of Indian cents desired the 1869/8 "overdate" in addition to the regular 1869. The "overdate" was considered to be about three times rarer. Now, careful study under high magnification, plus a better knowledge of the die-making process, has caused a rethinking of

The "State of the Art" in Numismatics

the situation, and many experts, including Thomas DeLorey (former senior authenticator for the American Numismatic Authentication Certification Service), believe that there is no such thing as an overdate in the 1869 Indian cent series, and that what used to be called the "overdate" variety refers to a specimen with a recut date, but not with the digit 8 under the final 9. The current (1986) issue of the *Guide Book* reflects this: "The 9 is doubled on some varieties of the 1869, and on others it appears to be over an 8, although it is probably only a doubled 9." The *Guide Book* is hedging a bit when it says *probably*, but the changing thought is nevertheless expressed.

Are there such things as 1917 Matte Proof Lincoln cents and Buffalo nickels? These are listed in the current *Guide Book*, but one authority with whom the present writer has talked stated, in effect, the following: "I was called upon to authenticate examples of these issues a few years ago, when a well-known coin firm had a couple of them for sale. At that time I said they were Matte Proofs, but since then I have refined my thinking and believe that they were simply business strikes, although with very nice surfaces."

This comment ties in with the writer's experience in which my firm was offered a 1917 Matte Proof Lincoln cent for consignment in an auction sale, but the consignment was declined, for none of the professionals on our staff, myself included, agreed that it was a Proof. "When in doubt, leave it out," as the old saying goes. Is there such a thing as a Matte Proof 1917 Lincoln cent or a 1917 Matte Proof Buffalo nickel? We have never seen one, but our mind is open, and if we see an unequivocal Proof we will then be convinced. Until then we'll be skeptical.

There is a changing face to numismatics, and each year research in our field presents some new discoveries, destroys some old icons, and clarifies past misconceptions or confusion. The "state of the art" continues to progress, as it should, and numismatists everywhere can be proud that their hobby is perhaps the best-documented and most carefully researched among all major collecting fields.

The "I Like It" Investment Theory

By Q. David Bowers — 1983

At a recent convention, a Mr. Denville, who had just disposed of his coin collection for a very large sum, registering a great profit in the transaction, was queried as to the secret of his investment success. "What formula did you use?" asked an eager listener, who himself had just entered the coin investment game.

"I didn't use any formula," Denville replied. "If I liked something, I bought it. If I didn't, I didn't buy it."

So often coin collectors and investors are motivated to buy what *someone else* likes, not what they themselves enjoy. The "I like it" theory of investment is a good one, and we dare say that it may be the best way to go. After hearing of Denville's success, we were prompted to ask two purchasers of Morgan silver dollars why they found the series to be of interest. In essence, their replies were as follows:

Buyer No. 1: "Morgan dollars have shown the best investment return since 1975, and all I am interested in is investment, so that's why I have been buying them. I am not a collector, so don't talk to me about art, beauty of design, and things like that. Show me numbers, for numbers count."

Buyer No. 2: "I like Morgan dollars because they are large, heavy, and very beautiful coins. I bought my first Morgan dollar, an 1885 Philadelphia Mint coin, a few years ago when I learned that it cost less than an Uncirculated 1885 Indian cent. I know that the Morgan dollar is much commoner than the Indian cent, but I still feel I got a lot of coin for my money. Since then I have bought three books on Morgan silver dollars and have read each of them. My objective is to get whatever I can afford in MS-65 condition, with the others being MS-60 to MS-63. Fortunately, quite a few of my silver dollars were bought years ago, so I already had most of the commoner dates in higher condition before the current price rise started. I bought a reprint copy of the *History of Nevada,* originally published in 1881, and have been leafing through it. There is a lot of information in there about the Comstock Lode, where the silver for many of these dollars was obtained."

It could be that Buyer No. 1 and Buyer No. 2 will each do equally well from an investment viewpoint, but it seems as though the second person is having more fun along the way.

At the American Numismatic Association Convention Show last August, a Wisconsin collector told your editor he was starting a set of nickel three-cent pieces of the 1865-1889 dates. "Why did you pick nickel three-cent pieces" was the inquiry, to which the following reply was given:

"My type set of United States coins is nearly finished, so I thought it would be interesting to specialize. Using the *Guide Book of United States Coins* as an authority, I leafed through the different series and studied their designs, mintages, and price levels. I concluded that nickel-three cent pieces were ideal to collect, for there are no rarities that are out of sight, there is a string of unbroken dates from 1865 through 1889, and there is also one interesting die variety, the 1887 over 6 overdate. I think low mintages are always appealing, and there are plenty of those, too. Ideally, I would like to get MS-65 and Proof-65 coins, but these seem to be high priced, with all of the demands from investors, so I have set my goal as MS-60 to MS-63. For the later dates, which turn up only in Proof condition for the most part, Proof-60 to Proof-63 will be aimed for.

"There is something interesting about collecting a three-cent piece, for it is an unusual denomination. When I finish this set, I am going to go for a set of 20-cent pieces, although I cherish no illusions about ever getting an 1876-CC. I did enjoy reading about the two that you offered in your auctions in autumn 1984."

This conversation reminded us of a telephone call received from a New Jersey gentleman, who stated that he had read *United States Pattern, Experimental and Trial Pieces* as well as *The History of United States Coinage* and had concluded that he wanted to own a 1792 half disme. He had no other pattern coins of any kind, nor did he possess any later regular-issue half dimes. The 1792 half disme was intriguing to him, and for this reason alone he desired to possess an example. We talked long about the availability of different pieces, with the result that he is now aiming for one in the Fine to Very Fine range.

The "I Like It" Investment Theory

The "I like it" theory of coin buying has a lot to recommend it. A parallel can be drawn to a New England collector of picture postcards of the 1900-1915 era. With literally hundreds of thousands of postcard views to choose from, and with a field that, unlike coins, typically does not fit into "complete" collections—for the variety is virtually endless—she simply buys cards that are interesting and attractive *to her*, with the theory that if she ever sells them, the same cards will be attractive to someone else.

If you were buying a home, would you pick a house that a real estate seller liked, or would you pick one that you and your family liked? If you were buying a painting to hang on the wall of your living room or office, would you buy a painting that an art gallery or an interior decorator said was pretty, or would you buy one that you enjoyed viewing? If you were buying an automobile, would you pick out one that captured your fancy, or would you close your eyes and tell the car salesman that you would take whatever he picked out?

The "I like it" theory of coin buying is no different. When buying coins, pick out what *you* like, not what someone else likes. Of course, it doesn't hurt to get a few opinions, and once you have narrowed your choices to some favorites, if you have questions about the market structure, the investment potential, the availability of certain conditions, or the like, then contact your favorite coin dealer and get some ideas. After all, that's what professional numismatists are in business for. But, the basic desire should come from you. Only in that way can you truly enjoy forming a numismatic holding, whether it be a specialized collection or an "investment portfolio."

The Secret of an Old Estate

By Michael Hodder 1988

The following narrative is typical in a way of experiences of just about any coin dealer you name. But, it does have an interesting "twist" to it—which certainly isn't typical!

Early in July last year, a couple arrived at our offices in New Hampshire, having driven hundreds of miles to keep an appointment made with Tom Becker of our staff. They owned, so they said, some "valuable coins" which had been rescued from an old trunk that once belonged to a long-departed ancestor.

After making his visitors comfortable, Tom asked to see the coins. It took him only a few minutes to realize that he would have to tell them their journey had been in vain, for, unfortunately, all of the coins were well-circulated common-date Liberty nickels, early Lincoln cents, Washington quarters, and the like, pieces of some slight value, but none worth anything significant over face value or bullion content.

The disappointing news was delivered, after which Tom was set to bid his guests farewell. But wait! They had another item, something old from the same estate, but it wasn't a coin, they said. As a courtesy, Tom said he would look it over. Soon, he was gazing at a relatively modern frame enclosing a printed reproduction of the signature of President Andrew Johnson. Above the signature was a silver medallion—nothing valuable, the visitors thought, but possibly a curiosity of the type one might find at a flea market.

At this point, Tom called me in, for he knew that I could glance at the medal and tell the visitor about it.

Before my eyes was the finest authentic, original 1865 Andrew Johnson 62mm. silver Indian peace medal I had ever seen, complete with its original ring mount! Only 90 such medals were reported as having been struck, and the specimen I was holding was a previously unknown survivor of that small mintage. Just think, if our visitors hadn't brought it with them, perhaps it would have been carelessly sold or traded away, and would have lost to the numismatic fraternity.

Following a close inspection, Tom and I both recognized that the medal we were holding was far finer than the specimen appearing in our sale of the David Dreyfuss Collection in 1986. As many present readers will recall, the Dreyfuss Collection, auctioned jointly with Joe Levine, was by far the finest presentation of American medals to cross the auction block in our generation. If it was desirable, chances are the Dreyfuss Collection had it—and in the finest available condition.

The Dreyfuss specimen of the Andrew Johnson Indian peace medal had been graded by us as Very Fine and it had sold for $5,720.

Tom and I graded the newly-discovered medal even finer, as About Uncirculated. After telling the couple what we knew about the medal, and showing the description of the Dreyfuss piece, they decided to consign it to our next available auction, which happened to be that scheduled for November 1987 in conjunction with the offering of the Ebenezer Milton Saunders Collection.

The sale date approached, and, as expected, the Andrew Johnson medal created quite a bit of pre-sale attention, including several telephone calls from a Midwestern client who was especially eager to acquire the piece. What it would sell for, we couldn't say. Perhaps the Dreyfuss piece had absorbed much of the market demand, and the new discovery would sell for less. But, we didn't think so, for its quality was superb and every time we offer a classic in a sale, there are more bidders than there are pieces available.

The medal came up for sale at the appointed time, and we were pleased to see that the winner was our Midwestern friend. Two days after the auction, Tom and I had the very pleasant task of telling the consignor couple that their unsuspected treasure more than repayed the time and trouble they spent to come to our office—for it had sold for $7,480!

A Trip to Colorado

By Q. David Bowers   1986

It was the Saturday after the Fourth of July, near the middle of the summer, when I boarded a TWA plane at Boston, destination St. Louis, connecting to another flight to Colorado Springs. A few hours later, on the second leg of the flight, the Front Range of the Rocky Mountains loomed up before the plane, and we touched down at the Colorado Springs Airport. Storm clouds were above, and the drive from the airport was with the windshield wipers on. However, summer afternoon storms in Colorado, like those in Hawaii, are usually ephemeral, and soon the skies were clear again. The occasion was a visit to American Numismatic Association Headquarters on the campus of Colorado College, to teach a class, "Introduction to Numismatics." For a number of years in the 1970s and early 1980s I taught the class, then called "All About Coins," but when I was president of the American Numismatic Association I stopped scheduled to teach, for my annual summer visit to A.N.A. Headquarters was occupied with other things—such as going over account books, visiting with the staff people there, and tending to A.N.A. business. Now, in July 1986, I was teaching again, and I looked forward to the experience. Fortunately, I had kept notes from several years earlier, so preparing an outline was a snap. To be sure, there were some changes—and as I contemplated talking about grading to my students, I knew I would have to say something about the intermediate grades AU–58, MS–61, MS–62, and so on which the A.N.A. Board of Governors had made official at a meeting a few days earlier.

The next day, Sunday, started with a brunch held at the Broadmoor Hotel in honor of Mr. and Mrs. Eric P. Newman. Eric, who hails from

St. Louis, was scheduled to be the keynote speaker at the introductory gathering of seminar students later in the day. About two dozen people attended the brunch, and words were spoken by A.N.A. President Florence Schook and by Ruthann Brettell, the executive director of the A.N.A.. On hand were A.N.A. department heads and instructors for the forthcoming seminar.

The Fine Arts Center was the site for a reception that evening, followed by welcoming talks to the over 160 students who were gathered in an auditorium. Ken Bressett was master of ceremonies and introduced the various speakers, noting that his first contact with Eric P. Newman came in the 1950s when he read something that Eric had written, and then wrote to him to ask what he knew about the history of New Hampshire pattern copper coins. Ken, a resident of New Hampshire at the time, was amazed to receive by return mail an actual New Hampshire copper cent, worth several thousand dollars then and worth much more now! "Not much is known about New Hampshire colonial coins," Eric said, "so I am sending one to you so you can study it and perhaps find out more about it." From this introduction, Eric and Ken became fast friends, eventually collaborating in the production of a book, *The Fantastic 1804 Dollar*, which today stands as one of the finest pieces of numismatic scholarship ever to reach print in book form.

Eric's talk that Sunday evening was titled "Numismatic Riddles." By means of slides projected on a screen, Eric illustrated and told of some of his research discoveries, including the first use of the term *dollar* on a coin or bank note in America, the discovery of the original sketches, by Benjamin Franklin, which proved that Franklin devised the mottos and motif of the 1776 Continental "dollar" (later also used on the 1787 Fugio cent), the fascinating process of "nature printing" on colonial currency, and other fascinating tidbits.

He told of the situation a number of years ago when the numismatic world was startled to learn of new die varieties of 1804 and, believe it or not, *1805* silver dollars. Prior to that time, no one thought that 1805-dated dollars existed. Eric told how he examined the coins, concluded that they were alterations from earlier dates, and were completely phony—worth nothing except as curiosities. The truth hurts, and the owner of the coins and also the prominent dealer involved in the sale of them responded with dark threats of lawsuits! The truth won out, and before long the matter was dropped.

About an hour later, Eric switched off the slide projector and took a seat, amidst a wave of enthusiastic applause. The Summer Seminar had started, and now a week of learning awaited the participants.

A Trip to Colorado

My own class, held in Armstrong Hall on the campus of Colorado College, attracted 26 students. As in years before, I gave each student a questionnaire to determine his or her numismatic experiences, interests, and preferences. One of my students had been collecting since 1950, while another had just begun his interest the month before. Ages of the participants ranged from members of the Young Numismatists Group, still in high school (one was in 6th grade), to grandparents, with a nice spread inbetween. Geographically, extremes were represented by students from Alaska, Mexico City, and New England. All in all it was quite a cosmopolitan group.

As a basic text we used *A Guide Book of United States Coins,* copies of which were furnished gratis by Western Publishing Co. supplementing this book were copies of *Coin World, Numismatic News,* and *The Coin Dealer Newsletter,* also furnished free of charge by the publishers.

On Monday, the class started at nine o'clock sharp. After introductory remarks, I started discussing the *Guide Book* in a way not too much different from the "Day Trip" series of articles I have been doing for the *Rare Coin Review.* Thinking that some students might question the reason for discussing colonial and early American coins, which are hardly in the mainstream of numismatics, I noted that if I were to spend the day on a "popular" subject—such as giving market recommendations for certain coins at certain price levels in certain grades—all the students would have when they returned home would be the knowledge of what one person thought was a good investment one summer day in 1986. They would have nothing of continuing useful value. I stated that the best way to invest wisely (having determined that investment was indeed an interest of the students, as indicated on the sheets I had them fill out) was to learn as much about numismatics. By understanding colonial early American coins, half cents and large cents, and other early issues, one can place such "popular" series as Morgan silver dollars in the proper context, I noted. This seemed to be what the students wanted, so we proceeded with a discussion of silver coins of the Massachusetts Bay Colony, through the Rosa Americana issues, the various copper coins of the states, and so on, right through to the start of the Philadelphia Mint in 1792 and the patterns connected with it. Along the way, I mentioned the interesting mottos that were reflective of the sentiment of the era, such as "Immune (or Immunis) Columbia" (referring to Columbia, or America, being immune from the problems of the rest of the world), "Rosa Americana" and "Utile Dulci" (found on Rosa Americana coins, "the American rose" and "the useful with the sweet"), "Mind Your

Business" (found on 1776 Continental and 1787 Fugio coins), "Liberty, Parent of Science and Industry" (a legend on the obverse of 1792 pattern coins), and so on, noting at the same time that certain coins, tokens, and medals of George Washington had interesting and tear-provoking legends, such as "He is in glory, the world in tears," "Time increases his fame," and so on.

Then came a discussion of half cents, large cents, and other early American pieces, interspersed with information about die preparation, methods of striking, and the fact that horsepower, in the literal sense of the word, was employed at the Mint, not to overlook the fact that early coin presses were truly hand-operated. By noon, when the class took a break for lunch, we had arrived at the topic of Liberty Head nickels. After lunch we progressed part way through American silver coins, by which time it was 2:30 in the afternoon. Arriving at that time to address the group were Adna Wilde and Bill Henderson. As the class was scheduled to go on a field trip to Cripple Creek the next day, Adna and Bill were on hand to discuss the background of what has been called "the world's greatest gold camp on earth." Adna, who served as president of the A.N.A. for the 1981–1983 term and who currently is treasurer, gave a slide talk on Lesher "dollars," telling how these pieces, listed on page 261 of the *Guide Book,* were made, the different varieties, and other fascinating information about them. Curiously, these coins, distributed in Victor, Colorado, a *gold* mining area, were made of *silver.* Lesher, who conceived them, was a silver miner thrown out of work in Georgetown, Colorado, who subsequently moved to Victor, still believing in the value of silver on the market, which by that time had declined to a low level. His octagonal "dollars" were an attempt to revive public interest in silver metal. The Treasury stepped in and seized the dies, and other complications developed, all of which were related in fascinating detail by the speaker.

Then came Bill Henderson's talk on the romance and adventure of the gold discoveries in Cripple Creek. "Gold is where you find it," they say and in the olden days luck often played the part in setting up a fortune. In one instance, a druggist threw his hat in the air, resolving to dig for gold wherever the hat landed. The result was a bonanza, which he named the Pharmacist Mine! In another instance, two brothers named Woods set about excavating the foundation for the Hotel Victor, but instead happened upon a rich vein of gold ore, laying the basis for the famous Gold Coin Mine, which went on to great fame—especially after Theodore Roosevelt visited it and also due to its prominent situation right

A Trip to Colorado

in the middle of downtown Victor. Stained glass windows were employed in the shaft house of the Gold Coin Mine, and right across the street from the operation was the Gold Coin Club, which furnished deluxe after-hours amusement facilities for the miners.

My students were delighted when Bill Henderson drew winners from students' names printed on slips of paper and passed out a number of colorful stock certificates from Cripple Creek and Victor mines, plus some interesting commemorative medals.

Before long it was after 4 pm, the class adjourned, and a number of us headed for A.N.A. Headquarters to board a bus for the Pikes Peak Cog Railway. On board were Mary Lou Barrett and Liz Arlin of the Bowers and Merena Galleries staff, who were in Colorado for the week to take the course on coin grading. Leaving the station at 5, the three-part train was at the 14,110-foot altitude summit by an hour and a half later. It was a clear day, the sun was still bright in the early evening, and one could see all the way to Kansas. Pikes Peak doesn't change, of course, so it wasn't much different from my last trip up the incline, which was in 1976. Our guide told us that there were just two cog railways in America, one being the Pikes Peak rig operated by diesel engines and the other being the steam-operated railroad up Mt. Washington in New Hampshire.

The next morning, Tuesday, my class boarded a bus and headed for Cripple Creek and Victor, with Adna Wilde and Bill Henderson joining me as tour guides. After a journey through the mountains, we arrived in Cripple Creek, alighted, and proceeded to visit the many tourist shops up and down the main street, Bennett Avenue. A recent addition to the line-up was a coin and antiques shop operated by Ken Hallenbeck, a member of the A.N.A. Board of Governors (and the contributor of an article to a recent *Rare Coin Review*.) The group split up, and some elected to visit the Old Homestead, a former bordello now converted to a museum, while others went to the Cripple Creek District Museum at the head of Myers Avenue, and still others went to different places. I lingered at the Long Hungry Trading Company on Bennett Avenue, where I bought several T-shirts, each made by hand as I watched, using the silk screen process (instead of the faster iron-on transfer process used by most tourist places). There was enough time to catch a number of other stores and shops, including Ken Hallenbeck's place, and to buy a few books at the Golden Leaves, a book store, where I found still another Cripple Creek volume to add to my library, *The Last Gold Rush*, by Raymond L. Drake—a rather nifty volume, one of the best I have seen on the subject, in fact.

We gathered for lunch at the Imperial Hotel, built in 1896, and were treated to a fine buffet, a welcome change from the food served at Colorado College during the seminar, which most of my students rated at a "two" or "three" (on a scale of ten)—the only negative I heard to an otherwise fine week of activity.

Following lunch, we boarded the bus and headed toward Victor, seven miles away. Unlike Cripple Creek, which has more tourist shops than can be easily counted, Victor is not much different from the "good old days," except that many of the buildings are abandoned or boarded up. The Gold Coin Club, which still is across the street from the Gold Coin Mine (except that the mine is in ruins, and all that remain are a few brick walls, piles of rubble, and a gaping shaft), had a "for sale" sign on it. I wonder what price they are asking? Certainly, this is one of the most historical of all buildings in the district. The New Victor Hotel, formerly a bank building, remains the most prominent building in the town and is largely empty, as is the building captioned "Victor Record" across the facade, where Lowell Thomas once worked. Owen Fulrodt's antique shop, named the Assay Office, had expanded to a second location since my last visit. I suggested that my students go there, for Owen always has on hand a lot of interesting bottles, mining artifacts, and other relics, including stock certificates. Also on the Victor tour was a stop at the Joseph Lesher House, owned by the American Numismatic Association, and recently restored by the A.N.A. to a comfortable interior, ideal for overnight lodging. According to a sheet given out by the A.N.A., rates are most reasonable, and A.N.A. members can use the house for only $50, the charge for a visit from one to three days.

By mid afternoon, quite thoroughly steeped in the lore of "the world's greatest gold camp," all of us boarded the bus and headed back to Colorado Springs.

I started my class the next day with a discussion of coin grading, pricing, and values, beginning with an explanation of the Sheldon system of numerical grading. To refresh my memory, I borrowed from Nancy Green, the A.N.A. librarian, a copy of Dr. William H. Sheldon's book, *Early American Cents,* published in 1949—the book which started it all. The numerical system, in which coins are rated from 1 to 70, was devised as a market formula for the pricing of large cents of the 1793-1814 era. The theory was that each die variety would be assigned a basal value. This basal value could be multiplied by the numerical grade. Thus, if a die variety had a basal value of $1, and it was in EF–40 grade, then the value of the coin could be computed by multiplying $1 times 40,

A Trip to Colorado

and coming up with $40. The reason that the numbers are from 1 to 70 and not some other system is that these fit the market structure of large cents at the time. As strange as it may seem today, an MS–60 cent in 1949 was worth only twice the price of a VF–30 cent! If Dr. Sheldon were devising the same scale today, if we had VF–30 for that range, then MS–60 would probably have to be MS–500!

Some of my readers may recall that when the A.N.A. Grading System was first formulated in the 1970s, there was much discussion about how illogical the Sheldon system was, for it had long fallen out of use as a pricing formula. However, logic has never prevented people from making decisions, and the Sheldon market formula system of numbers from 1 to 70 was thrown in place, now to cover all coins from half cents to double eagles. Thus, today in 1986 we have the rather illogical situation that the grade of Very Fine begins at VF–20 and goes all the way up until you are just short of EF–40, or a span of 19 numbers, whereas within a short span of just 10 numbers are now crammed MS–60, MS–61, MS–62, MS–63, MS–64, and so on all the way through to MS–70!

Another part of my classroom presentation was a discussion of coin market cycles, popularity booms and busts, and trends over the years. "Those who do not learn the lessons of history are condemned to repeat its mistakes," Santayana said, and, heeding this advice, I have always felt that the best way to understand today is to learn what went on before.

What makes a coin valuable? This was another topic of discussion, and my students and I discussed such considerations as face value, intrinsic value, design, rarity, popularity, grade, and so on.

Then came a discussion of market values, advertising policies, and the like. In one instance, a silver dollar in MS–65 with a market value in the $1,200 range was advertised in a current periodical for less than $100! "There is no Santa Claus in numismatics," Lee F. Hewitt, publisher of the *Numismatic Scrapbook Magazine,* said years ago, and I have repeated this piece of advice many times. However, there are always catchpenny ads which appeal to the bargain-seeker, who, somehow, feels that coins for which leading dealers pay $800 or $900 can be purchased retail for $100! Of course, the day of reckoning comes when bargain seeker the pieces are offered for sale.

As the end of Wednesday afternoon approached, I turned my class over to Ken Bressett, the A.N.A. director of education, who continued the discussion for the remaining two hours and also two days later on Friday, with the intervening day, Thursday, being devoted to a trip to the

Denver Mint. I hopped aboard another TWA plane, went to St. Louis, connected to Boston, and at the rather quiet and traffic-free hour of 2:30 a.m., Thursday, arrived back in Wolfeboro, to continue working the following day on details for our September auction sale (The Princeton Collection and the Dr. Charles Ingle Collection). All in all, my five days in Colorado were among the most active and intense of the year and, as always, were an exhilarating experience.

Let's Talk About Auction Sales

By Q. David Bowers   1986

The following article and the accompanying introductions are from *The Numismatic Investment Journal*, Volume 4, Number 6, published at 151 Elm Street, New Canaan, Connecticut 06840. The introductory paragraphs, given below in italic type, are by Ray Mercer, co-editor of the publication. The text (set in regular type) is by our own Q. David Bowers. The article follows:

Few of us can ignore the seemingly endless parade of rare coin auction reports, articles, and advertisements that steadily march through the pages of each passing issue of "Coin World" and "Numismatic News." Rare coin auctions have long established themselves to be a thrilling part of our industry and they command a dedicated following of dealers, collectors, and investors who eagerly await each new swing of the auctioneer's gavel to certify the capture of yet another prized lot.

If you find the glamor and excitement inherent to the numismatic auction scene to be a contagious spark towards igniting your imagination, you may rest assured you're not alone! A week seldom slips by that I don't receive an anxious inquiry from a collector/investor who wants to learn more about the mechanics involved for participating in one of these fascinating events.

Because of this growing interest on the part of many of our readers, Jim Iacovo and I decided to devote this entire issue of the "Numismatic Investment Journal" to the alluring subject of rare coin auctions. Not only did we wish to highlight the overall complexion of this fast-paced method of sale, but we also wanted to answer some of the more common questions normally asked by the budding auction enthusiast.

So, after much thought, we decided to contact Q. David Bowers (of Bowers and Merena Galleries, Inc., Box 1224, Wolfeboro, NH 03894) and inquire if he would be kind enough to provide us with an article suitable for our readers.

Both Jim and I have a great amount of respect for his well documented expertise on the subject of rare coins, his proven writing abilities, and the flair for professionalism Bowers and Merena Galleries, Inc. displays when conducting their auction sales. Since Dave is a subscriber to the NIJ, we also knew he would have a good feel as to what our readers have come to expect from our publication in regards to its educational content and purpose. Needless to state, we were not disappointed.

One of the best ways to acquire a solid understanding of a specific area of a marketplace is to solicit the insights of a true expert. Frankly, I cannot think of anyone who would honestly argue about Dave's deserved recognition in this field. Although the NIJ commonly interviews various members of our numismatic community, we are frequently hard pressed to turn over an entire issue to just one individual. Fortunately, we were able to make a happy exception in this case.

Before I completely turn this printing of the NIJ over to Dave, I would like to personally thank him for taking the time out from his busy schedule to write this article. It is a very kind AND informative gesture on his part. I'm sure you'll enjoy reading it as much as I did.

Let's Talk About Auction Sales
By Q. David Bowers

Auctions are a vital part of the coin hobby. Indeed, from the standpoint of news value, auction action captures more headlines than any other field of commercial activity. When my firm sold the finest known specimen of the 1787 Brasher gold doubloon for $725,000 in 1979, thus setting a world's record auction price for a single coin—a record which still stands today—the event made headlines everywhere.

Similarly, the recent sale by Superior Galleries of the 1913 Liberty Head nickel for a record $385,000 captured the imagination of numismatists all across the country. And, the auctions held by Stack's, Heritage, McIntire, Kurt Krueger, Rarcoa, NASCA, Paramount, Mid-America, Williams Gallery, Joe Lepczyk, Kagin's, Devonshire, Coinhunter, Harmer Rooke, Joe Siegel, and others offer a wide variety of coinage—ranging from "ordinary" pieces to headline-grabbing rarities. Even the well-known art auction houses of Sotheby's and Christie's get in the act occasionally with coin sales. In addition to these, there are other auctioneers who are active in the United States, Europe, Asia, and Australia who boast a host of coin sales.

A few months ago, in my firm's catalogue of the Milton G. Cohen Collection sale, I spent a few pages discussing auctions. I did this after realizing that while many collectors read news articles about auctions, there are thousands of numismatists who don't participate in such events.

Why is this? The answers are multiple. First, while the very term "auction" implies competition and excitement, not everyone desires this. Many collectors prefer to order coins on approval from a trusted professional, take a few days to consider them, and then "play or pass."

One cannot do this with an auction. Once you have examined a lot prior to bidding, then capture it in a spirited contest at the sale itself, the coin is yours to keep. If you decide the morning after that you paid too much, or that there was a nick on the rim you didn't notice, or simply, that you don't want to own the coin, you are out of luck. An exception, of course, would be a counterfeit coin—which can be returned. But, nearly all coin sellers state that sales to floor bidders are final.

Further, most coin auctioneers state that auction sales are not approval sales, and returns will be accepted from mail bidders only if some flagrant error has been made in the cataloguing. Such differences of opinion as to whether a coin is MS-63 or MS-65, for example, generally do not constitute grounds for returning a piece. So, the participant in a coin auction has to know what he or she is doing.

Knowledge is the Key

This requirement for *knowledge* separates the men from the boys or the women from the girls. In today's market it is well-known that a large percentage of buyers simply don't know what they are doing. They are investors who, like sheep, like to follow a leader—or follow investment recommendations. If Investment Advisor X says that a given coin is worth $500, then it will be purchased, for, somehow, the statement is believed. The same buyer would probably be hesitant to bid $500, or even $400 for the same piece in an auction sale. Why? The logic and psychology is complex, but the reasoning may go something like this: If it goes for $400, then there must be something wrong with it! If it goes for $600, then the price is too much! In other words, it is a no-win situation for the buyer who is not knowledgeable.

The truth is somewhat different. Coin auctions offer the opportunity for the *astute* collector to make excellent buys. If this were not the case, then dealers would not attend auction sales nor would leading collectors use the auction route to add to their cabinets. I have yet to meet *anyone* who has formed a great collection of coins who has not bid in auction sales either personally or through an agent. Think about it.

A True Test of Value

Auctions are perhaps the truest test of coin values. One can talk about "Bid" and "Ask" prices in various numismatic publications, one can even see "bid" and "ask" prices on the teletype, but do actual transactions occur at these figures? Too often, we read a "bid" price for an MS-65 coin represents not the price at which you or I can sell an MS-65 coin for but, rather, some wishful thinking as to what someone *might* pay *if* a "wonder coin" is presented. If you go into the marketplace with a half dozen examples of Coin A or B and want to sell them at the "bid" price, you might be out of luck. Everyone might agree that they are MS-65, but no one will come forth with a check.

The bottom line is that a coin is worth what someone will pay for it. An auction price, assuming that the sale is conducted in a professional manner and that reserves are disclosed, and also assuming that the catalogue is widely distributed and that the sale is publicized, represents what a given coin, token, medal, or piece of paper money is worth in a given moment of time. For example, if I were to state to you that a certain colonial coin in Very Fine grade fetched $1,200 at a recent sale, you would be hard pressed to argue that it was only worth $500 or, conversely, it was worth $3,000. Rather, $1,200 represents the current market value at the moment.

In his superb *Encyclopedia of United States Half Cents,* Walter Breen states the same thing:

"What of prices? I have no better answer at the moment than to list top coins of each variety known to me, together with their auction records. In a market that is far more unstable than it was in previous decades, this seems to be the only sensible procedure. Values will be established by subsequent auction results. Fixed-price lists too often represent dealers' dreams; the coins may or may not change hands at stated values . . ."

I believe I write from an unbiased viewpoint when I state that auctions are not always the best way to acquire pieces, nor are they the worst. Rather, auctions represent a *different* area—an area that should

Let's Talk About Auction Sales

be explored. I have conducted auction sales for many years—since 1957—and I have been selling coins on a fixed-price basis for even a longer time (since 1953) and have handled just about everything in the book. I have often seen coins at auction sell for much more—sometimes for multiples more—than the same pieces could have been bought for over a dealer's counter. At the same time, I have seen some mighty good values at auctions—pieces which represented fortunate acquisitions for the buyers.

I suspect that a relatively small percentage of the active coin buyers in the United States bid in auctions. As noted, many of these coin buyers are not knowledgeable and like to follow the advice of investment advisors, so this gives one explanation. Others may be afraid of the terms of sale (once you buy it, you own it). But, if you have confidence in what you are doing, it seems to me that you are missing much of what the coin market has to offer if you are not an active auction participant.

Just What is an "Auction"?

Auction sales are an important part of the numismatic spectrum. Over the past years most of the great collections to be sold were dispersed through the auction route. The term "auction," by the way, covers several different forms of competition. In numismatics, the two most popular are mail bid sales and "regular" auctions.

Mail bid sales are often listings of a dealer's inventory or other items on which bids are taken. The pieces which receive satisfactory bids (in the estimation of the person holding the sale) are sold. They are not "auctions" in the normal sense of the word but, like most human endeavors, there are exceptions.

The type of sale which receives the most publicity and through which important collections are dispersed is the "regular" auction, which combines public and mail order bid participation, whereby coins are sold to the highest bidder, unless a reserve is disclosed. Some coins go for record prices, others sell right at market levels, and still others are bargains, but all are sold.

The coin market is interesting, perhaps unique, in this regard. The field of antique car auctions, as reported in *Old Cars* (a weekly newspaper), often sees the situation that just a percentage of the items presented for auction actually sell. The unsold cars go back to the owners. In the fields of art, antiques, and the like, it is often the case that just 60%, 70%, or some other figure shy of 100% as noted as the sale's realization.

In coin auctions, all or nearly all items sell. Thus, as stated, a coin auction furnishes an accurate record of current market valuations. However, there are exceptions and anyone attending a large auction and "waiting it out" is apt to snatch a few bargains. Conversely, if two people "just have to own" a particular rarity, it may zoom to far over the regular price.

Let me digress for a moment to state that anyone interested in behind-the-scenes auction procedures would do well to investigate a subscription to the *Maine Antique Digest*, published in Waldoboro, Maine. This monthly publication, edited by Sam Pennington, pulls no punches, bars no holds, and contains lots of information concerning auctions that you're not apt to find anywhere else! Coin auctions, unfortunately, aren't covered—but antique auctions are. The philosophies are the same in many instances and this publication contains an enormous amount of good reading!

Auction "Fever"

There are a lot of interesting stories that can be told with regard to auction sales. A number of years ago, the New Netherlands Coin Company conducted an auction in which some Uncirculated examples of early Lincoln cents were offered on an individual basis. A 1915 Philadelphia Mint cent surprised spectators by selling for four or five times what everyone thought it would fetch. Later, it developed that both bidders were competing for what they thought was a different lot! The auction record price was publicized (without explanation of the bidding mistake), and, overnight, the price of the 1915 Lincoln cent in Uncirculated grade multiplied in catalogues and reference books!

In another instance, I recall offering a 1909-S V.D.B. cent in one of my own auction catalogues. I attended the sale and was amazed as the price went over current retail levels, then double retail, and then even further. Both buyers were people I knew, so after the sale I asked them for the rationale of their bidding. Both stated that they wanted a coin pedigreed from the sale and illustrated in the catalogue, and this was more important than buying it for a reasonable price!

Similarly, in our sale of the Garrett Collection for The Johns Hopkins University, 1979-1981, a common Washington-Carver commemorative half dollar, worth perhaps $15 at the time, sold for several hundred dollars because of its pedigree! The *New York Times* illustrated and featured this otherwise common coin, sold at a spectacular price, in one of the articles concerning the event.

Let's Talk About Auction Sales

How to be a Smart Bidder

How should one participate in an auction? In my opinion, it is best to plan in advance. I recommend contacting different auction firms and requesting sample copies of their catalogues, but please bear in mind that often a charge must be paid. Review the catalogues, determine the type of coins offered, and then subscribe to the catalogues you find to be best. If you have a specialty—such as tokens, medals, obsolete paper money, or the like—you may find that one or two firms issue specialized catalogues. If your interests are simply the general United States series, then you have a very wide selection. In any event, I recommend that you subscribe to multiple auction catalogues so that you can get a "feel for the market." After a sale takes place, you will receive a copy of the prices realized list, which will guide you in future bidding.

Grading often varies at auctions—as it does in mail and over-the-counter sales. It could be that what one auctioneer calls MS-65, you might call MS-60. Sometimes the opposite is true, strange as it may seem. I recall a few years ago noting that a competitor was getting unbelievable prices for Extremely Fine and AU coins. It turned out that dealers and collectors attending the sale were grading them as Uncirculated and paying Uncirculated prices. So, the prices realized list was a bit misleading. In the long run, the coins brought what they were worth.

Rick Sundman, the numismatic manager of Littleton Rare Coins, once told me of a curious auction sale to which he was invited to consign. According to Rick, the sale was being conducted by a newly-formed auction house in desperate need of consignments. As a last-straw measure, the auctioneer said that dealers could consign their unsold remainders and could assign whatever grades they wanted to them! Rick Sundman declined to participate. However, this does illustrate that what you see imprinted in an auction catalogue may not necessarily agree with what your in-person inspection might show. Accordingly, it would be advisable to acquaint yourself with the grading practices of the auctioneer. The best way, of course, is to attend the sale personally and to examine the lots. If this is not possible, then a trusted dealer friend or experienced collector can participate for you.

While it is possible to return coins in some sales (depending upon the terms of sale in the catalogue), this is much more difficult than not bidding on the pieces in the first place!

The concept of letting a dealer bid for you should be explored. Chances are, if you have been buying coins for at least a year or two, you have developed some friendships with leading dealers. Many of these leading dealers attend auction sales and execute bids on behalf of clients, sometimes charging a fee (such as 5%) for doing this. But, the fee is worth it, for the dealer views each lot through his own eyes and lends his expertise to any conversation he has with you concerning how much you should bid. In each sale we conduct, numerous dealers attend to bid on behalf of their clients. This is a mutually beneficial situation. We really appreciate the dealers' business, and the dealers' clients are getting a good deal, too.

A typical auction firm will issue a catalogue describing each lot in detail. If you have a question about a piece, that question can often be answered on the telephone. If you make your request early enough, and if you are known to the auctioneer, an arrangement may be made whereby the coin can be sent to your bank for inspection, providing that the coin is returned the same day and that you pay postage and insurance both ways.

Before each auction, there is a lot viewing period during which each lot can be personally inspected. Most auctioneers firmly state that anyone who has had a chance to view lots beforehand, or anyone who is a floor bidder, cannot return a coin for any reason whatsoever, with the exception of authenticity. In other words, if you examine a piece in person or if you bid on it as a floor participant, and if you later think that MS-65 described in the catalogue was really only MS-60, you are out of luck. So, do your homework earlier, not later!

Participation in an auction sale can be by mail or in person. Be sure to read the Terms of Sale in the catalogue carefully before bidding either way, for you are legally bound to those terms, and they are put into the catalogue for a specific purpose—not just for entertaining reading. Do not take them lightly or fail to read them!

If you bid by mail the auctioneer (my firm included) may grant a reduction if competition permits. That is, if for a given coin the two highest bids are $850 and $1,000, and if there is no floor participation for a particular lot, the $1,000 bidder will not be charged the full limit of his bid but, rather, will be charged some advance over $850, perhaps $900 or $925. But, not all companies follow this practice. In any event, it is best not to count on this, for it is often the case that if you bid $1,000 you will be charged $1,000—for the underbids might be very close to that figure.

I have seen many strange things happen in this regard. In a recent auction sale, the two highest bids we received for the same lot were each $311. So, we had to honor the first bid received. The chances of such

Let's Talk About Auction Sales

a precise bid being entered on one lot are probably less than one in several hundred, but it did happen.

It is a policy of most auction firms to charge a buyer's fee. This fee is added to your invoice and should be considered by you as part of the cost of the coin. For example, if you bid $1,000 on a coin and the buyer's fee is 10%, then your invoice will show $1,100. If $1,100 is the most you want to pay for this coin, then stop bidding at the $1,000 level, for this is equal to $1,100 when all is said and done. If you bid up to the $1,100 level, then an extra 10% or a further $110 will appear on your invoice, instead of paying $1,100 you will pay $1,210.

The art market furnished the origin for the buyer's fee. Beginning in the 1980s, it became popular in numismatics. Now it is nearly universally used. The way I view it is that the buyer's fee is not an extra cost of any kind if you simply adjust your bidding levels accordingly. I note however, that there are many who disagree with my statement. For example, when auction prices are reported in *Coin World*, the buyer's fee is not added. Thus, earlier this year, when the 1913 Liberty Head nickel was sold by Superior Galleries for $350,000 plus a 10% buyer's fee, *Coin World* reported that it had sold for $350,000, while *Numismatic News* headlined the price as $385,000. I personally prefer reporting the buyer's fee as part of the auction transaction, for that shows what someone actually paid for the coin. But, opinions differ on this subject.

In Massachusetts, one auctioneer in the field of antiques (a gentleman who does not auction coins) has referred to the buyer's fee as a "penalty," as if there is something unfair about people who charge the fee. Be that as it may, if you adjust your bids accordingly in advance, there is no reason why you should ever pay more for a coin because of a buyer's fee.

Mail Bids

If you plan to bid by mail, send in your bid sheet as early as you can. As noted in my previous $311 tie bid example, preference is usually given to the earliest bid received. If you are a new bidder, references should be listed, and mailing your bid sheet early gives the firm a chance to check them out. Such references, by the way, should include other dealers with whom you have done business on an auction basis, in addition to banking credentials.

If you wait until the last few days to mail your bid sheet, your bids may not reach the auctioneer until after the sale is concluded and the coins have been sold to others! When the catalogue first arrives, note the sale date carefully, for if you are a busy person, days on the calendar have a way of zipping by. In the case of last minute bids, you may be able to bid by telegram or Mailgram, but telephone the auction house to determine if this alternative is open to you.

Most auction houses will require a deposit on mail bids if the bidder is not known to them. The reason for this is some potential bidders feel that auctions are a "game," and they submit bids without any serious intent of honoring them. A deposit requirement shortstops this problem and is a benefit for other bidders at the sale for it eliminates competition that is not real.

Some auction firms give you the opportunity to check a box for an optional 10% or 20% increase in your bids. In this instance the auction house will "stretch" your bids by this amount, but only if it is necessary to capture a lot.

Time and time again, I have seen people state "I will pay $1,000 for that coin," then to have the piece to sell at auction for $1,050 to someone else. The collector then later tells the auctioneer, "You know I would have paid just a bit more!"

As Abe Kosoff, the late auctioneer who handled many sales, observed, it is difficult to spend someone else's money. How much is "a little bit more?" If the auctioneer had taken it upon himself to bid $2,000 for the coin, some people would have said, "That's fine, I am glad you got it for me." However, another buyer might indignantly say, "$2,000 is a ridiculous price! The coin isn't worth that to me," and then not honor the bid. So, the auctioneer *must* know your limits.

As noted, the provision for a 10% or 20% increase enables a slight stretching. However, the logic concerning this is questionable, for it could be argued that instead of bidding $1,000 and saying that the bid should be stretched by 10% if necessary, one could just as easily bid $1,100 to begin with. However, there seems to be a popular psychological aspect to it, and the 10% to 20% increase feature is a popular one.

Years ago, before the 1950s, dealers would accept "buy" bids. In other words, a well-known client would simply say to the auctioneer, "Whatever the lot goes for, buy it for me." As Abe Kosoff wrote in his *Coin World* column years ago, this caused great problems during rising periods in the market, when pieces that everyone expected to go for a certain price all of a sudden went for double or triple the value. And, then there is the situation if two or three good clients each put in a "buy" bid, who takes precedence? To my knowledge, this "buy" feature is not used by any coin auctioneers in the United States today.

Let's Talk About Auction Sales

Bidding Tips

It is important not to bid more than you are prepared to pay. For example, if you have $1,000 in your checking account and want to spend no more than this, don't bid on $10,000 worth of coins—for if you get them all or nearly all, you are legally bound to pay for them! I observe that some firms, including your own, have a provision whereby you can bid on a larger number of coins but limit your total purchases to a given amount, such as $1,000. Again, read the Terms of Sale to find this out. Or, if you submit your bids through an agent, such as a trusted dealer, you can simply give the dealer all the bids you want but tell him to stop bidding for your account once you have spent your limit.

There are probably as many bidding strategies as there are bidders. A typical auction catalogue may contain many hundreds if not many thousands of lots. Sometimes these are in order by various series and dates, but at other times they are grouped by consignments or are in mixed order. I feel it is best if you spend several hours studying the catalogue when you first receive it—postponing the formulation of bids until you have had a chance to review the entire catalogue from cover to cover.

While you are initially scanning the catalogue, make marks on the pages or make other notes of pieces that fit your particular interests. Sometimes the same type or variety of coin may be offered in several different places throughout the catalogue. If there seems to be a difference in the description, pick which single lot you would like best. Some auction houses give you the right to bid on several similar lots, with the assurance that you will be successful on no more than one. However, this is not a universal practice, so, again, you have to check the Terms of Sale.

One situation which all auctioneers have observed—and I believe it was James Risk of Coin Galleries who first publicized it in print—is the curious procedure of having a bidder state for example, "If I am not successful on Lot No. 412 at $800, then buy Lot 113 for me at $600." Of course, by the time the auctioneer knows what is going on with Lot 412, Lot 113 has long since been sold, but people sometimes don't stop to think about this!

A few years ago, after reviewing questions received from bidders, Karl Hirtzinger, who manages Auctions by Bowers and Merena, Inc., started keeping a list of questions most often asked by bidders. He came up with some ideas, which to me, seem valuable to everyone.

One of his thoughts is to use a worksheet, not the actual bid sheet, to first compile your bids. By doing this, you can check back and forth throughout the catalogue, make changes and revisions, and update your thinking until the last moment. Very few people know at the outset whether they want to bid precisely $825, or $370, or $11,600 on a single lot. If you are the typical bidder, chances are your ideas may change. Perhaps what you think the first day you received the catalogue might not be what you think after you sleep on it overnight.

In my own experience, I received a catalogue from a rare book dealer offering a Lafayette historical item for $6,000. I read the catalogue description carefully, was enticed by it, and was resolved to "go for it." Then I slept on it, considered the catalogue description carefully, and concluded that while the item was interesting, the design of it was such that it would not be particularly appealing from an aesthetic viewpoint. Even though there was no question concerning its rarity, I decided not to bid at all on the item.

By using a worksheet, you can change your thinking as often as you want and no one will know the difference. I recommend that you use a pen and write very clearly. Often I have seen bid sheets in which it is difficult to distinguish the number "1" from a "7," or a "7" from a "9." Likewise, be sure your name and address are clear. Give your telephone number, so if the auctioneer has a question you can be easily contacted by day or night.

The preceding precaution might seem elementary, but as I noted in our Milton G. Cohen Collection commentary, I recall receiving a bid sheet which had in the name and address portion on the top, the following message:

"Dave—here are my bids on silver dollars. I hope I win a few—Bob."

Unfortunately, there was not a clear cancellation on the outside of the envelope, nor did "Bob" state his address. As I know a number of people named "Bob," I hadn't the faintest idea which one was bidding on silver dollars! So, the bid sheet had to be ignored, and a customer/friend had to be disappointed.

When you bid, be aware of current price levels. While high and low ranges sometimes occur, many items sell within market ranges. If a popular Morgan silver dollar or commemorative generally brings $500 on the retail market, the chances aren't very good that a bid of, say, $300 will make you the owner. Conversely, there is no particular point in bidding $800 for it if you can buy one somewhere else for $500, unless you like the pedigree, toning, or some other aspect which differentiates the piece.

Let's Talk About Auction Sales

Continuing my example, if you want to buy a $500 commemorative or Morgan dollar and the piece in the auction fits your requirements exactly, then I recommend bidding in the $500 range. If you don't want to go through the bother of considering a piece in a later auction (when the price might be higher if the market is rising), then you might want to stretch your bid to $550 or $600.

Of course, there are exceptions, as the previously mentioned 1909-S V.D.B. experience indicates. I have seen many instances in our sales where a coin that I thought would sell for $500 sells for $2,000 or even more. Usually this happens when the piece is a rare die variety, or with a truly rare piece that has a modest catalogue listing. There are sleepers out there and these are the pieces that often amaze everyone with their selling price.

There is no harm in bargain hunting, so I do not mean to dissuade anyone from putting in low bids. But, if the bids are very low, you are just wasting your valuable time as well as the time of the auctioneer. In order to realize the most success in your acquisitions, you should keep current values in mind when you bid and you will achieve the best results.

And yet there is the possibility that something very special that you want may arise at auction, an item that has not been on the market for years! Just as a fair maiden was never won by a faint heart, a prize rarity was never captured by a reluctant bidder.

For instance, what would happen if a Gem Uncirculated 1849-O half dime were to cross the auction block? Here is a coin I have never seen in some 30 years of handling United States coins, a coin which is not priced in the *Guide Book,* and which in this grade might be one-of-kind. Would such a thing bring the "type coin" price, a few thousand dollars? Or would it bring $10,000, $50,000, or more? One in just Good condition catalogues for $30, in EF-40 it lists for $450, but there are no catalogue listings for MS-60, let alone Gem Uncirculated, MS-67.

In such an instance, you would be well advised to "go the whole nine yards" (editor's note: and keep going past the hot dog stand and into the parking lot!) and pay whatever you think you can afford, for your failure to capture the piece in this particular instance probably equates to you never owning an example for the rest of your life. If you pay $50,000 for it, it will be a surprising figure and a headline-getting price, but on the other hand, you will have something no one else has!

This points out the value of research! Do some studying, particularly on rare pieces, *before* placing your bids. There is not too much homework you can do before bidding on a 1946 Liberty Walking half dollar in MS-65 condition as the market activity of this calibre of coin is quite well documented. But, the 1849-O half dime is something else entirely and there are many other examples that could be cited.

Floor Bidding

If you plan to attend a sale in person, when you do your homework it would be a good idea to put some price notations in your catalgoue. If you have the will power to do it, you might consider listing your top bids. However, since catalogues have a way of being looked at by others, I feel it would not be a good idea to simply write "$1,500" next to a lot you want in the catalogue. You might want to devise some sort of a code. One dealer used the word *Charleston* as a letter substitution. Thus, by using this code, C would equal 1, H would equal 2, and so on. $1,500 could simply be written as CLNN and no one would be the wiser.

Often when writing an introduction to an auction catalogue I suggest that collectors and dealers pay the going price. I even advise them to stretch a bit if the item is particularly elusive or if the coin in question has been eagerly sought after by them for some time. With this in mind, if you plan to attend a sale in person, during the lot viewing process why not check out some coins that are not in the mainstream of your collecting specialty but, at an appropriate price, might still prove to be a good buy?

For example, there is nothing more frustrating than to be a silver dollar specialist who has looked only at Morgan and Peace dollars, and to be sitting in the auction room when a gorgeous Liberty Seated silver dollar comes up, only then to realize that you did not take the time to look at the lot before the sale!

As sales to floor bidders are usually final, it is important to study each piece carefully on the obverse, reverse, and edge. Except in the case of counterfeits, it is essential you understand the fact that if you buy it, you almost always own it. Bearing this in mind, if you have a question, ask a representative of the auctioneer to help you. That's what they are there for and no auctioneer wants his clients to acquire pieces they don't desire. At the same time, all auctioneers want people who acquire pieces to pay for them promptly and to enjoy their purchases.

Bidding strategy at the sale itself has furnished the topic for endless discussions. Should I sit in the front row? Or, will I better know what is going on if I sit in the very back? Or, perhaps somewhere on the side would be best. I know people who subscribe to each of these theories,

Let's Talk About Auction Sales

each believing it is best. As an auctioneer, I prefer that you sit in the front or the middle, for it makes it easier to catch your bids, and mistakes are minimized. I suppose my own feeling is that if I trusted the auctioneer and I wanted to be sure that my competition was "real," then I might sit in the back to watch the action.

At an auction of antiques (not coins) held a few years ago in the West, a mysterious but apparently well-heeled buyer was sitting in the sale and capturing most everything. After the sale, some of the dealers and collectors in attendance went over to meet Mr. Big. Apparently the gentleman did not want to talk to anyone, for he had headed toward an exit, but not before he was "collared" by some onlookers. It turns out he was a relative of the auctioneer—and that the sales weren't real at all. Happily, I know of no instances like this at all—not even one—in the rare coin auction field. But, before attending a sale it certainly would pay to check the reputation of the auctioneer. The best way to do this is to consult with old-time collectors who have had experience.

Most auction houses furnish bidders with paddles or cards with printed numbers. Generally, if you watch someone raise his or her paddle in the air, you will know who the bidder is, but you might not always know who the buyer is—for the buyer may be someone else. At the Garrett Collection sale in 1979 the successful bidder on the $725,000 Brasher doubloon was not the actual buyer, for the real owner wanted to remain anonymous, so he placed his bid through his attorney. I have seen this happen numerous times. Indeed, this is one reason why collectors will often place their bids through a trusted dealer.

In contrast, the underbidder, a leading Midwestern dealer, wanted everyone to know that he wanted and could afford the 1787 Brasher doubloon, so he stood up and called out his bids loudly. There is no harm with such publicity, and anyone who wants to bid hundreds of thousands of dollars on a single item in my auctions can do all the shouting he wants in my sales room!

Some bidders will flick their paddles almost unnoticeably, while others will hold them up in the air like a banner. Personal preference is the key. But, be sure the auctioneer knows what you are doing. And, if the auctioneer misses your bid, call out right at the time the lot is being sold—for if you wait two or three lots later, it may be too late. Generally, the auctioneer at his discretion may reopen a lot if he feels that a legitimate mistake has been made on the auction floor, but he will not do this on a consistent basis for the same bidder who isn't paying attention. Be alert! And, another reason for being alert is to avoid mistakes—like the 1915 Lincoln cent mentioned earlier.

After the sale, check with the accounting department of the firm and make payment. You may wish to take the coins with you, as satisfactory payment or references are given. Or you may wish to have the auctioneer ship the coins to your home or office. Unless you have a resale permit, you will be liable for city or state sales tax in the area in which the auction was held. Calculate such things beforehand, for they add to the cost of the coin and may affect the price you want to pay.

Your Role as a Seller

What about selling coins? First of all, auction isn't the only way to sell. Indeed, auction sales undoubtedly account for a very minor fraction of all coin transactions. Each year in the United States approximately $500 million worth of coins change hands by the fixed-price route—through investment companies, bullion dealers, rare coin dealers, and the like. The Professional Numismatists Guild alone numbers close to 200 dealers. If one assumes that the dealers have average retail sales of $1 million each—and this figure may be low as an average—that equates to $200 million worth of retail sales per year, or about four times the auction activity, and, this is just for the PNG. On the other hand, yearly auction activity is usually in the $50 million range.

I would not recommend selling bullion coins at auction, for by the time you pay the seller's fee, the "spread" on the transaction is apt to be less than if you simply sold them to someone with a bid and ask posting. Similarly, certain varieties of common-date gold coins, even if they are worth more than bullion value, might be best sold to a bid and ask situation.

Low value collections are not of interest to most auctioneers. There is not much excitement, for example, for a set of Jefferson nickels picked from circulation, nor does a cigar box full of worn Lincoln cents from 1930 up attract much notice. If you have an accumulation rather than a collection, your best bet is to go to a local coin dealer, and even he or she may wish to "cherry pick" the finer items.

If you have a group of scarce and rare coins, auction may be a good route for you. By exposing your coins in an auction catalogue, thousands of potential bidders can become acquainted with them. On the other hand, in a private sale, most people would not have the patience to offer their collection to more than three or four people—because of the time necessary to show their collection, security precautions, and so on.

There is no hard and fast rule on this. Again, I feel I can write in an unbiased manner, for I am involved in both auctioning coins and selling them by direct sale. In general, I suggest that auction is a good way to sell scarce and rare coins or a meaningful collection, especially one that will attract attention. On the other hand, a miscellaneous collection or accumulation is probably best sold privately, as are such things as modern rolls and Proof sets and the like.

Finding the Right Auctioneer

How to choose an auctioneer? I am not unbiased in this area, for I would be pleased to stand up on a soapbox and extol the virtues of my company. At the same time, I realize that my distinguished competitors will likewise say that in each instance they may be "best," "do the greatest job," "get the highest prices realized," and so on. Similarly, a while back I noticed three companies each boldly proclaiming to be "America's largest rare coin dealer" or "the world's largest rare coin dealer." It is important to you, as a prospective auction consignor, to look beyond such hype and do some investigation on your own. Here are some questions you should ask:

What is the commission rate? What do I get for this rate? Are there any extra charges? Are illustrations extra? What about color and black and white photography? What about advertising? It is a practice for some auction houses to give a "minimum price" or cut-rate fee, and then charge extra to bring the service back up to "normal." Find this out in advance.

Once the auction takes place, when will the settlement date be? How will I receive payment? Can I receive a portion of the expected realization in advance? If so, what interest rates are charged? What is the financial reputation of the firm? Does the company have adequate insurance? How can I be sure that my valued coins and other numismatic items are in truly safe hands?

Does the auction house allow reserves? Can I bid on my own coins? What does the auctioneer think of my particular consignment, and what is the anticipated market for it? What happens if someone bidding on my coins fails to pay his auction bill? Am I responsible? Are there any areas in which I am *not* protected?

What type of coins has the firm handled in the past? Does the company specialize only in certain areas or does it offer many different services? How large is the staff and what are the qualifications of the individual staff members?

What is the reputation of the firm? What do past consignors think of the performance of the auction house? Is the company familiar with die-varieties, great rarities, and obscure coins—as well as normal common ones? Does the company have a research department? What do the firm's catalogues look like? How much space is devoted to certain coins? Are the descriptions appealing? Are the descriptions authoritative? What is the quality of the mailing list? Does it contain proven bidders? How many catalogues will be mailed? What type of advertising will be done for the catalogue featuring my coins?

Who will be the auctioneer when the sale takes place? In what town or city will the event be held? What are the facilities like?

I suggest that each of the preceding questions be investigated—and you may well think of other questions in addition. I have seen many unusual situations arise from lack of care in this regard. A couple of years ago, I and another member of the Auctions by Bowers and Merena staff traveled to a distant city to visit with the heirs to a very large collection of United States and world coins. Our firm offered a 10 percent commission rate to sell the pieces, stating that they would be presented in a "grand format;" color-illustrated catalogue with no expense spared when it came to advertising, publicity, and the like.

While the owners of the coins seemed to be very impressed with our track record, the appearance of our past catalogues, our reputation, and other factors, there was one problem: a competitor had offered to do it for no commission rate at all! It was stated that the competitor's profit would be determined only by the buyer's fee.

In calculating this particular project, I figured that our actual cost of advertising, insurance, photography, catalogue preparation, and the hundreds of other things that go into making a successful sale would be approximately 16% of the prices realized. The buyer's fee would take care of 10%, and the 10% charged to the consignor; yielding approximately 20% totally, would leave us a profit margin of about 4%. So I knew that no other firm could offer the same degree of service and care, and mail it to so many different names, and do all the other aspects of a "full program" for just the buyer's fee alone.

To make a long story short, the coins were awarded to a company whose main expertise was not in coins but rather, in art and furniture. The sale came and went, and instead of realizing the approximately $1.5 million that the heirs hoped for, (and which I felt could be achieved with *proper* presentation), only about half that amount was obtained! Dealers at the sale had a field day, for few collectors had received a copy of the catalogue! I later reviewed a copy of the prices realized and noted that many issues sold for fractions of what I felt they could be sold for by my firm or by one of my strong numismatically-oriented competitors. Virtually no advertising was placed by the other auction firm. And, apparently only about 2,500 catalogues were mailed—and many of these went to people who were not proven buyers of the type of coins being offered.

When I quoted my commission rate, I figured on a mailing basis of 11,000 catalogues. If the same seller had come to me and said, "Would you auction my coins at no charge to me, the seller, if you will do very little advertising, if you will distribute only 2,500 catalogues, and if you will give most auction lots (including expensive coins) a simple one-line description?", I would theoretically like to say "yes." With such a short-cut approach, my firm probably would have made more money this way than by my original proposal to charge 10%! But, in reality I would not have said "yes," for I feel we have our reputation to protect and consider. But, this example does show that the auction commission charge means very little; it is the eventual prices realized that count.

It's the Bottom Line that Counts

To expand upon this further, if an auctioneer sells a coin for $1,000 hammer price and charges you 10%, thus netting you $900, it might be a much better deal than if another auctioneer sells your coin for $600 and charges you no fee at all—netting you $600. If you were considering having surgery done, or having an architect design your house, or having your portrait painted, I cannot envision you saying "I am looking for the cheapest rate." Rather such considerations as past performance would be more important. So it should be with coins as well. As I believe John Ruskin said, "The bitterness of poor quality lasts much longer than the sweetness of low price."

Advantages and Disadvantages

As is true of any other method of selling, there are advantages and disadvantages of selling by auction. The disadvantage is that you do not know precisely what your coins will bring until the moment of the sale. Although most firms do offer cash advances, it usually takes several months from the time you consign your coins until after the sale is held before you receive your money.

Some prospective consignors have hesitated to sell their coins fearing tax consequences. In my opinion, the present tax rates in the United

States on capital gains are sufficiently low that this should not be a factor in anyone's mind. It would be far better, in my opinion, to sell your coins, receive money that you can put in a bank account and earn interest on, and pay the low tax—than to have tax evasion on your conscience and, besides, have a bunch of cash or unaccounted-for funds which you cannot invest at today's attractive rates! Put $10,000 worth of auction proceeds to work at current rates, and you will have $20,000 in just a few years. Why deny yourself this advantage?

There are some aesthetic considerations to selling at auction. A finely-prepared catalogue can be a memorial to you and your collecting activities. Most people who have spent many years collecting coins enjoy the pride and satisfaction that comes with recognition when their collections are sold. Unquestionably, such names as Garrett, Dunham, Jenks, Eliasberg, and others would not be as well known—or not known at all—had it not been for the fame attached to their collections, especially at the time of the sale. Conversely, collectors enjoy owning coins with a "name" attached to them, and a pedigree—your pedigree—can actually give a coin an added value. Often people will desire "souvenirs" of an important offering.

There are many fine firms engaged in the coin auction business, and many of them have been quite successful over a span of years. It is my recommendation that you do some investigation before making any decisions. Weigh the advantages of each and every one, and determine which is best for you. Foremost in your mind should be the net price realized when all is said and done, but do not overlook the ethics of the people involved, the enjoyment of having a nice transaction with people whom you trust and enjoy your relation to, and so on.

As noted, do not worry too much about the commission, assuming that an auctioneer will do a good job for you. Stated simply, it would be better to pay a 50% commission to a firm who sold your collection for, say, $100,000 than to pay no commission at all to a firm who did a poor job and sold your collection for just $30,000! Of course, no one is going to charge you 50%, but this does serve to prove a point. You probably have spent many years building your collection. To me it seems to make sense to spend more than just a few minutes selecting the firm to sell your coins!

Right now, as you read these words, you may be a coin buyer, not a coin seller. If you have not experimented with the auction route, why not try placing some bids by mail or, as suggested earlier, consult with a trusted dealer advisor and have him or her represent you? In the

Let's Talk About Auction Sales

meantime, get acquainted with different auction firms. Subscribe to several different catalogues. That way, when the time comes to sell your coins it won't be an experiment—you will be an "expert" and can make a decision based upon experience.

Auctions are a vital, wonderful part of the coin hobby. Why not get acquainted with it?

Sunny Jim and the 1912-S Nickel

By David W. Lange   1986

"Let's get the cars going all right first and toot our horn afterward."[1]

It was thus that Mayor James S. "Sunny Jim" Rolph, Jr. inaugurated service on the San Francisco Municipal Railway, the city's new publicly owned streetcar system. Rolph's protests against the pomp and ceremony were in vain however, for, while the Municipal Band may have been silenced by his words, the public could not be. The crowd that had gathered on that Saturday noon were not to be relieved of their high spirits. San Francisco was a city reborn from the ashes only six years past, and this day marked the ultimate legacy of that tragedy. As the earthquake and fire of 1906 had largely witnessed the demise of the cable car lines and the emergence of the electric streetcar as the dominant mode of transportation in the city, so would this day witness the operation of the first publicly owned street railway in the nation. The date was December 28, 1912, and San Francisco was a city alive.

It seems difficult in 1986 to imagine the population of any city becoming so excited over the inauguration of a municipally owned and operated transportation system. It must be remembered, however, that this was the era of Progressivism, the era of crusading "muckrakers" such as Theodore Roosevelt and Ida Tarbell. Upton Sinclair's novel, *The Jungle*, had been published only a few years earlier, and there still existed in urban America a general distrust of industrialists and unrestrained free enterprise. While the trend in recent years has been toward the deregulation of industry in the interest of competition, the feeling was pervasive amongst many that government intervention in industries serving the public was necessary to protect society from the "malefactors of great wealth." It was with this spirit that the people of San Francisco were infused on that day nearly seventy-five years ago when the first cars of the new Municipal Railway rolled out of the carbarn at Geary Street and Presidio Avenue and headed east toward their rendezvous with the mayor.

Wresting control of the street railway lines from the exclusive ownership of private companies had been no easy matter. For decades, the owners had relied upon their influence with city politicians to have their franchises renewed time after time. Furthermore, public apathy toward the various proposals for a publicly owned street railway had resulted in the defeat of several bond issues. It was only with the growing nationwide trend toward the regulation of public service industries that the people were prepared to end the abuses and poor service which had been practiced by the street railway companies at their expense.

In a special election held on December 30, 1909, a measure passed providing for a bond issue to finance the construction of an electric railway along Geary Street. This would supplant the existing railway being operated by the Geary Street, Park and Ocean Railroad. The privately owned company brought the matter to court claiming a violation of its franchise rights. However, as the disputed franchise had expired in 1903, the city emerged victorious. Cable car service on Geary Street was terminated in May of 1912, and the city acquired all track and equipment belonging to the Geary Street, Park and Ocean Railroad at a price determined by the value of capital investment plus interest.

An estimated 50,000 persons cheered Mayor Rolph as he ascended the rear platform of the first car which was set to lead the procession from the intersection of Geary, Kearny, and Market Streets. All eyes were focused upon him as he prepared to begin the official ceremony. Sunny Jim was at his best in such situations, and this was his day. Having just completed the first of his twenty years as Mayor of San Francisco, Rolph was to preside over the many similar occasions as the Municipal Railway was extended throughout the city in succeeding years.

Ironically, Rolph was originally skeptical of the proposal to build a publicly owned street railway. His views on the matter had resulted in some lingering resentment on the part of certain city officials and public figures. Later on in the day, he would find himself having to defend his administration's position on public ownership in response to remarks made by J.J. Pratt, president of the Public Ownership Association. However, that was to be later. For the time being, the attitude of the day was "all for one" toward the Municipal Railway, and Sunny Jim was its biggest booster.

Sunny Jim and the 1912-S Nickel

The crowd anxiously awaited their chance to board the shiny, new cars. One man, however, must have believed that the wait was an undue inconvenience, as he attempted to board a car by climbing through its open window. His effort to inaugurate service a few minutes early was aborted by Sergeant J.J. Farrell of the San Francisco Police Department, who withdrew the man by his legs. "You can't get in that way," barked Sergeant Farrell at the offender. The man fired back, "Let me alone. Who owns the cars, anyway?"[2]

Joining Mayor Rolph on the platform of the first car was City Treasurer John E. MacDougald. Smiling broadly, Sunny Jim reached out and handed to MacDougald a bright, shiny new nickel. The story of what occurred next is told in an article which appeared in a newspaper the previous day:

The cars of the Municipal Railway will begin running at 12:30 tomorrow, and Mayor Rolph is to pay the first fare as a passenger. That particular nickel has been already spoken for by Treasurer McDougald [sic], who will substitute another for it that he be allowed to make proper arrangements for its preservation and display in his office of the first coin earned by the Municipal Railway.[3]

That nickel was, in fact, one of the first forty pieces coined of that denomination at the San Francisco Mint, which had begun striking the coins on Christmas Eve, just four days previous. The coin used by Rolph had been forwarded to him by Thomas P. Burns, Acting Treasurer of the United States Sub-Treasury. Members of the Board of Supervisors of San Francisco, who were to follow the lead car carrying Mayor Rolph and MacDougald, would also pay their fares with the new nickels.

Upon seeing the Municipal Railway earn its first five-cent fare, the crowd cheered and demanded a speech. Stepping back to the sixth car where the gathering was the thickest, Sunny Jim saluted the citizens of San Francisco and their vision:

"It is in reality the people's road, built by the people and with the people's money. The first cable road in the country was built in San Francisco, and now the first municipal railway of the country is built in San Francisco. Our operation of this road will be closely watched by the whole country. It must prove successful."[4]

Returning to the first car, Rolph instructed Conductor Nathan Rahn and Motorman Eugene Clisbee to get things rolling. The men attended to their jobs eagerly. There were many who had been blacklisted by the privately owned street railways for participating in strikes. Thus it was with a certain sense of satisfaction that these new public employees began their duties.

As cars began traveling up Geary Street toward Union Square, the Municipal Band was finally permitted to play. However, the music could scarcely be heard above the noise of the spectators, those unable to board the crowded cars following on foot. A policeman rode aboard each car. As the procession approached the elegant St. Francis Hotel, the guests of that establishment were alerted to its arrival by the hotel's wailing siren. All along the route, newsboys and others had been creating souvenirs by placing cents on top of the rails to have them flattened by the new cars. The guests of the St. Francis, in view of their station, instead placed silver pieces upon the rails. Two wealthy miners from Nevada bested them all by each flattening a gold eagle!

Those residents of the hotel who could find a place aboard the overloaded cars went along for the ride, each paying with yet another of the new nickels. These had apparently been secured on special order by the management of the hotel as a courtesy to its exclusive clientele.

First to receive a 1912-S nickel in change was an attorney named Timothy E. Healy, who was given one piece in exchange for a dime presented to the conductor.

The parade of streetcars continued on to the carbarn at Presidio Avenue, the mayor there being cheered by Municipal Railway employees. The crowd that had gathered then set off firecrackers and joined the procession as it continued on to Tenth Avenue and Golden Gate Park.

The return trip to Market Street was much the same. The enthusiasm did not abate, and Rolph continued to receive the public's acknowledgements throughout the ride. Finally, the starting point was achieved by the lead car around three o'clock.

By all accounts, the day had been a huge success. The superintendent of the Municipal Railway, Thomas A. Cashin, estimated that at least one hundred persons had been crowded onto each outbound and inbound car for a total ridership for the day of 20,000 or more.

The story is still a successful one, as the San Francisco Municipal Railway continues in service today. Althought many of the streetcar lines which were added to the system in subsequent years have since been replaced by diesel buses or trolley coaches, San Francisco still utilizes electric streetcars in regular service. This tradition is celebrated annually in the Summer Trolley Festival. Each year, from June to October, old streetcars from around the world, including San Francisco's own car Number One, make the run along Market Street in tribute to the past and the present. While the nickel fare is history, the system lives on. 1987 will mark the 75th anniversary of the Municipal Railway and will probably witness a special celebration.

Sunny Jim and the 1912-S Nickel

Sunny Jim Rolph was to be Mayor of San Francisco from 1912 to 1931, a record which still stands. While his years in office are remembered by few today, his name lives on in legend. He shares with such mayors as Jimmy Walker of New York and "Big Bill" Thompson of Chicago that peculiar kind of fame so prevalent in the 1920s, a fame based more on notability than capability.

Nevertheless, Rolph, more than anyone else, is associated with the inauguration and the expansion of Muni, as the system is now called. He remains a colorful figure and part of San Francisco's folklore.

And what of that first 1912-S nickel? While it may have once hung in the City Treasurer's office, a search made in recent years turned up no trace of the coin. Was it lost? Stolen? Misplaced?

Perhaps, it no longer exists. Perhaps, it does exist and is in the possession of someone who does not know its significance. Whatever the truth, the coin's present whereabouts is unknown.

While this particular coin may be no longer available, any collector can own a specimen of the 1912-S nickel. This date, while a key coin in the Liberty Head series, is not terribly expensive in the lower grades. In grades Very Fine and above, it becomes genuinely scarce and is priced in the three and four figures.

However, the desirability of this coin as the first nickel struck at the San Francisco Mint and the only S-Mint nickel with the Liberty Head design seems to justify the coin's price.

It is an authentic piece of history and one of the most interesting issues of American coinage. The 1912-S nickel that you hold in your hand may be one of those dropped into the fare box of a new municipal streetcar on that afternoon way back when the City of San Francisco got its first wheels. In fact, it may even have been the one paid by Sunny Jim himself.

Appendix

The law of February 12, 1873, which provided for a general revision of our coinage system, included a directive on the procurement and utilization of bullion for the minor coinage of bronze and copper nickel. Section 29 of this act, wherein this directive may be found, includes also the stipulation that such minor coinage may be produced only at the Philadelphia Mint.

The exact reason for this latter provision is not specified. However, one possibility seems likely. Minor coins, being made from base metals, were viewed by Congress as token pieces, struck for the sake of convenience rather than to be presented as a legal tender. In the years immediately following the conclusion of the Civil War, minor coins had been produced in great quantities which resulted in a distressing overabundance. This matter had been settled through legislation in 1871 by providing for their redemption in lawful money when presented in sums of not less than twenty dollars. With this experience fresh in its collective memory, Congress probably wished to restrict the coinage of minor pieces to the parent facility at Philadelphia where it could be more readily controlled.

This presented little hardship at the time, as minor coins circulated primarily in the northeastern states. They circulated not at all in the Far West, where the inflated economy offered little need for anything of lesser value than a dime. However, as the West became less of a frontier, commerce there began to evolve into something more akin to that encountered in the East. The extension of the railroad brought down the cost of articles sent across the country, thereby providing a need for small change. Although paper money would be scorned for many years to come, by the end of the 19th century, western cities had become receptive to the one-cent and five-cent coins, and these were regularly shipped from Philadelphia.

In view of this development, legislation was passed April 24, 1906 amending Section 29 of the Act of 1873 to read that:

For the purchase of metal for the minor coinage authorized by this act a sum not exceeding two hundred thousand dollars in lawful money of the United States shall, upon the recommendation of the Director of the Mint, and in such sums as he may designate, with the approval of the Secretary of the Treasury, be transferred to the credit of the Superintendents of the Mints at Philadelphia, San Francisco, Denver, and New Orleans, at which establishments, until otherwise provided by law, such coinage shall be carried on.[5]

The first coinage of minor pieces by the San Franciso Mint occurred in 1908, a total of 1,115,000 cents being struck there during the month of December. Five-cent pieces were not produced by any branch mint until 1912 when the mint at Denver coined 8,474,000 examples. For reasons unknown, the coinage of nickels at the San Francisco Mint was delayed until December 24, 1912. A mere 238,000 pieces were produced during the final week of that year, all of these bearing Barber's portrait of Liberty.

Footnotes

[1] *San Francisco Examiner,* December 28, 1912.
[2] *Ibid.*
[3] *Ibid.,* December 27, 1912.
[4] *The People's Railway,* page 27.
[5] *Fractional Money,* pages 357-358.

Bibliography

Carothers, Neil. *Fractional Money.* New York, NY. John Wiley & Sons, 1930.

Coin World, "Coin World Almanac." Sidney, OH, Amos Press, Fourth Edition, 1984.

Perles, Anthony. *The People's Railway.* Glendale, CA, Interurban Press, 1981.

United States Treasury Department. *Annual Report of the Director of the Mint.* Washington, D.C., Government Printing Office, 1914.

San Francisco Examiner. December 27, 1912 and December 28, 1912.

The preceding article originally appeared in *"The Journal of the Pacific Coast Numismatic Society,"* issue of April 1986. Readers desiring to join or learn more about the Pacific Coast Numismatic Society, which was founded in 1915, are encouraged to write to PCNS, 610 Arlington Avenue, Berkeley, California 94707.

Some Barber Silver Rarities

| By Andrew W. Pollock III | 1986 |

The following article, by Massachusetts numismatist [Ed. Note: Now a member of the Bowers and Merena staff] Andrew W. Pollock III, delves into an interesting area of American coinage: Barber dimes, quarters, and half dollars from 1892 to 1916. In your editor's opinion, certain Barber coins are considerably scarcer in Uncirculated grade—particularly in upper echelons of the Uncirculated classification—than auction appearances make them out to be. The reason for this is that, until recent times, grading often was optimistic or careless and, in any event, it was not as strict as today.

Your editor recalls, for example, an experience in which noted collector Ray Byrne purchased a long string of Barber quarter dollars in "Uncirculated" grade at auction. Upon receiving them he showed them to me, and we both agreed that many of the pieces were Extremely Fine or AU at best—and yet this was a "name" sale conducted by a leading auctioneer. I suspect that not more than one in ten "Uncirculated" coins of several decades ago would qualify as MS-65 by today's standards.

Andrew Pollock's study contains some interesting findings; witness the availability and price of the 1901-O quarter in comparison to the famous 1901-S, for example.

Introduction

In the autumn of 1985 I undertook the study of the rarity of Mint State specimens of Charles Barber's U.S. silver coinage of 1892-1916. It was my plan to thoroughly investigate this series by surveying a group of nearly

500 auction catalogues and to bring my findings to the attention of the numismatic community.

Prior to starting this project I anticipated that I might find several rarities. Two years previously I had surveyed over 300 auction sales in a general study of all denominations of Mint State U.S. Liberty Seated silver coins issued between 1837-1891, and succeeded in finding well over 100 date/mintmark combinations that I regard as being rare in Mint State (probably 25 or fewer Mint State specimens extant). Early in 1985, I had completed a similar study on all denominations of Mint State U.S. gold coins 1838-1907, and had found over 500 rare dates. Much to my disappointment, however, after having completed my study of Barber's silver coins, the number of rarities I was able to find in the series was very small, and the rarest of them, the 1894-S dime (really a branch mint Proof) and the 1901-S quarter have been recognized as rarities for a long time. Nonetheless, there are a few surprises in this series which have served to make my study worthwhile.

Methodology

I divided my investigation of the Barber coins into two phases. In the first phase, I surveyed about 250 auction catalogues for the appearance of coins of each date and mintmark in the series which all together comprises 222 different members. I carefully noted all appearances of Mint State specimens in a ledger. In the event that I recorded 25 appearances of a single date/mintmark combination, I removed the page representing this coin from my ledger, and discontinued studying it; this was the fate of most of the different issues. At the completion of the first phase of my study, only 18 issues of the original 222 remained on my list for further evaluation. In the second phase of my study, I surveyed an additional group of auction catalogues (bringing up the total to about 500). I continued to enumerate all Mint State appearances of the 18 different dates that had survived the selection process of phase 1. If as many as 45 appearances were recorded (comprising entries of coins in both phase 1 and 2), consideration of these too were discontinued. In this paper, I've chosen to discuss only those coins of which I found fewer than 40 appearances at the end of phase 2 of my study. There are two dates of dimes, five quarter dollars, and two half dollars.

The Rarities

1894-S 10c: This is the only great rarity in the series, and technically doesn't belong in a study of Uncirculated coins because it is regarded as a branch mint Proof. However, no study on the rarity of Barber coins would be complete without some mention of this date. Walter Breen lists 12 specimens in his book, Encyclopedia of U.S. and Colonial Proof Coins, some of them in worn condition. In my survey, I was able to find five appearances representing four coins. One of the coins on my list, offered in a 1953 sale, is of doubtful authenticity according to Breen's book. The coin in Rarcoa's section of Auction '80 sold for $145,000.

1896-O 10c: This coin was the second most infrequently offered dime in my study, and narrowly edged out the 1898-S and 1902-S dimes. I was able to find only 35 auction appearances. It was plated in 19 of these sales. According to the 1986 Guide Book of U.S. Coins, it is priced lower than a few other dates such as the 1897-O, 1901-S, 1903-S, and 1904-S dimes in Uncirculated condition.

This coin is representative of the Barber silver coinage 'rarities.' Nearly all Barber coins, excepting the 1894-S dime, exist in substantial quantities in Mint State. Even the rarest dates in this series are probably only R5 on the Sheldon scale (between 31-75 specimens extant); this rarity level probably even includes the celebrated 1901-S quarter.

1899-S, 25c: This turned out to be the third most infrequently offered quarter in my study. I found only 34 auction appearances. It was plated in these sales only 13 times. The earliest sale in which I could find this coin plated was 1976. Several other dates in this series are listed in the 1986 Guide Book as having higher prices.

1900-O 25c: This coin is tied with the 1914-S as being the fourth most infrequently offered quarter dollar. In my survey I found 39 auction appearances. In only 12 sales was this coin plated. The price for this issue appears to be only about $100 above the type coin price.

1901-O 25c: This is the second most infrequently offered quarter, and the third most infrequently offered Barber coin in my survey. I was only able to find 27 appearances at auction, and in these sales it was plated 17 times, which is a very good ratio when compared to some of the previously discussed dates. Based on my study of auction catalogues the 1901-O does not seem to be offered much more frequently than the famous 1901-S 25c, but is priced at less than 10% the value of the 1901-S in Mint State.

1901-S 25c: This is the second most infrequently offered coin in the entire Barber series, and the rarest quarter in my survey. I found 23 auction appearances, and it was plated in nearly all of them. The 23 appearances represent a maximum of only 18 coins because some of the coins appeared in more than one sale. I was able to find a few reappearing coins by comparing the illustrations in the auction catalogues.

The 1901-S has been called the rarest 20th century silver coin, and some numismatic writers have suggested that it may be the rarest 20th century coin. However, in so far as we regard only Mint State coins, there appear to be several 20th century gold pieces of equal or greater rarity; among these are: 1915-S $5; 1913-S $10; 1933 $10; 1921 $20; and 1927-D $20.

1914-S 25c: This is tied with the 1900-O as being the fourth most infrequently offered quarter. In my survey I was able to find 39 auction appearances. The coin was plated in 22 of these sales. This date narrowly edged out the 1902-O and 1904-O quarters which were offered only slightly more frequently. The rarity of this date seems to be better appreciated than that of many others, and it commands a price comparable to the 1901-O 25c.

1903 50c: This is the second most infrequently offered half dollar in my study, and the only Philadelphia coin included among the rarities listed in this article. I found only 38 auction appearances, and in these sales it was illustrated only 5 times. It is a totally unappreciated date. It sells for the value of a regular type coin, and thus is out-priced by numerous other dates according to the 1986 *Guide Book*.

1904-S 50c: This is the most infrequently offered half dollar in my survey. I was able to find only 35 auction appearances. It was illustrated in 24 of these sales. The rarity of this date seems to be well appreciated as it is priced in the 1986 *Guide Book* above all but a few other issues.

Anomalous Issues

Originally, when I first started work on this project, I expected that many of the coins with high catalogue values would prove to be more infrequently offered than was actually the case. It would be reasonable to anticipate that many such coins would be presented high on the list of rarities presented above. Although coins like the 1894-S 10c, and the 1901-S 25c, are included in this paper, many other valuable dates are conspicuously absent. The 1895-S half dollars are all very valuable, yet were all screened out during phase 1 of my study, indicating that I was able to find 25 appearances of each of these coins before even beginning the second half of my survey.

This strange situation demands an attempt at explanation. I can present but two hypotheses. Firstly, it may be that these very expensive coins, on account of their great value and scarcity (supposed or real) are sold at auction with greater regularity than most other dates. This would give a numismatist studying auction catalogues a somewhat distorted perception of the availability of these dates. Secondly, it could simply be that some of these expensive coins are over-rated and are really more common than anyone had previously thought.

Conclusion

The Barber series of U.S. silver coins doesn't contain the number of great rarities as do the preceding Liberty Seated series or earlier issues. Nonetheless, my research has suggested that there are some dates and mintmarks that have not received the recognition that should be accorded to them. Perhaps future research will bring to light other such rare dates that I've somehow overlooked.

Money and Wealth

By Q. David Bowers 1983

A few weeks ago a friend of mine, an executive with a leading New York bank, reminded me—or at least prompted me to think—that there is a difference between *money* and *wealth*. Money is a medium of exchange. Coins and currency are familiar examples. Money can be a store of value, but generally only on a *temporary* basis.

On the other hand, Webster's *New Collegiate Dictionary* defines wealth as the "abundance of valuable material possessions or resources."

Two years ago, S.S., a Midwest accountant who numbers among his clients several successful surgeons who earn several hundred thousand dollars per year each, came to me with a problem. Actually, his clients had the problem. Although they were earning *money*, lots of it, they were not able to accumulate much in the way of *wealth* due to high taxation and other considerations. Perhaps coin investment offered an alternative. Several discussions ensued.

An officer associated with one of America's leading banks, one of America's top 10 in fact, recently mentioned a similar problem. It seems as though the bank has many clients with lots of money. Try as they may, money left on deposit earning interest simply hasn't gone anywhere, especially when the effects of inflation are deducted. The stock market has produced some winners, especially for those on the inside track, of innovative companies, but often the investor has finished last, so to speak, for when a given stock receives a lot of publicity then it might be the time to *sell*, not to buy. In any event, the customers of this particular bank were not making fortunes on their stock portfolios. Perhaps coin investment would be an interesting alternative. Discussions are now in progress.

A few months ago *Forbes* ran an article giving a list of the 400 wealthiest people in the United States. A quick analysis showed that the majority of wealth is possessed by investors, innovators, or the heirs of such people. I am not aware of any great American fortune which has been made by collecting a salary, deducting living expenses (which always seem to rise proportionately with salary increases!), and then putting the balance in a bank on interest.

Recently I revised my book, *High Profits from Rare Coin Investment*. This book first appeared in print in 1974. Undoubtedly many of you who are reading these words now purchased the first edition. Back then I mused that 1974 certainly was not as ideal for coin buying as was 1964 or 1954. I could look back with hindsight, as could anyone, and determine that in 1964 all sorts of things should have been purchased. But, reality was the present: 1974.

Now it is 1983, and 1974 was nine years ago. Today, we look at the world of numismatics around us and consider that most everything is "fully priced." Back in 1974 people felt the same way. They also felt the same way in 1964 and in 1954, and, probably, in 1894!

If you were to look at the *Wall Street Journal* today you could easily rationalize that all stocks are selling for precisely what they are worth. Someone knows more than you do concerning any given stock, and if the security should be worth more then it would be.

Using such thinking one might well head to the nearest bank and put money on deposit. After all, drawing interest of 5% or 6%, or even 9% or so in other financial instruments, is a sure thing. Or, is it? As such interest is taxable at the highest income rate, those earning high salaries, who happen to be those in the best positions to make large deposits are penalized the most. The net result may well be a return on your investment of 3% or 4%.

What about coins? Historically, going back several decades in recent times, selected choice and rare coins have appreciated in value from 15% per year to 30% per year depending on what you read. An average group of coins, selected to be representative, increased in value from $1,000 in 1948 to over $100,000 today, as outlined in my *High Profits from Rare Coin Investment* book. On a dollar-for-dollar basis the strongest gains have come in the past decade.

Drawing upon studies in economics and practical experience in the rare coin business I wrote a study of coin price cycles which was

Money and Wealth

published in 1963, the first such exposition ever made in numismatics. Since that time I have observed several more cycles, with a recent peak occurring in the year 1979, continuing through March 1980. While some people like to predict coin prices on a mathematical basis, drawing upon such "hard" numbers as mintage figures and the extrapolation of prices (if a coin was worth $20 in 1972, $40 in 1974, $80 in 1976, it will continue doubling every two years forever), I feel that the major factor affecting coin price cycles is psychology. To predict the prices of coins in the future it is important to go beyond mintage figures, to go beyond price movements, to go beyond specials and promotions, to go beyond what most people are predicting. Rather, it is important to take into consideration the complex and interrelated factors of demand, supply, condition, price levels, appeal, rarity, and so on, adding a knowledge of what has gone before in the coin market, to come up with what *might* occur in the future.

The recommendations and suggestions made in 1974 in my *High Profits from Rare Coin Investment*, if followed, probably would have made a fortune for anyone who invested a substantial amount of money at the time. At least I have not heard to the contrary from any of the many people who purchased the book!

Now it is 1983. Where do we go from here? Are all the bargains already purchased, or is there truly an opportunity for growth in coin investment?

My own feeling is that in order to acquire great *wealth* the person earning large amounts of *money* today must find a way to convert the money to something that will increase in value at a rate outpacing inflation, *sharply* outpacing it if possible. Historically coins have been such a vehicle.

And yet one must be careful with rare coin investment. Unfortunately, anyone can hand up a sign saying "Professional Rare Coin Dealer." A few years ago, when there was an intense interest in gold and silver, an interest stronger than the interest today, I often read advertisements in airline magazines and other popular publications offering groups of coins for investment. Frequently the advertisement would be signed by a company which I had never heard of, which was not a member of the Professional Numismatists Guild, and which simply was not known in the dealer community. Such firms were merely sales organizations, often buying coins at full retail (or close to it) from other dealers, adding a generous mark-up, and in some instances raising the grade by a few points. The effect on the customers does not have to be stated here. Obviously, buyers of such groups had a severe handicap. If the coin market did well, they might do well also, but if they paid $500 for a coin worth only $300, then it would be a long time before they broke even. A doctor showed me a group of coins he purchased from such a sales organization. He was especially proud of his 1824 "Brilliant Uncirculated" large cent for which he had paid $3,000. The only problem was that the cent was not Uncirculated, it was Extremely Fine, whizzed (given an artificial lustre by a wire brush process) and recolored. To add insult to injury, a magnifying glass showed that it once had been holed at the top but had been plugged. The true value of the coin? Probably about $20 to $40!

"But, my sales representative told me that these were very good values and that the grading is guaranteed," my visitor related. Exactly what the grading was guaranteed to be, I didn't figure out, but, suffice it to say, he really had been "had." Fortunately in this instance, he did not abandon the field of rare coins, but, rather, sought to spend his next investment money by purchasing books and subscriptions. Today the doctor, a resident of Southern California, has a beautiful collection of large size United States currency and has nearly completed a type set of copper, nickel, and silver coins (and is eyeing gold).

Another type of numismatic come-on is exemplified by advertisements in popular publications for modern medals and tokens which resemble genuine United States commemorative regular coins but which really aren't (but which are priced as if they were!). Still another popular advertising activity is to feature a group of Morgan or Peace dollars of common dates, available in vast quantities in the coin market of course, and to say that "a rare treasure has been found," or "a momentus occasion in American history is about to happen" (as a bag is opened and distributed on a limited basis to the fortunate people who send in three times what they are worth!). Arlyn Sieber, editor of *Numismatic News*, wrote to me in November concerning misleading silver dollar advertisements which one of my clients had mailed me and which I had forwarded to him (knowing of the interest of that publication in exposing such things). "My file is bulging with these items," Arlyn wrote. He went on to say that the problem was not with *Numismatic News* readers, most of whom were numismatically aware and would not buy such things anyway, but, rather, with the American public who believed whatever they saw in print.

There is a happy side to all of this, at least in some instances. The

Money and Wealth

doctor who got burned with his "Uncirculated" 1824 cent and other purchases paid this as the price of admission to get acquainted with coins. Similarly, someone paying three or four times the going price for a common-date Morgan dollar, thinking they are getting the buy of the century, may use this coin as a passport to learning more about coins and, eventually, joining the American Numismatic Association and becoming knowledgeable on the subject. Years later, the initial overpriced purchase might not make that much difference.

The point of all this is that all sorts of things have been written in the name of coin "investment" and "bargains." In our last *Review* issue we advertised a complete set of Jefferson nickels in truly Uncirculated grade for $259. The advertising message was not that strong, indeed it was conservative: "Jefferson nickels, long overlooked, are considered by many to have potential for the future. Uncirculated Jefferson nickel sets sold for $200 15 years ago, and the typical set was not as nice as the one we offer now."

A new client from Connecticut talked to me about the Jefferson nickel sets. "I would like to buy a set, but can you guarantee it will be worth $1,000 within a few years?"

I told him that I could make no such guarantees, but that perhaps within a decade or two it *might* achieve such a value.

"I have with me a newsletter with investment recommendations which are very spectacular," he went on to tell me. He then mentioned that he had ordered several of the recommendations from the writer of the newsletter.

Our firm lost out on the sale of a set of Jefferson nickels. Perhaps the description was too conservative. Perhaps the title should have read: "Will Be Worth $1,000 in 10 Years!!!" Then we could have sold the sets not for $259 but perhaps $359!

Numismatic history is littered with many best-selling investment guides which, by using mintage figures and mathematical concepts, predicted prices for the future. Harry Forman once wrote that "anyone can make predictions." And, anyone can. Just like anyone can hand out a shingle saying "I am the largest, best, and finest professional rare coin dealer."

It is important to go beyond what you see in print and to think for yourself. Does the dealer have a fine reputation? What are his or her professional qualifications?

Seeking to limit an unduly large influx of members which might not be qualified, the International Association of Professional Numismatists a number of years ago required applicants to submit the last half dozen or so catalogues or publications issued by the firm. It was found that many could not come close to meeting this requirement.

While I do not claim that Bowers and Merena Galleries is the best rare coin firm ever invented, I do feel that we have a professional standing second to none and can stand the closest inspection and scrutiny. I feel that competition is healthy, and I have always encouraged our clients to find out about other rare coin firms and to patronize locations where they found the best values. And yet, I cannot help but be annoyed when I consider certain competition to be unfair—the offering of "bargains" which, upon inspection, prove to be vastly overgraded. Although it would be nice to think that certain popular numismatic publications screen their advertisers and check on the quality of the values listed, apparently such is not the case. Time and time again pieces will be offered at fractions of what correctly-graded coins will sell for. Customer complaints to the publications are nipped in the bud by fast refund checks. All this means is that alert buyers are protected if they are knowledgeable enough to make a request to get their money back. Those who have faith in the advertisement, based upon the publication in which it appeared, and who do not question the grading or have it checked are apt to be taken to the cleaners, as the saying goes.

So, for starters, when considering increasing your wealth through the medium of coin investment, be particular concerning the source of your acquisitions. Be fussy, about grading, and don't overpay.

In 1983 the coin market is, in my opinion, at the bottom of a cycle. In fact, the cycle bottom may not last throughout 1983, as prices tend to be firming. Ray Merena has spent thousands of dollars advertising to *buy* coins in popular publications, and yet the amount of *correctly* graded material he has been receiving at prices he can pay in order to pass along good buys to our clients has been small. Clearly, there is very little quality material overhanging the market.

And yet, psychology being what it is, there is much less interest in coin investment now than there was during the giddy nothing-can-go-wrong days of 1979 and early 1980. If you are inclined to think with the crowd, then you are the type who will buy stocks at the top of the market after they are vastly publicized and everyone else has bought them. You are the type who will head right for the coins that are most heavily advertised and promoted and buy all you can. But, contrary thinking has always produced better results than this.

When asked the secret of his tremendous success in the stock market, Bernard Baruch said that when others were paying ridiculously high

Money and Wealth

prices for stocks he would sell them his. Conversely, when people were willing to sell stocks at very reasonable prices, he was a buyer. Baruch was not a crowd-follower. He marched to the beat of a different drum. He thought for himself.

As unspectacular (is this really a word?) as this may seem, the best way to accumulate wealth via rare coins is to build a meaningful collection. At least this has been the key to the greatest profits I have seen in the past. And, in 30 years in numismatics I have much experience to consider for I have had transactions with tens of thousands of numismatists. You won't see many advertisements trumpeting that you should build a collection, for a collection often involves acquiring scarce and rare items which are devilishly difficult to obtain and which are seldom promoted. And, there isn't anything romantic about plodding along month after month adding a coin here and there to a growing collection. It is far more spectacular to make a telephone call and buy in one fell swoop a jugful of coins advertised to be rare (but which probably aren't).

I feel that 1983 will offer opportunities greater than have been available in recent years. If you begin a collection in 1983 you will have a head start, in my opinion, over anyone who joins numismatics in later years. I feel that 1983 to the coin field is what 1976, 1966, and other "down cycle" years were. In retrospect such years, representing the bottoms of their markets, proved to be the very best times to buy.

Just as our Jefferson nickel sets sold themselves—we were completely sold out within two weeks of the time our *Review* was distributed—Bowers and Merena Galleries does not have to depend upon meaningless price predictions or promotions to sell truly scarce and rare coins. Such pieces sell in a steady stream to clients who know our firm and who have traded with us for many years, some going back as far as 1953.

If you have money and want to convert it to *wealth*, then consider rare coins. I don't recommend borrowing against your vital assets, nor do I recommend cashing in all of the other investments you have. But, you may agree, as many have that a certain percentage of your assets *carefully* invested in the field of rare coins may be a good idea. If any generally-available investment medium has even come close to the record posted by rare coins in recent decades, I have yet to learn about it! Perhaps this says something about the future.

Auction Catalogues as Collectors' Items

By Richard A. Bagg, Ph.D.   *1983*

The often repeated phrase "buy the book before the coin" was made famous by Aaron R. Feldman, a prominent coin dealer of the 1950s and 1960s. It is very important that collectors obtain as much information as possible before setting out to purchase coins. Surely, Mr. Feldman included auction catalogues as sources of numismatic information that would make coin collecting a more enjoyable and interesting pursuit and, eventually, would aid the collector in making wise purchase decisions.

Auction catalogues are useful numismatic documents for several reasons. First, the prices realized lists, especially for auctions held in recent times, serve as indications of market value. It is important, however, to remember that scanning price lists must be combined with reading in detail the auction lot descriptions, or, better yet, with the knowledge of having seen the coins personally. Two pieces could each be described as "Brilliant Uncirculated" and if one was a superb piece, but the other was overgraded, and if one was listed at $500 and the second was listed at $200, the truth would be that each probably sold for what it was worth, not that the $200 piece was a great bargain. This situation is not unique to auction catalogues. Fixed price lists and advertisements are even worse. "Know your dealer before you buy the coin" is another good saying to remember!

Second, past ownership can sometimes be determined. Such information makes a coin more exciting to own. Unquestionably, many of the record prices paid in our Garrett Collection series of auctions

(1979-1981) can be attributed to the fact that certain pieces were pedigreed back to the time that T. Harrison Garrett bought them in the 1880s. There is always something special about owning a coin which has belonged to a prominent numismatist of the past.

Third, some auction catalogues provide historical information which further enhances the value of a coin and the buyer's appreciation of it.

Several thousand auction catalogues have been produced by various coin dealers since Edward Cogan, "the father of the coin trade in America," first issued one in 1858. Although a handful of catalogues were produced prior to that year, Cogan's first sale is considered by many numismatic bibliophiles to represent the true beginning of coin auctions in this country. Since that time a number of dealers have each held upwards of 200 sales during their careers, which in some instances have spanned a half century or more. B. Max Mehl's activities commenced in 1903 and ended with his death in 1957, for example.

With so many auction sales having taken place in the past, the task of the auction catalogue collector is to choose which sales are most important, informationally, for one's purposes. Another consideration is a financial one. Recently, auction catalogues of the 19th and early 20th centuries have enjoyed great success at book auctions, with one notable example fetching $9,000, a world's record for a coin book. The subject was a rare and desirable Chapman auction catalogue with photographic plates depicting the W.H. Hunter Collection auctioned in 1920.

Fortunately, many catalogues which contain valuable information from a collector's point of view are from the 20th century and are relatively inexpensive. In the past few decades numerous great collections have come on the market and have wrought great changes in the numismatic scene. Occurring during the lifetimes of many of our present readers, such sales as Garrett, Fairfield, The United States Gold Coin Collection, and others held by our firm have had a profound influence, as have sales held by others. One specialist in the Hard Times tokens series related to the writer that the offering of pieces in the Garrett Collection caused more awareness of the 1833-1844 token field than any other event in recent history!

A good starting point for a collection of auction catalogues is to obtain, usually by subscription, publications produced by various firms which have been in the coin business for a number of years. Such subscriptions are usually available for a nominal fee. For under $50 most auction houses will send you their output for a year. Of course, the quality

Auction Catalogues as Collectors' Items

and quantity of the output varies, so subscriptions are difficult to compare. Suffice it to say, however, that coin auction catalogue subscriptions cost much less than comparable subscriptions for art and antique auction catalogues. By comparison coin catalogues are a bargain!

Equally important are catalogues from firms who no longer hold sales but who were held in high esteem in the recent past because of the quality and presentation of numismatic material offered. These firms include the New Netherlands Coin Company, Lester Merkin, Abe Kosoff, B. Max Mehl and others.

Both 19th and 20th century catalogues can be obtained from many sources. In recent years a popular way has been to bid in book auctions which are held occasionally by such firms as Bourne, Durst, Katen, Kolbe, and Wilson. Sometimes modern catalogues are grouped in large lots and sell for just a few dollars each, often for even far less.

In the writer's opinion a good starting point for a collection of modern auction catalogues is B. Max Mehl's famous William Forrester Dunham Sale held in 1941. Mehl was known for his lavish presentations of the great collections which came his way for auction. His colorful descriptions created a demand for many of the rarities that are offered today. A copy of the Dunham catalogue now costs in the $100 range.

In addition to Mehl, the firm of Stack's and the team of Abe Kosoff and Abner Kreisberg (the Numismatic Gallery) issued many important catalogues. Volumes describing the Flanagan, "Bell," Menjou, "Lee," and "The World's Greatest Collection," among others, are highly desired today.

Often collectors do not wish their names to be used when coins are sold. It was later revealed that "The World's Greatest Collection" belonged to F.C.C. Boyd, a famous dealer who owned the Union News Company. The "Memorable Collection" was owned by Jake Shapiro, who used the name "Jake Bell" in his business. The separately offered "Bell" Collection also belonged to him. The "Lee" Collection consisted of duplicates from the cabinet of Louis E. Eliasberg, Sr., the name given to the sale being his initials.

Important catalogues of the 1950s were produced by the New Netherlands Coin Company and were written by the scholarly John J. Ford, Jr., with the assistance of Walter Breen as research associate. These catalogues are to the present writer the most important from that decade as they provide accurate descriptions and a wealth of historical information.

The 1960s saw the addition of catalogues produced by Lester Merkin, Paramount, Rarcoa, and other firms. I regret that the Merkin catalogues are no longer produced for they were especially interesting and provided much information on United States coins for the connoisseur. During the 1970s still other firms produced splendid catalogues of great collections for public sale. Years from now numismatists will isolate many of these as classics.

Many of the catalogues previously mentioned provide a wealth of information for the serious collector and can be obtained for a few dollars each. Sometimes when collections are liquidated, groupings of catalogues from the past 10 or 20 years can be had for little more than the effort to take them away. Perhaps these represent some of the greatest true bargains in numismatics!

No article on the subject of auction catalogues would be complete without mentioning a volume which appeared on the market last August, *United States Numismatic Literature, Volume I,* by John W. Adams (whom I had the pleasure of working with earlier in the year concerning the disposal of his 1794 large cent collection). The first of a projected three volumes, the relatively expensive ($85) but very informative book discusses in detail catalogues from the 19th century. Biographies are given of the Chapmans, J.W. Scott, J.W. Haseltine, W.H. Strobridge, W. Elliot Woodward, and other luminaries of the era. Come to think of it, perhaps the Adams book in itself will be a collectors' item, for only 500 copies were produced, and each is a signed limited edition!. . . .

Collecting auction catalogues? An interesting possibility! Why not consider it.

Profit and Pleasure In Coin Collecting

By Q. David Bowers   1985

I f you had asked me the question: "Why do you collect coins?" back in 1953, when I began my numismatic interest, I am not sure what my answer would have been. I am certain it would not have been "to make a profit" or "to invest."

To me, there is something magical about coins—tangible links with the past. When Robert Rusbar, the tax collector in my hometown of Forty Fort, Pennsylvania, diverted my attention from his collection of rocks and minerals (a hobby interest of mine at the time) to show me his album of Lincoln cents, I was fascinated. Before then, Lincoln cents were Lincoln cents and nothing more. Actually, probably I called them "pennies," but I don't remember. Strangely enough I had never heard of a mintmark and had given no thought as to where such pieces were produced.

Within a half hour of my introduction to numismatics, Bob Rusbar spread out in front of me some Lincoln cents from pocket change. I then discovered that some pieces had a D or S under the date. Excited, I went home, eager to start finding rarities, especially a few 1909-S V.D.B. cents, for Bob Rusbar showed me his (a piece in Uncirculated grade) and told me he had paid the awesome sum of $10 for it which, stated more spectacularly, was a thousand times face value! I was absolutely positive that within the next few days I would have a handful of them, not Uncirculated, but still nice enough to be worth a few dollars each.

Going to the Forty Fort State Bank (which, I understand, has since been merged into some larger banking corporation and no longer exists the same entity), I exchanged $5 or $10 for a bunch of "penny" rolls in red wrappers. Using the two Whitman folders which Bob Rusbar gave me, I quickly began to fill in the various dates. Before long, I had them all the way back to the early 1930s, except for 1931-S, which I never did find. From that point to earlier times there were scattered issues. I was excited when I found my first 1909 V.D.B. (unfortunately not with an S, however!), a coin in what I later would call Extremely Fine condition. Then I found another, then another. By the time a week or two of penny-searching had been completed, I had a whole handful of 1909 V.D.B. cents. They were common in circulation at the time. Fearful that I would tie up too much of my capital, I spent them. Soon, my Lincoln cent set lacked just a dozen or so pieces.

Not satisfied with Lincoln cents, I expanded my numismatic world to include nickels, dimes, quarters, and half dollars. This happened not all at once but over a period of several months. In one of my books I told how in a single afternoon standing at a counter at the Forty Fort State Bank, I put together a complete set of Liberty Walking half dollars from 1916 through 1947—yes, including the varieties of 1921 and the 1938-D. Duplicates of some of the scarce pieces were obtained but not kept.

Somehow, I became acquainted with George Williams, who lived in neighboring Kingston and who maintained an insurance agency in his home. George, who was secretary of the Wilkes-Barre (the largest city in the area) Coin Club, took me under his wing and shepherded me to a meeting of the organization. By that time a few more months had passed and I had become a "dealer" of sorts. Of course, my early deals weren't very impressive. My initial activities consisted of running advertisements in the local newspapers to seek Indian cents, Columbian half dollars, and other obsolete pieces. I was rather successful, and over a period of time I amassed quite a few.

For some reason or other I thought if I placed some advertisements in the West I would find all sorts of rare coins that did not circulate in Pennsylvania, where I lived. So, a few inexpensive classified advertisements were placed in Colorado. Days went by, the mailman came and went, and no serious replies were received. End one Western advertising campaign.

At my first coin club meeting, George Williams versed me in coin club etiquette. Being a dealer, I should not bid at the club auction unless no collectors were bidding. So, if I wanted something for my collection I would bid on it (and state so while bidding), but if I were buying it strictly for "commercial purposes," I would wait until there was no floor activity, then I would step in. Coins were apt to sell for very little in comparison to later values. I recall paying $5 for an 1879 Liberty Seated half dollar which, if I had kept it (which I didn't), would have been worth the best part of $5,000 30 years later!

A Choice Uncirculated Indian cent would cost $1 or so, except that the word "choice" wasn't used. A coin was either Uncirculated or something else—like Very Fine or Extremely Fine. If a club member wanted a Proof set but had forgotten to order one the preceding year, then chances were good that another member would sell him one at issue price or for just a little more. There was never an effort to get "top dollar," although club members were human then as they are now, and some wanted more than others.

I should mention that my viewing of Robert Rusbar's collection of Lincoln cents was not my first encounter with coins, for many years earlier I had acquired an 1892 or 1893 Columbian silver dollar from my maternal grandfather, Chester A. Garrett. This was probably around the end of World War II, so perhaps in an advertisement I could say "in numismatics since 1945"! However, that really didn't count.

As my interest in coins grew, my fascination grew even more. I sought the stories behind coins and eagerly devoured whatever books I could find on the subject. I learned that a veritable gold mine of information was available in back issues of the two leading periodicals of the time, *The Numismatist* and the *Numismatic Scrapbook Magazine*. Further, such back issues were apt to be available free (at club meetings) or for just a few cents each if ordered through the mail.

As years went on, my business prospered, I went to college, I met up with Jim Ruddy and formed the Empire Coin Company, auctions were conducted, rarities were handled, and in general I became very much in the mainstream of the numismatic scene. By 1957, Maurice M. Gould, writing in *The Numismatist,* referred to me as a "well-known dealer." In retrospect, I don't know whether I was deserving of that appellation or not, but it certainly pleased me!

All of the while, I continued learning about coins. I found that $25 spent on a book was apt to bring more pleasure and, ultimately more profit, than the same funds expended on a coin. A coin is a coin is a coin, a poet might have said, but a book represents knowledge.

Profits were made, not by investing in coins but by buying and selling them. I have always felt that it is my customers who should make the investment profits. The function of a dealer is to act as a middleman, to buy from someone who wants to sell and to sell to someone who wants to buy. Considering expenses, profits are often marginal—a $100 transaction probably typically yielded less than $5 net profit at the time, but volume made up for it.

I soon found that profits kept the business going, but true pleasures in numismatics were derived from things other than the coins themselves. People were and are important. When I was a youngster, I received no end of kindness from established old-line dealers, who were willing to help me with my purchases, extend to me trade discounts, give me information, and otherwise encourage my efforts. Customers were likewise friendly. While the occasional customer might "give me a hard time" or try to browbeat me in some sort of a transaction, 99.4% were true gentlemen—the type of people you would enjoy having lunch or dinner with or hearing their life stories. I am happy to say that the same is true today.

With the advent of the 1960s, coins became what some people called an "industry." *Coin World* made its appearance, the Teletype circuit—make that plural, circuits—were wired in, prices jumped, the number of dealers multiplied, and no longer was the hobby a close-knit fraternity.

Today, while I hesitate to use the term "industry" for the coin hobby, for I feel that hobby is a more descriptive name, there is no question that in terms of money changing hands, coins are a big business. One has but to go to a major convention and see hundreds of dealers handling an aggregate of millions of dollars worth of coins. I still have to pause and think how marvelous it was that one single section of our Garrett Collection auction alone brought over $10 million for coins listed in a single catalogue. This is more money then realized by *all* auctions ever held by B. Max Mehl and the Chapman brothers combined!

Today, in 1985, the market is more like the "good old days" than it has been in many years. True, the Teletype is still here, *Coin World* and *Numismatic News* are published weekly, rarities bring tens of thousands or hundreds of thousands of dollars, and a lot is going on, but there also seems to be a return to basic numismatics.

When I speak of "the good old days," I am reminded of archivist Otto Bettmann's statement that "the good old days are not so good after all," or, perhaps he put it more strongly, "the good old days were terrible." Well, in numismatics the days gone by certainly were enjoyable and create many memories now, but many of today's opportunities simply did not exist then.

One has to pay more for coins now—much more—but there are compensating differences. Take, for example, numismatic books. Back in the

Profit and Pleasure in Coin Collecting

early 1950s, the number of significant numismatic books pertaining to the American series, and currently in print, could be counted on the fingers of both hands. Now, in 1985, there are literally dozens of worthwhile volumes. Published knowledge is more readily available than ever before.

Some new directions have been taken in research. For example, David Akers a few years ago compiled listings of gold coin auction appearances. His set of books is useful to the scholar, dealer, and collector alike. One of these days, similar volumes may be available for Liberty Seated, Barber, and other coins.

Morgan silver dollars, admittedly probably the most popular of all 19th-century American series, have been studied forward, backwards, and upside down—with many fine volumes in print concerning them. I venture to say that if you wanted to make Xerox copies of all the information published during the past 20 years on a single issue such as an 1881-S silver dollar, not a rare date, you would have a few dozen pages! All of this makes coin collecting fun and vastly expands the enjoyment of a coin beyond the coin itself. One does not necessarily have to own a coin to enjoy it; one can vicariously appreciate it through the medium of the printed word.

I have never owned a 1703 British five-guinea gold piece with VIGO on it (although a client treated me to the sight of one at his bank recently), but my life is richer for having read its fascinating history. Similarly, I have never owned a Simon Petition crown. Nor have I ever owned the unique 1849 $20, which reposes in the Smithsonian Institution, but I have enjoyed reading about it and seeing the coin during visits to that museum.

I have never met Christian Gobrecht or James B. Longacre, but both of these people have come alive through the articles and paragraphs written about them. Similarly, Augustus Saint-Gaudens, who spent much of his life in Cornish, New Hampshire, not far (about two hours away by car) from my office, is almost a friend, although he died in 1907.

I am often asked if coins hold pleasure for me, now that my firm has handled just about every rarity in the book, has auctioned many remarkable collections, and has been involved otherwise in the hobby for a long time. My answer is that I enjoy every hour of every day in my profession. Once one goes back a few years in history, no two coins encountered are apt to be similar. Each one is different, each one has its own characteristics, and each one is a challenge to evaluate, describe, and present for sale.

Numismatist's Lakeside Companion

In my *Adventures With Rare Coins* book I noted that coins have many appeals, including art, history, romance, and investment. I am not a coin investor for, as noted, my function is buying, selling, and trading coins for my clients. I do collect some pieces, which I have photographed and stored in a bank vault. Included are such esoteric series as United States large cents with counterstamps on them, nickel-size brass tokens with inscriptions such as GOOD FOR ONE TUNE, and copper coins of Vermont of the 1785-1788 era. None of these series would be even an also-ran on the "best investments list" of any self-respecting investment newsletter! In fact, if someone suggested that one seriously approach counterstamped large cents from an investment viewpoint, he would be laughed at. This is not particularly important to me. If I buy a best-selling book at the local book store I do not expect that my $12.95 "investment" will increase in value next year. In fact, the used book will probably be worth very little. Likewise, I have no illusions that my counterstamped large cents will ever be worth more than I paid for them, especially if one considers the hundreds of hours of effort I have spent in their study. But, profit isn't everything. Enjoyment is important. Each of these little counterstamped coins has its own story to tell.

Other writers have agreed with me: pleasure is an important reason for getting involved in numismatics. Last year our firm bought a numismatic library of an old-time New England dealer, cartons of books that are still packed away save for a slim volume, *Coin Collectors' Guide*, which I extracted from the top of a box recently. This pamphlet, written by Deane Sears and Martin Rywell and published in 1961, gives some thoughts which I reprint herewith:

"Collecting, or the accumulation of anything, tends to satisfy a need. Many desires motivate collecting, and the collector may even be unaware of the real reason. Among the motivations for coin collecting may be the need for relaxation; the drive for knowledge, the want to have something no one else has; or the symbolic craving for collecting metallic disks that represent purchasing power.

"A hobby is a pleasure in which one takes an absorbing interest because it fascinates and shuts out immediate problems . . . . A coin may tell you the state which issued it, the territories of the state, the succession of rulers, the pretensions of the rulers, the battles, the sieges, the victories, the economic pattern, the artistic style, and the religion. History is traced on coins as well as religion. History is traced on coins as well as geography. Illustrations are drawn from mythology, geography, religion, government, customs, philosophy, art, history as the caval-

Profit and Pleasure in Coin Collecting

cade of time passes. History's pageant parades through our imagination and the process pushes the past closer and makes it clearer.

"Not only is it an intellectual pursuit, but also coin collecting trains us in the habit of close observation to detect detail. It develops accuracy and description and demands methodical arrangement. If offers the profit of economic gain because it is an excellent monetary investment.

"Divest coin collecting of all other considerations and it offers a relief for those physically or mentally tired. Coin collecting is a sanctuary safe from the stress and strain of a distraught world. To locate and to obtain a wanted coin to complete a collection represents a challenge with the ensuing satisfaction of fulfillment. How each coin was acquired sews a sentimental attachment to the collection. The confirmed collector soon seeks absolute perfection in his coin collection.

"In coin collecting you meet people who have the same hobby and thus you develop new friendships. Coin collecting is a hobby that the family can share and is an antidote to discipline and routine. It is planned relaxation and provides an interest in life often when none existed."

Of the many preceding sentences by Messrs. Sears and Rywell, most are devoted to pleasure and the challenge of collecting. Only one, "It offers the profit of economic gain because it is an excellent monetary investment," discusses a financial aspect.

In another book, *Investing for Pleasure and Profit*, by John Peterson (published by Dow-Jones & Company, publishers of *The Wall Street Journal*), an interesting "warning" is given:

"A warning: collecting can become a passion. If the beginner collector chooses his area wisely, finds a field that will amaze, interest, and intrigue him, and knows the pleasure of becoming absorbed in his pursuit—well, his life will be dramatically changed. He'll become a person in demand for his expertise. That, of course, is one of the pleasurable benefits. A benefit, too, that can lead to sometimes as much profit as his collecting activities themselves."

Obviously, you are interested in coins or you would not be receiving this *Rare Coin Review* issue. But, have you stopped to think about *why* you are interested? Have you stopped to consider what numismatics can offer you besides the chance to acquire specific pieces for your collection? To me, numismatics has meant a very rewarding life, one filled with many enjoyments, many fine people, many wonderful experiences. The hobby invites you to likewise sample its pleasures.

Robert Gilmor, Jr. and the Cradle Age of American Numismatics

By Joel J. Orosz, Ph.D.   1985/86

On November 30, 1848, Robert Gilmor, Jr., one of Baltimore's most prominent citizens, quietly passed away. Gilmor had been a man of taste and wealth. His town residence, his country place, and even his sister-in-law's home groaned under the weight of 50 years of active collecting. The foremost American cabinet of the fine arts was to be found within these walls, including canvases by Cole, Poussin and Cuyp. Less spectacular, but equally valuable, was his massive accumulation of thousands of autographs. Politicians, power brokers, poets—Gilmor had the signatures of everyone from Jefferson to Louis XIV to Wordsworth. And he was a numismatist par excellence—not only did his cabinet contain Greek and Roman coins, but also a nearly complete set, by date, of U.S. coinage, and even an example of the celebrated Brasher doubloon. The formation of Gilmor's coin cabinet would be of interest merely because of its scope and its early date, but there is more. Gilmor built his collection, in part, by having pieces extra-legally coined for him at the United States Mint. The saga of Gilmor and his cozy relations with Adam Eckfeldt, Chief Coiner of the Mint, illuminates much, not only about the Gilmor Collection, but also about the early history of numismatics in America.

Robert Gilmor, Jr. was born in St. Mary's County, Maryland, on September 24, 1774. He was a fortunate infant, for Robert, Sr. was a man of talent and ambition. Already he was making a good living as a merchant; eventually he would become the principal partner in the firm of Bingham, Inglis & Gilmor, importers and retailers specializing in the coffee trade. He was a partner in the first bank established in Baltimore, and he spearheaded the fund-raising efforts to build the fortifications at Whetstone Point, better known to posterity as Fort McHenry.[1] Robert, Sr. was also ambitious for Robert, Jr. and his younger son, William. He provided a stimulating environment for them. In 1797, for instance, they dined with Louis Philippe, the future king of France.[2] Robert, Sr. sent Robert, Jr. to Amsterdam and Marseilles for his education. It was there that the youngster began to acquire a taste for art. In 1799, both Robert and his brother became partners in their father's firm, thereafter logically known as Robert Gilmor & Sons.

Robert, Jr. had hardly joined the firm before his father sent him back to Europe, on a "grand tour" that mixed business with pleasure. He was gone from May 16, 1799 to October 1, 1801, traveling to Scotland, England, Holland, Belgium, France, Italy, Austria, and Prussia.[3] While on this trip his interest in numismatics was awakened by a visit to the Imperial Cabinet of Natural History in Vienna. Robert excitedly wrote to his brother:

The Cabinet of Medals is extremely valuable, and contains gold medals of a size I had no conception of—one of them is worth instrinsically it is said 1,500 guineas. There were several of 150 to 300 ducats value, but the large one just mentioned weighs 12 pounds.[4]

In fact, Gilmor probably began gathering his coin collection on this trip, for shortly before he returned he wrote his brother: "The materials I have collected both for the improvement of art and science will I trust be a rich fund for my friends as well as myself to draw pleasure and instruction from."[5]

Gilmor returned to America with his tastes formed, and with the means to satisfy them. He turned first to art, where he already had the nucleus of a collection, having purchased several paintings in Belgium and Holland. Landscapes were his special passion. He commissioned so many of them that one scholar concluded that he was "probably America's most prominent patron of landscape painting during the first three decades of the 19th century."[6] By the time of his death, Gilmor's art collection was reputed to be America's finest. More than that, it was a school. Gilmor opened it up to budding artists for study, and Horatio Greenough, among others, took his early training at Gilmor's home.[7]

Gilmor soon reached a position of equal prominence in the field of autograph collecting. The 1820s was the watershed decade for this hobby. James Monroe, "the last of the cocked hats," was in the White House. The Marquis de Lafayette made his triumphal return visit in 1824. In 1826

Robert Gilmor, Jr.

came the 50th anniversary of the Declaration of Independence and the extraordinary confluence of the deaths of ex-Presidents Jefferson and Adams on July 4. The revolutionary generation was passing, and everyone, it seemed, wanted to preserve its relics—and so began the craze for autographs. No one indulged in this mania more than Robert Gilmor, Jr. By 1832, he had published a catalogue of his holdings which enumerated 1,244 autographs (624 of which were American). A second catalogue, issued in 1841, listed approximately 1,700 "foreign" autographs alone.[8] In 1845 he became the second collector to complete a set of the signers of the Declaration of Independence.[9] It is small wonder that a contemporary author rated the Gilmor Collection as one of the three most valuable in America.[10]

The outburst of nostalgia for America's brilliant revolutionary past gave the infant hobby of numismatics an enormous boost. Each old coin was a tangible piece of history, a direct link to an earlier, more glorious time. What had been the domain of a select few collectors now became attractive to a wider audience. Interestingly, a by-product of the hero's welcome accorded to Lafayette added fuel to this fire. During and after his visit, hundreds of cents and half dollars (among other coins) were counterstamped in the center with a small image of Lafayette on one side, and George Washington on the other. These circulated widely, and for the first time, many Americans noticed coins as something beyond a mere medium of exhange. Historical societies and museums, which had always collected coins, were spurred by the new spirit, and redoubled their efforts to capture these pieces of American history.

Robert Gilmor, Jr., even as he was accumulating art and autographs, was very much a part of the emerging numismatic scene. As early as 1821, we find him writing a "Mr. Bogard" in New York on matters numismatic.[11] Gilmor wrote that he had received a box of medals that "Bogard" had picked up for him at the New York Customs House, but complained that one gold medal was missing. "Presuming you were present when the box was opened," wrote Gilmor, "your testimony to the (manufacturer?) will enable me to claim of him a deduction of the . . .cost of one of these medals, 11 guineas."[12] If only one of the medals cost 11 guineas, Gilmor was spending a considerable sum on his numismatic collection, according to the standards of the time.

By that same year, Robert had managed to form a connection at the United States Mint who would help him build his coin collection for the next two decades. 1821 also happened to mark the 50th wedding anniversary of the Robert, Jr.'s parents, Robert, Sr. and Louisa.

Robert, Jr. was by now one of the leading businessmen in America, and he apparently took a short trip to Philadelphia to use his influence on Mint Director Robert Patterson and Chief Coiner Adam Eckfeldt. Gilmor wanted something very special to honor his parent's golden wedding anniversary, and he got it: the second private medal struck by the United States Mint.[13] The first had honored the great Dr. Benjamin Rush, signer of the Declaration of Independence; now the second would commemorate the conjugal bliss of Robert's parents. The medal itself, which features busts of Mr. and Mrs. Gilmor on the obverse and a putto on the reverse, is not particularly outstanding as a work of art, but it is important as a piece of evidence, for it clearly proves a connection between the Baltimore collector and the top echelons of the Mint. Anyone with enough "pull" to have a private medal struck at the Mint would also have the potential to persuade the chief coiner to surreptitiously recoin his desiderata. As we shall see Robert was actively engaging in such activities before 1841.

Even as Robert was taking part in these shenanigans, a group of men in Washington was casting covetous glances at his collections. Who these men were, and what they were doing, makes a fascinating story. The tale begins, oddly enough with a Briton in Genoa. James Smithson, the wealthy but illegitimate son of the Duke of Northumberland, died in Genoa in 1829. the curious terms of his will provided for the establishment, at Washington, DC, of the "Smithsonian Institution," for the "increase and diffusion of knowledge among men." The American Congress was bewildered by this unexpected bequest. Ought it to be accepted at all? Would not acceptance of foreign charity besmirch our pride as a sovereign nation? Such objections were overcome, but, then, what sort of institution was the Smithsonian to be? A national university? A school of agriculture? A museum? A library? An observatory? A research institution? The debate dragged on for years.

As the rhetorical fireworks continued, Joel Robert Poinsett (1799-1851), the sitting Secretary of War, quietly, almost deviously, entered the fray. Poinsett's plan was simple; he would found an organization called the National Institute for the Promotion of Science, create a huge museum under its care, and then present it to Congress as a *fait accompli*. Congress would then hand over the Smithson bequest to the National Institute, and the issue would be settled. By May 1840 a constitution for the National Institute had been written, and within a year the United States government's National Cabinet of Curiosities and the specimens from the United States Exploring Expedition to the Southern Pacific were under the Institute's care.[14] Congress, however, was not yet prepared to award the Smithson bequest to the National Institute.

To help Congress make up its mind, Poinsett determined to enroll prominent patrons from all over the country. Accordingly, around the middle of 1840, Gilmor was offered a corresponding membership in the National Institute. He was enthusiastic in his reply, saying, "It will afford me much pleasure to render any service in my power to so valuable an Institution, and one so long wanted in this country as a nucleus of an immense National Collection or Museum..."[15] But Poinsett hoped for more than a general expression of support; he wanted donations of money and material. So, early in 1841, he tried again, sending a copy of the Institute's *Proceedings* to Gilmor. The Baltimore collector's reply to Poinsett is dated April 14, 1841. It is a remarkably candid letter, one which sheds much light on the state of numismatics in the 1840s and which also details a few of the Mint's clandestine activities.

After a page and one-half of general conversation with Poinsett, Gilmor got down to brass tacks:

One result, good it may be thought, issues from the perusal of the "Proceedings" I have just received, and that is that it induces me to suggest to the Society the forming *without delay* of [as] complete a collection of the coinage of the Mint, and the earlier one [sic] of [the] several states, as a[n] [interesting?] part of its historical department.

Several significant facts emerge from this brief passage. First, Gilmor obviously recognized the historical importance of both colonial and United States Mint coinage. Second, his interest transcended those of a mere curio collector, for he advocated a systematic collection of coinage for historical purposes. Finally, he clearly felt a sense of urgency in recommending that the work begin immediately. Gilmor continued:

I believe no other person but myself ever thought of making such a one, which I began many years ago and have collected every gold, silver and copper coin issued from the Mint, which was to be had, but strange as it may seem, I could more easily make a complete collection of Greek and Roman coins than American, notwithstanding the recent establishment of the Mint—with all my industry and perseverance, I am yet deficient in seven gold coins (an eagle of 1802 among them), 10 silver ones and three copper[.] Hence my expression above, "without delay." So many of our gold and silver coins have been banished [from] the country by the balance of trade, that sometimes a whole years [sic] coinage of half dollars disappears.[17]

Gilmor's first statement is ambiguous. Was he unaware of the collecting activities of his contemporaries Joseph Mickley and Matthew Stickney, or did he feel that they were not collecting systematically?[18] Equally unclear is his statement that he began collecting "many years ago." Did he begin on his return from Europe in 1801, or was it later? There can be no doubt, however, that collecting American coinage was a difficult task, for the early issues were elusive, even in 1841. Imagine how difficult it must have been for Gilmor, with no dealers, no reference books, and practically no auctions on which to rely! The bulk of his prizes must have been plucked from circulation as they came over the counter at Robert Gilmor & Sons. Even worse, as he observed at the end of the passage, American gold and silver coins were worth a premium if converted into bullion, so thousands of desirable specimens were annually disappearing into the melting pot. Yet, despite these handicaps, Gilmor had assembled a set of United States coinage by date that was nearly complete! He had undoubtedly paid no attention to mintmarks; virtually no one did, until Augustus Heaton called attention to them more than 50 years later.[19] The lack of reference books certainly plagued Gilmor, for he was searching for "an eagle of 1802," which never existed! It is tantalizing to speculate about the gaps in the Gilmor cabinet. Was he missing the 1815 and 1822 half eagles? The 1802 half dime? The 1799 cent? Or was there a "common" issue or two that proved elusive?

Our pioneer numismatist had much more to say on the subject:
The Mint has aided me considerably, and has even provided my desiderata from the old dies, when I require it—Mr. Eckfeldt of the Mint has been of great service to me, and was stimulated by my attempt to commence one for the Mint itself, which realy [sic] ought not to be without a specimen of every one of its coins—by timely attention to the subject whoever has charge of the Department may soon make a considerable advance towards obtaining those in circulation, but no time should be lost, as the old gold coin is gradually disappearing by being coined into the new. The Mint would no doubt aid you in this, and coin your deficiencies.[20]

This is by far the most interesting part of the letter. For one thing, Gilmor claimed to be the father of the Mint Cabinet, now the National Numismatic Collection of the Smithsonian Institution. We probably will never know if Gilmor really did inspire Eckfeldt and DuBois to begin the collection; if so, he has never received the proper credit.[21] However, there is one verifiable bombshell in this passage. Never before have we found contemporary proof that the Mint was striking fancy pieces for collectors. But here, Gilmor quite casually mentions that the Mint had "provided my desiderata from the old dies, when I require it." And he even named the provider: Adam Eckfeldt, the aged former chief coiner. This seems highly plausible. Gilmor had had connections at the Mint at least since 1821, and he undoubtedly knew Eckfeldt well. Moreover, there was a neat coincidence, for Gilmor was building his collection while Eckfeldt and DuBois were assembling the Mint Cabinet. It would be beneficial to all concerned if the Mint were to recoin certain rarities and trade them to Gilmor for his duplicates. Thus Gilmor and Eckfeldt had a symbiotic, if somewhat underhanded, relationship.

It is important to remember, however, that Gilmor's "admissions" with regard to coining were not a confession to wrongdoing. They were made, quite openly, to a man who only a month before had been the Secretary of War—along with the recommendation that he follow the same practice! Clearly Gilmor felt that in recoining, neither the Mint nor the collector was doing anything wrong. The stigma of impropriety that later generations would apply to recoining did not exist in 1841. In its place was a serene confidence that "the Mint would no doubt...coin your deficiencies."

Gilmor had a final recommendation for Poinsett:

P.S. Would it not also be worthwhile to make a collection of the old Continental money—(paper I mean)—It has lessons historical, and so far interesting, besides having in many cases the autographs of many of our patriots—[22]

The autograph collector in Gilmor was speaking here. Paper money was a natural complement to coined money, and even more interesting when treated as an autograph-bearing document as well. Surprisingly, however, Gilmor does not seem to have formed such a collection himself.

Gilmor's suggestions to Poinsett unfortunately fell on deaf ears. The National Institute did collect a few coins, but only haphazardly. In the meantime, Poinsett's efforts to capture the Smithson endowment failed, and the National Institute went into a prolonged decline, finally expiring in 1862. It was then completely absorbed by the Smithsonian Institution. Ironically, although Gilmor's idea of a numismatic collection for the National Institute never came to pass, the Smithsonian, by combining the elements of the National Institute and the Mint Cabinet, established the National Numismatic Collection, which may well include some pieces which once belonged to Gilmor.

Gilmor's letter to Poinsett makes it clear that he was still in possession of his numismatic collection in 1841, a point which was previously unclear.[23] Moreover, Gilmor was also the owner of one of the greatest prizes in all of American numismatics, the legendary Brasher doubloon.[24] Just how he came to own it is unclear, but it seems likely that the doubloon may have been redeemed at the Mint as bullion, during the 1830s where it was saved by Eckfeldt or DuBois, and then sold or traded to Gilmor. This is a more plausible explanation than one which suggests that it was cashed in at a bank or used for payment at Robert Gilmor & Sons. At any rate, the doubloon was in the Gilmor cabinet by 1840, for in that year another pioneer numismatist, William G. Stearns of Boston, described it in a letter to a "Dr. Bowditch" in England. The letter is dated March 18, 1840, and in it, Stearns has this to say about the Brasher:

There is also a gold coin of New York, of the value of about $10, but I know nothing of the place of its coinage, or its history. *Obverse,* the arms of New York. *Reverse,* the arms of the United States. The only specimen within my knowledge, is in the possession of Mr. Gilmor of Baltimore. I have not seen the coin, and do not even know its date.[25]

As of this writing, Stearns' letter provides the earliest documented case of a Brasher doubloon being held by a private collector. Thanks to the enterprising research of Carl W.A. Carlson, we now know the pedigree for this coin from Gilmor to the present owner, and what a pedigree it is! The Gilmor Brasher has been handled by such great dealers as Lyman Low and B. Max Mehl, and has graced the cabinets of such notable collectors as Robert Coulton Davis, James Ten Eyck, and eventually the immortal Virgil Brand. Its last appearance in the marketplace was as Lot No. 1433 in Auction '79, where the piece realized $435,000.[26]

Of the hundreds of coins that once comprised Robert Gilmor, Jr.'s cabinet, this is one of only three that we can trace to his ownership with confidence. That it was once a massive accumulation there can be no doubt. In addition to his enumeration of the collection of his letter to Poinsett, Gilmor left behind a ledger of what he called his "Pictures, Statues, and Medals Account." There were two columns, one headed "Amount," for the sum actually spent on his collection, and the other headed "Actual Value" presumably, an estimate of what the collections would realize at auction. At the height of his activities, in 1841, he lists an "Amount" of $27,602 and an "Actual Value" of $20,000.[27] If accurate, these figures suggest enormous collections in the fields of art and numismatics; autographs being in a separate account. Truly, Robert Gilmor, Jr. was one of the foremost collectors of his generation.

The Gilmor Collection, one of the earliest systematic accumulations of American coinage, is now thoroughly dispersed. Of the hundreds, perhaps thousands of coins that comprised it, we can trace only one, the "Ten Eyck-Brand" Brasher doubloon, down to the present. What happened to the others?

A partial answer is found in Emmanuel Joseph Attinelli's classic work, *Numisgraphics,* a bibliography of American numismatic auction catalogues before 1876. Attinelli lists a sale of paintings, statuary, and engravings from Gilmor's art collection, dated March 8, 1849, in which offering No. 143 was a "Lot of Greek and Roman Coins."[28] Attinelli added parenthetically:

This gentleman had at one time one of the largest and finest collections of his day, which he disposed of at a private sale. "From the Gilmor Collection" was a recommendation, which immediately gave high character to a coin or medal.[29]

Was there a catalogue issued for this private sale? Attinelli was unaware of one, and the author has been unable to find one. Hence the exact contents of the Gilmor Collection may remain forever a mystery. The date of the sale may be at least reduced to a range. Gilmor still owned his coins when he wrote to Poinsett in 1841, but Attinelli says he sold them before his death in 1848. It may be possible to refine the date further, for in his ledgers, the "Actual Value" of his Pictures, Statues, and Medals dips from $20,000 in 1841 to $15,000 in 1842 to $10,000 in 1843. Therefore, it is likely that the coin sale was held between 1841 and 1843.[30]

Where did the coins go? The Mint undoubtedly would have wished to fill some gaps in its cabinet at the Gilmor sale, but its tiny budget for acquisitions must have prevented its officers from buying much. A more likely buyer was Robert's good friend, Mendes I. Cohen (1796-1879), a Baltimore banker and numismatist of renown. It is possible that Cohen bought several of Gilmor's coins. However, he probably did not purchase the Gilmor Collection *en bloc,* for the 1875 auction of the Cohen Collection, catalogued by Edward Cogan, was not nearly as complete as the Gilmor Collection in United States issues. It does not seem probable that any significant number of the coins went to the National Institute, for the Institute held only 70 United States coins and 160 ancient Greek and Roman pieces.[31]

Carl Carlson speculates that the sale was indeed a private one, hence no catalogue would have been printed. It is his opinion that most of the Gilmor Collection was purchased by Joseph Mickley, with a few "heirloom" coins retained by the Gilmor family. This cannot be proved, but it certainly is plausible. It would explain how Mickley was able to build so comprehensive a collection, and it might also suggest a source for Mickley's genuine 1822 half eagle, which he eventually sold, through W. Elliot Woodward, to William Sumner Appleton. In any case, given the small number of serious collectors in the early 1840s, Mickley appears to be the "prime suspect" as the purchaser.[32]

So it seems reasonable that the sale was held between 1841 and 1843, and that Joseph Mickley bought most of the collection. There is, however, a contradictory piece of evidence. William Harvey Strobridge, the much-respected and scholarly early coin dealer, catalogued the collection of E.J. Snow, which was sold at auction March 19-21, 1878. It was Strobridge's 29th and final sale, for blindness, induced by his exhaustive cataloguing of the George Stenz Collection three years earlier, overtook him shortly thereafter.

In his introduction to the Snow sale, Strobridge had this to say:
About 20 years ago [1858], Mr. E.J. Snow, of Baltimore, and the writer, who soon after became a resident of that city, commenced life together as amateurs and collectors of "rare old coins;" we followed our pursuit in great harmony until the breaking out of the war in 1861. Returning to New York in that year, I brought with me all of Mr. Snow's American coins . . .The great Gilmour [sic] collection was then breaking up, and out of it I had obtained many valuable pieces, among them the pattern groat of Edward I, No. 272 of this catalogue, and the Indian Peace Medal of George II, No. 490, of which I have never seen another example.[33]

Strobridge's chance mention of the "Gilmour" Collection allows us to positively identify two more pieces that were in Robert, Jr.'s cabinet. But it seems to contradict our chronology, for Strobridge appears to suggest that the main body of the collection was sold around the year 1861. This hardly squares with Attinelli's testimony, however, which holds that Gilmor held a private sale before his death, and that his heirs sold his Greek and Roman coins shortly after his passing.

Upon closer examination of all of the evidence, it is possible to construct a sequence of events that fits all of the known facts. Admittedly, it is highly conjectural, but it may suffice until such time as better evidence is found.

Robert Gilmor, Jr.

We know from Gilmor's letter to Poinsett that his coin collection was nearly complete as of 1841, lacking, by his own count, seven gold coins, 10 silver coins and three copper pieces. Perhaps over the next year, he was able to substantially complete his date run, or, more likely, he found the remaining gaps impossible to fill. In either case, it is likely that Robert tired of the chase, and decided to sell the lion's share of his collection, including his date runs of U.S. Mint issues, but not including his Greek and Roman coins, nor certain "special" pieces, like the Brasher doubloon, the pattern groat of Edward I, and the Indian Peace Medal of George II (probably either Betts 396 or 401). Therefore, in 1842 or 1843, Robert Gilmor, Jr. privately sold the bulk of his collection to one or more collectors; it is possible that Joseph Mickley bought it *en bloc*.

Gilmor died in 1848, and his heirs decided to dispose of the Greek and Roman coins, which they did in the sale of March 8, 1849 cited by Attinelli. They retained Robert's "special" coins, however, as heirloom keepsakes of their uncle. They owned these coins until 1861, when the impending crisis of the Civil War loomed over their heads. Living as they did in the border town of Baltimore, they were vulnerable to the armies of both sides in the conflict. It would be prudent, therefore, to convert the "heirloom" coins into cash, which could be easily hidden. How many "heirloom" coins were sold in 1861? It is impossible to say, but if the two we know of were representative of their quality, the collection would certainly merit Strobridge's description of it: "great."

We know, however, that at least one of the "heirloom" coins was retained by the Gilmor family, at least until 1886: Robert's Brasher doubloon. There may have been others as well. As to the ultimate fate of the groat and the Indian Peace Medal, the author has been unable to trace them. The answer may be found in a copy of the Snow Collection catalogue, for it was common practice in the 19th century for sale attendees to annotate catalogues with prices and names of purchasers. If such a catalogue were to be found, it might yet be possible to trace the subsequent history of these two pieces. The author would be grateful for any information anyone might provide on this point.

We do know what became of Gilmor's Brasher doubloon. That passed, apparently through inheritance, to Robert's great-nephew, Harry Gilmor (1838-1883). Although it cannot be proved conclusively, it seems very likely that Lyman Low purchased the Brasher doubloon from Harry's heirs; at any rate, the doubloon appeared as Lot 524 in Low's June 27, 1886 sale of the John T. Raymond Collection.[34] If, as seems very likely, Low purchased the Brasher from Harry's heirs, he may have purchased other "heirloom" coins inherited from Robert, Jr. as well. This much can be reconstructed; the full story is probably lost forever.

One thing, however, can be indisputably concluded from the existing evidence: it is time for the name of Robert Gilmor, Jr. to be elevated to the front rank of antebellum collectors, along with Mickley and Stickney. It is to these pioneers that we owe gratitude for saving countless coins from the melting pot, for gathering pieces that would pass from sale to sale, collection to collection, down through the generations. Perhaps that well-worn piece filling a hole in your album once served a similar function in Robert Gilmor, Jr.'s cabinet. Add to such tantalizing musings the question of which pieces were missing, which were struck surreptitiously at the Mint and the fact that much of the story remains unknown, and Gilmor's history becomes mesmerizing as well as important, a riddle that will always fascinate because it will never be completely solved.

FOOTNOTES

1 Lyman Abbot, et. al., Eds., *The National Cyclopedia of American Biography* (New York: James T. White & Co., 1909), Vol. XI, pp., 401-402. Alternatively, Francis C. Haber maintains that it was Dorchester County. See Haber, "Robert Gilmor, Jr.—Pioneer American Autograph Collector," Manuscripts 7 (Fall 1954), p. 13.

2 Louis Phillipe, Diary of My Travels in America, Trans. by Stephen Becker. (New York: Delacorte Press, 1977), p. 19.

3 William Gilmor (Robert, Jr.'s brother), "Family Record for the Use of My Children and their Successors," Ms. No. 387, Box No. 2, Robert Gilmor Papers, Maryland Historical Society.

4 Robert Gilmor, Jr. to William Gilmor, June 27, 1801. "Robert Gilmor, Letters Written to His Brother in America in the Years 1800 and 1801," Ms. No. 387, Box No. 1, Vol. 4, Letter 47. Robert Gilmor Papers. Maryland Historical Society.

5 Ibid., Letter 51, August 8, 1801.

6 Lillian B. Miller, *Patrons and Patriotism: The Encouragement of the Fine Arts in the United States, 1790-1860* (Chicago: University of Chicago Press, 1966), p. 150.

7 Ibid., p. 131.

8 Robert Gilmor, Jr., "Catalog of the Collection of Autographs in the Possession of Robert Gilmor of Baltimore, 1832," and "Catalog of the Collection of Autographs in the Possession of Robert Gilmor of Baltimore, 1841." Both in the collection of the Maryland Historical Society.

9 The first was William B. Sprague of Albany. See Haber, "Robert Gilmor, Jr.," p. 14.

10 Reverend S. Gilman, "A Week Among the Autographs" in Caroline H. Gilman, *The Poetry of Travelling in the United States* (New York: S. Colman, 1838), Reprint ed., Upper Saddle River, N.J.: Literature House Gregg Press, 1970, pp. 374-75.

11 "Mr. Bogard" was probably John G. Bogert, a member of the New York Historical Society and an early numismatist in New York. Bogert was for a time the Chairman of the Committee on Coins and Medals of the New York Historical Society. See *Minutes* of

Robert Gilmor, Jr.

the New York Historical Society, August 12, 1817 and June 9, 1818, at the New York Historical Society.

12 Robert Gilmor, Jr. to "Mr. Bogard" August 9, 1821. Misc. Mss.—Gilmor, New York Historical Society. If "Mr. Bogard" was indeed John Bogert, the mystery of the missing medal may be explicable. On February 19, 1822 Bogert resigned from the New York Historical Society. He had in fact been asked to resign because an investigative committee found he had stolen coins from the Society's cabinet. Perhaps Robert Gilmor, Jr. was another of his victims. See New York Historical Society *Minutes*, August 14, 1821; November 13, 1821; December 11, 1821; and February 19, 1822.

13 The author is indebted to Carl W.A. Carlson for information relating to the Gilmor anniversary medal. See Carlson, "Brasher Doubloon Research Revealing," *Coin World* Vol. 23 (August 25, 1982), pp. 1, 28, 54 and 59. The Gilmor anniversary medal itself is fairly rare; a reasonable estimate of the surviving specimens is 50 to 75 examples.

14 The United States government owned a collection of objects it had acquired from various sources, including gifts from foreign governments and spoils of war, which was known as the National Cabinet of Curiosities. The government also held a massive collection of the flora and fauna of the South Pacific and other maritime areas, which had been collected by the United States Exploring Expedition, a naval squadron which had circumnavigated the globe from 1838 to 1842 on a voyage of scientific discovery.

15 Robert Gilmor, Jr. to Francis Markoe, Jr., September 28, 1840. Record Unit 7058, National Institute Records, Box 2, Smithsonian Institution Archives.

16 Robert Gilmor, Jr. to Joel Roberts Poinsett, April 14, 1841. Joel Roberts Poinsett Papers. Historical Society of Pennsylvania. Among his many other accomplishments, Poinsett is credited with introducing the poinsettia to America, hence it was named in his honor.

17 Ibid.

18 The Pennsylvanian Joseph J. Mickley (1799-1878), was among the earliest serious numismatists in America. Mickley began collecting coins in 1816 by forming a date run of large cents. A burglary in 1867 made him decide to dispose of the balance of his collection, which he did on October 28, 1867, in a sale catalogue by W. Elliot Woodward. The auction realized $13,308.17, an enormous sum for a coin sale at that time. Matthew Stickney (1805-1894) of Salem, Massachusetts, began collecting coins around the year 1819. Among his other accomplishments, he was the first private collector to own an 1804 silver dollar. Stickney's magnificent collection was auctioned in Philadelphia on June 25-29, 1907 by Henry Chapman. See Q. David Bowers' *The History of United States Coinage as Illustrated by the Garrett Collection* (Los Angeles: Bowers and Ruddy Galleries, Inc., 1979), pp. 13-14 and 149-150; Emmanuel J. Attinelli, *Numisgraphics, or a List of Catalogues in Which Occur Coins or Medals, Which Have Been Sold by Auction in the United States* (New York: 1876), Reprint ed., *A Bibliography of Numismatic Auction Catalogues, 1828-1875.* (Lawrence, Mass.: Quarterman Publications, Inc. 1976), pp. 48-49; Eric P. Newman and Kenneth Bressett, *The Fantastic 1804 Silver dollar* (Racine: Whitman Publishing Company, 1962), pp. 71-72.

19 Augustus Heaton (1844-1930), an artist, poet, architect and numismatist, authored a slim volume entitled *A Treatise on the Coinage of the United States Branch Mints in 1893.* This little book had a big effect, for soon numismatists were avidly collecting branch mint pieces they had formerly ignored. An excellent summary of "Heaton's Mint Marks" can be found in Bowers' *The History of United States Coinage*, pp. 49-52.

20 Gilmor to Poinsett, April 14, 1841, previously cited.

21 Adam Eckfeldt (1769-1852) began his long association with the United States Mint in 1792. As Chief Coiner from 1814 to 1839, Eckfeldt was perfectly capable of striking delicacies for Gilmor. Even after his retirement in 1839, Eckfeldt spent much of his time at the

— *133* —

Mint, offering advice and even occasional volunteer labor. Eckfeldt saved the first coins for the Mint Cabinet, then turned that duty over to William E. DuBois (1810-1881), who held a series of posts at the Mint beginning in 1833. DuBois eventually became Assayer.

22 Gilmor to Poinsett, April 14, 1841, previously cited.

23 Carl W.A. Carlson, in his previously cited *Coin World* article, says that by 1840 it is probable that Robert Gilmor, Jr.'s coin collection was in the possession of his son, also named Robert. This is erroneous on two counts. First, as we have seen, Robert, Jr. was still in possession of his coins in 1841, and second, Robert, Jr. and his wife were childless. The third Robert Gilmor (1808-1875), whom Carlson mentions was the son of Robert Jr.'s brother William (ca. 1775-1829), thus was Robert, Jr.'s nephew. See Carlson, "Brasher Doubloon Research," p. 28, and "Gilmor Family Genealogy," Ms. No. 387, Box 2, Robert Gilmor Papers, Maryland Historical Society.

24 The discussion that follows owes much to the pioneering research of Carl W.A. Carlson, who meticulously pieced together the story of Gilmor's Brasher and its pedigree. See "Brasher Doubloon Research," p. 28 and p. 54 for the full story.

25 William G. Stearns to "Dr. Bowditch," March 18, 1840. Printed in *The American Journal of Numismatics* 7 (October, 1872), p.36. Stearns' collection, much added to by his descendants C.H. and George M. Stearns, was sold by Mayflower Coin Auctions on December 2 and 3, 1966.

26 The following, with minor corrections, is the pedigree given by Carl Carlson in "Brasher Doubloon Research":
 1. Acquired by Robert Gilmor, Jr. before 1840, possibly from the U.S. Mint.
 2. Presumably passed by inheritance to Robert Gilmor (1810-1875), Robert Jr.'s nephew; thence presumably passed by inheritance to Harry Gilmor (1838-1883), Robert Jr.'s great-nephew.
 3. Purchased in 1886 by Lyman Low for about $100.
 4. Offered as Lot #524 in Low's June 27, 1887 sale of the John T. Raymond Collection (failed to reach reserve and was bought back by Low)
 5. Sold by private treaty to Harold P. Newlin of Philadelphia in 1887.
 6. Sold by private treaty in 1887 or 1888 to Robert Coulton Davis of Philadelphia.
 7. Listed in the 1889 "sale" of the Robert Coulton David Collection, which was never actually auctioned.
 8. Sold by private treaty to John G. Mills.
 9. Passed privately from the Mills collection to James Ten Eyck.
 10. Purchased by Virgil Brand in B. Max Mehl's sale of the Ten Eyck Collection in 1922.
 11. Passed from the Brand estate to the Capitol Coin Company.
 12. Sold on behalf of Capitol Coin Company's successors, the Coin and Currency Institute, as Lot 1433 in RARCOA's session of Auction '79, to Walter Perschke of Numisco, for $435,000.

27 Robert Gilmor, Jr. "Private Memoranda Relating to the Affairs of Robert Gilmor," Ms. Box 1, Robert Gilmor Papers, Maryland Historical Society.

28 Attinelli, *A Bibliography of Numismatic Auction Catalogues*, p.8.

29 Ibid.

30 Robert Gilmor, Jr. "Private Memoranda" previously cited.

31 Vladimir Clain-Stefanelli, *History of the National Numismatic Collections*, Contributions from the Museum of History and Technology, Paper 31 (Washington, DC, Smithsonian Institution, 1970), p.67. According to Stefanelli, the institute possessed 1,810 medieval and modern bronze and silver coins, but at least 853 of them probably came from a donor other than Gilmor.

Robert Gilmor, Jr.

32 Conversation with Carl W.A. Carlson, September, 1985. See also, Carl Carlson, "Research Extends Half Eagle Pedigrees," *Coin World* 26 (August 7, 1985), p. 57.

33 William Harvey Strobridge, *Catalogue of the Snow Collection of Modern Silver Medals and Coins With a Copious Appendix*, New York: March 19-21, 1878, 60 pp. The quoted sections were reproduced in Cal Wilson, *Auction sale XV, Important Numismatic Books*, January 16-17, 1987, p. 89.

34 See Carlson, "Brasher Doubloon Research," p. 28 and p. 54.

Acknowledgements: This article could not have been written without the generous help of several individuals. Q. David Bowers gave innumerable suggestions for further research and provided invaluable introductions to other numismatic scholars. Carl W.A. Carlson made available research he had conducted into the history of the Gilmor anniversary medal and Gilmor's Brasher doubloon. Mr. Carlson also conversed with me at length on this subject, unselfishly sharing his own insights. John J. Ford and David Enders Tripp shared their wide-ranging numismatic expertise with me. I am indebted to the unselfish aid all four of these gentlemen provided me.

I also owe thanks to two librarians: Krista Hesselbein of *Coin World,* and Nancy Green of the American Numismatic Association, for promptly and cheerfully finding everything I needed.

The Pleasures of Book Collecting

By Armand Champa   1988

The following article is by Armand Champa, a well-known collector of numismatic literature. Indeed, his library of reference books, auction catalogues and, numismatic periodicals is one of the finest ever formed.

Rare Coin Review readers may recall that in 1972 we had the pleasure of handling Armand Champa's coin collection at auction. After selling his coins, his interest turned to numismatic literature.

The Beginning

I cannot remember how I got started collecting numismatic literature, but I do remember back around 1966 or 1967 a local coin dealer called me and asked if I would be interested in a large group of catalogues. In the lot were approximately 75 by B. Max Mehl, a bunch of Bolender catalogues amounting to about 60 copies, and a further 60 copies of catalogues issued by Barney Bluestone, an old-time dealer in Syracuse, New York.

I asked him how much he wanted, and he said that $1 dollar each would take the group. I told him I would pay 50c each, and he told me to come down and pick them up. Holy cow—almost 200 catalogues for $100!

Years later, all of these became duplicates and were sold in connection with the Bowers and Ruddy Galleries sale of the Dr. Curtis Paxman Collection and other properties (1974). However, by this time I had been at it for quite a while and had a large library.

Right after my purchase of the B. Max Mehl catalogues in 1966 or 1967, I went through each of these auctions and discovered that Mehl did not handle more than three specimens of 1877 pattern half dollars in all of the auctions I surveyed. In his major sales, which were put up in large-sized catalogues bearing such names as Atwater, Dunham, Neil, Roach, Farouk, Ten Eyck, Granberg, Griffin, Manning, Roe, Green, Geiss, and Conover, not one had even a single 1877 pattern half dollar! The largest pattern collection Mehl ever had was the Olson Collection, which contained approximately 625 lots, including many great rarities. Would you believe that there was just one 1877 pattern half dollar!

Armed with this information I sent out want lists to several of the leading coin dealers of the day, including Bowers and Ruddy Galleries, the predecessor of Bowers and Merena Galleries—seeking to buy any and all 1877 pattern half dollars. Readers of this article know the rest of the story: I went from one success to another, by a lot of searching acquired many really great pieces, and all of these were eventually catalogued for auction by Dave Bowers and sold in 1972.

My Love for Books

I have a great love for numismatic books and related literature. My feeling on the subject can be summed up by a commentary by Mr. Charles Feinberg, as printed in a catalogue issued by Sotheby's on December 15, 1986:

"One lives by mistakes and learns by experience at auctions—experiences that are good and bad. You've got to make up your mind before the auction, how badly you want an item regardless of what the appraisers give you as an indication of an item's worth. You in your own mind have to decide what you can afford.

"The only regrets I have are the items I didn't get, the ones that got away—these are my lasting regrets. Collecting has brought me welcomes and honors—books have brought me a full life, but I've had the best enjoyment from chasing books at auctions."

In my own library, my pride and joy, and a great rarity, is Raphael P. Thian's personal copy of the *Register of the Confederate States Treasury Notes*, published in Washington in 1880. This deluxe copy came along with Thian's album of Confederate States of America currency notes and was acquired from the son of the late Herman Englehardt, who years ago was a dealer in California. Englehardt had acquired the album in 1962 from two granddaughters of Thian. A second copy of this work, not as nice, is in my library, and I have learned that a third copy is

The Pleasures of Book Collecting

possessed by the Harvard University Library in Cambridge, Massachusetts. John J. Ford, Jr. also possesses one. Just five copies were made, to my knowledge.

If this book were a coin I would compare it with and call it my "Brasher doubloon." So far as the value today is concerned, books have not achieved even remotely near the prices achieved by coins, but still a copy of the Thian book was appraised at $20,000 several years ago, and I suspect that a value of $30,000 may be correct today.

Another prize book in my library, right at the top of my list, is the 16-page pamphlet by Dr. Edward Maris on the subject of 1794 large cents, the second edition, 1870. I know of only two other copies: examples in the Ford Collection and in the American Numismatic Society Library. So far as I know, this book has appeared at auction only two times, both being Lyman H. Low auctions, May 9, 1887 and October 13, 1906.

I also have the first edition of this book, 1869, which is also rare, but not in the category of the second edition. I have traced eight auction appearances of this book, most of them being years ago, but two of them being in relatively modern times in sales conducted by George Kolbe.

Another book pertaining to Maris is the sale of Dr. Maris' collection on June 21, 1886, the edition with six photographic plates. This deluxe edition is wider and taller in format than other editions seen. I have traced just three other examples with certainty: the Harry Bass Collection copy (from the Fuld Library), the John Adams Collection, and the Del Bland Collection (from my sale of Lester Merkin's library, although it was Richard Picker's copy). The American Numismatic Society Library, which has nearly everything, does not possess a copy.

Sets of *The Numismatist*

Another great rarity in my library is Dr. William Lee's *The Currency of the Confederate States of America*, with photographic plates, published in Washington in 1875. I know of just five copies extant, including two in institutions: The Library of Congress and the American Numismatic Society.

Another pride and joy of mine is my set of *The Numismatist*, especially the first six volumes from 1888 through 1893. These are great rarities. In 1927 in *The Numismatist*, Farran Zerbe wrote concerning these early volumes:

"The original Dr. Heath set was purchased by me from the Heath estate when I took over *The Numismatist* following his death. At the time Mr. W.W.C. Wilson purchased the set from me; on his death it was given to the American Numismatic Association. This set is bound in cloth. I parted with it only because I previously purchased a finer set bound in three-quarters Morocco with gilt edges, at the Zabriski Sale. It is the finest set extant." (The Zabriski set is now in my library.)

A note in *The Numismatist* two years earlier, in 1925, traced the location of just six complete sets; volumes owned by the following: Elliott Smith, Julius Guttag, Farran Zerbe (Heath's set), Robert Earl, William Stone, and the Art Institute of Chicago.

Today, in 1988, I know of the following who own sets: Harry Bass, The American Numismatic Society, The American Numismatic Association, John Adams, Byron Johnson, John Pittman, John J. Ford, Jr., Eric P. Newman, and myself. I am not sure of the location of a set offered in an auction by Jess Peters in 1975, a set which formerly belonged to Ray Byrne and earlier was in the M. Perlmutter library.

To give you an idea of how rare and desirable the first six volumes of *The Numismatist* are, I relate to you that in B. Max Mehl's 107th sale, the Philpot Collection, the ten highest priced coins sold for: Lot 111 at $165, Lot 174 $168, Lot 657 $178, Lot 932 $187, Lot 1794 $210, Lot 656 $210, Lot 1001 $235, Lot 1899 $325, Lot 2139 $390 and, Lot 1372 $477.50. In the same sale, Lot 2017, a set of *The Numismatist* from 1888 to 1892 brought $585!

Another great rarity is *Ormsby's Bank-Note Engraving,* published in New York in 1852. This large-sized volume is illustrated with engravings of designs and vignettes used to make bank notes of the period. I have traced the whereabouts of just seven copies, and of these five have the original covers. The late Herbert Melnick once cut apart a copy to sell the plates individually.

J.J. Mickley

Another highlight of my collection is Joseph J. Mickley's personal diary. This, of course, is unique. I acquired it in November 1980 from George Kolbe, who sent me a nice letter telling of some of the important numismatic entries in the diary. Included were the following:

August 15, 1866: Mickley went to the Mint and got a Proof example of the new five-cent piece design.

September 14, 1866: Bought three dies from the son-in-law of George Eckfeldt.

April 13, 1867: Mickley's coin robbery.

April 18, 1867: Placed United States coins in the Mint for safekeeping.

The Pleasures of Book Collecting

April 24, 1867: Mr. Idler and his son-in-law (John Haseltine) visited to talk about buying.

April 30, 1867: Sold collection to W.E. Woodward.

May 17, 1867: Bought $10,000 worth of bonds (must be the price obtained for the collection).

September 27, 1867: Received from Woodward a catalogue of the collection.

November 2, 1867: "Learned that the 1804 silver dollar sold for $750, "which I considered an enormous price. It was bought by Mr. Lillienthal of New York."

December 30, 1867: Went to the Mint and got the two pattern five-cent pieces.

This particular diary was the subject of an article by George Kolbe, printed in *Coin World,* January 14, 1981, which stated, in part:

"Joseph J. Mickley is the name well-known to students and serious collectors of American coins. William DuBois, assayer of the Philadelphia Mint, referred to him in an 1871 *American Journal of Numismatics* as 'The Father of American Numismatics.'

"Mickley was certainly one of America's earliest and best known collectors. Born in 1799, his search as a young man for a one-cent piece of his birth year aroused his collecting interest—the story itself has become a legend in American numismatics. His life spanned nearly 80 years, almost from the beginnings of American coinage to a time when the collecting and study of these early coins had become a popular pastime.

"As a young man, he was practically alone in his collecting interests. He was always ready to show his collection to friends or strangers and did much to popularize the hobby. He was instrumental in the founding of the first numismatic society of the United States. Surprisingly, he left us with only one published work, which was titled: *Dates of United States Coins and Their Degrees of Rarity,* published in 1858 . . . .

"DuBois made a fascinating comment: 'The journal that Mr. Mickley has kept all his life has been diligently kept up abroad.' What a find that journal would be! There have always been unanswered questions and speculations concerning Mickley.

"Well, you guessed it! Recently I have the extremely good fortune to acquire a key volume of the Mickley journals covering the period 1866 to 1869. Numismatically speaking, this period was a turning point in Mickley's life. In early 1867 the major portion of his collection of foreign coins and his United States duplicates were stolen from his home.

This loss made him fearful of being robbed again, and he decided to dispose of his collection.

"His coins were placed in the vault at Philadelphia Mint for safekeeping, and shortly thereafter the entire collection was sold to the eminent antiquarian and coin dealer, W.P. Elliot Woodward... The Mickley auction grossed slightly over $13,000, which was an immense sum at the time. The 1804 silver dollar sold for $750, a record price. In his journal, Mickley expressed astonishment at such a high price. How much did Woodward pay Mickley for the collection? This is one of the questions that for years has been a matter of much conjecture. Q. David Bowers, in his indispensible work *The History of United States Coinage as Illustrated by the Garrett Collection* mentions that estimates have ranged from $12,000 to $16,000.

"Well, ladies and gentlemen, the Mickley journal suggests that the purchase price for the collection was $10,000. Shortly after Woodward took possession of the collection, Mickley notes in the journal that he purchased $10,000 worth of bonds. It is possible that this does not represent the total selling price, but that seems unlikely, especially in view of Mickley's fear of being robbed...

"Other portions of the journal detail his friendship with Colonel M.I. Cohen, another well known early collector, and covers some aspects of his relationship with Philadelphia Mint officials..."

As part of my Mickley memorabilia I have one of 60 deluxe copies issued of Woodward's sale of the Mickley Collection on October 28, 1867. My copy was once the property of C.P. Nichols.

Aaron Feldman's Advice

Aaron Feldman, the dealer, now deceased, whose motto was "Buy the book before the coin," got me started in collecting books and catalogues in a big way. He urged me to go about it seriously and to acquire rare pieces.

I've always liked bargains, so when I would deal with Aaron Feldman I would sometimes wait for the last day of the American Numismatic Association Convention to visit his table, at which time I would often name my own price for things I needed, if he didn't want to carry the books back home.

I am very proud of my complete set of the *American Journal of Numismatics*, originally one of two sets possessed by Q. David Bowers. This set went into the library of the Empire Coin Company, then to Paramount International Coin Corporation, then to Hank Spangenberger, and

The Pleasures of Book Collecting

then to me. I had this set bound in full Morocco leather with slip covers. John Adams stated in his book that a complete set of catalogues issued by the Chapman Brothers, catalogues in both the large and small size, each with plates, would rank among the great desiderata of American numismatics. I accepted his challenge to complete this set. Today I am missing only the McCoy Sale, and I doubt if this sale indeed exists with plates.

Further on the subject of the Chapman Brothers, I have Henry Chapman's personal copies of sales he attended, conducted by Thomas Elder and sales conducted by his brother, S. Hudson, each with handwritten prices and names of buyers. I also have the bid books of the Chapmans which they assembled when they attended Frossard's sales from 1879 to 1901, as well as numerous other similar volumes.

A unique and quite interesting item in my library is Henry Chapman's *Black List of Men Reported Bad*, compiled in Philadelphia, around 1918, and consisting of 26 pages lettered A through Z, with the names and addresses of 159 men reported "bad"—along with the dealers who reported them. Tipped in is a letter from Chapman to G.C. Arnold inquiring why Arnold reported a certain collector, with Arnold's handwritten response at the bottom. Some of the better known names which appear on this "bad" list are: Dr. George P. French, William B. Tennett, B.P. Wright—and someone else even reported G.C. Arnold!

Among dealers who provided information and reported names to Chapman were Morey, Low, Elder, Green, and Hesslein.

Of course, in today's world such a list could not be issued, but back then it was the thing to do. In fact, scattered mentions of "bad" credit risks appear in many different numismatic publications. It is fair to point out that a person who was considered "bad" by one person might have had his own story to tell about the person doing the reporting.

In the 1930s Lee F. Hewitt set up a numismatic credit bureau on the same philosophy. This furnished the foundation for *The Numismatic Scrapbook Magazine*. One of Hewitt's early printing efforts was the *Illinois Trader*, which consisted of six issues printed in 1932. Lee Hewitt gave me his own personal set, saying he wanted it to rest in my library. This was just six months before he died. He told me that not many copies were saved, and that he knew of no other complete set in existence.

The various counterfeit detectors issued by Laban Heath have been popular with collectors. These came in small and large size. In my collection I am proud of a deluxe presentation copy given to J.R. Kendrick, superintendent of the Concord Railroad, and another copy given to Charles F. Conant, who at one time was assistant secretary of the Treasury.

My library contains a complete set of 113 catalogues issued over a long period of time by W. Elliot Woodward and is the only such run known to exist. Most of these sales were issued without plates. However, 34 plated sales were issued by Woodward. My set is bound in 59 volumes, with the 113 sales in 25 bound volumes, and the 34 plated sales bound in 34 volumes.

A popular set is that of B. Max Mehl's auction catalogues. My complete set is one of only three or four known, although several collectors are nearing completion.

Auction Catalogue Rarities

Occasionally I'm asked my opinion of the rarest United States auction catalogues issued with photographic plates. I consider that such a list would include the following, not in any particular order of rarity. Those marked with an asterisk are not in the American Numismatic Society library: J.M. Henderson sale by S.H. Chapman, May 27, 1921; F.D. Simpson Collection sale by S. Hudson Chapman, June 9, 1924; William H. Woodin sale, by Edgar H. Adams, February 10, 1911; Col. Davis Collection sale by Thomas L. Elder, April 30, 1920; *H.O. Granberg Collection sale by Wayte Raymond, May 19, 1915; George Woodside Collection sale by New York Coin & Stamp Company, April 23, 1892; *William H. Woodin Collection sale by Thomas L. Elder, March 2, 1911; *Dr. Edward Maris Collection sale, H.P. Smith, June 1, 1886; *Colin King Collection sale by the Chapman brothers, April 5, 1892; Charles Zug Collection sale by S. Hudson Chapman, October 22, 1909; Gehring Collection sale by Thomas L. Elder, August 26, 1921; *William Schleicher Collection sale, by S. Hudson Chapman, October 9, 1919; Foster Ladner Collection sale by the U.S. Coin Company, November 20, 1914; and *Ralph Barker Collection sale by the Chapman brothers, July 7, 1904.

Other Highlights

There are many other highlights of my library, including rare auction catalogues issued by firms not already mentioned, deluxe or limited editions of reference works by Adams-Woodin, Valentine, Browning, Marvin, Hetrich-Guttag, and others; a complete set of Frossard's *Numisma;* Edgar H. Adams' notebook on early United States silver coins, obtained from John J. Ford, Jr., and earlier owned by F.C.C. Boyd; Adams' notebook on Hard Times tokens from the same source; and various

The Pleasures of Book Collecting

counterfeit detectors and banknote reporters.

The search for rare numismatic literature has been a challenging one, and scarcely a year goes by without several surprises occurring. One thing about numismatic literature is that many fine books, auction catalogues, and other periodicals are continually being produced, so it is also fun to keep my library up to date by adding things I consider to be relevant or important.

The Great 1942/1 Dime Search

By Tom LaMarre   1988

"It would appear that either a 1941 dime was by some accident restruck in 1942, or a die was given one blow with a 1941 hub and finished with a 1942 hub. There is no way of telling how this occurred by examining the coin, of course, since there is no way of ascertaining whether there is only one such coin or a number in existence."

That was Chief Engraver John R. Sinnock's initial reaction to the 1942/1 dime when *Numismatic Scrapbook Magazine* sent the discovery piece to him in 1943. Collectors learned of the coin in the May 1943 issue of the magazine, which said, "Numismatists won't have to be told to take the second look at every 1942 dime that passes through their hands."

Arnold Cohn of Kingston, New York found the first specimen of the overdate in circulation in February 1943. News of the discovery started a frenzied scramble for the coins. Most of the dimes were found in New York State and vicinity. It was rumored that a cashier of the New York subway lines removed more than 1,000 of the 1942/1 dimes from circulation in 1943 and 1944. The findings indicated that the entire coinage from the overdate die was distributed through the New York City Federal Reserve Bank. Unfortunately, most of the dimes circulated for at least a few months before being spotted by collectors. Uncirculated specimens are rare.

In the early years of the Mint, it was common practice to repunch the date on serviceable dies at the end of the year. Many overdate dimes were struck: 1798/7, 1811/09, 1823/2, and 1824/2. However, the practice of repunching dies had been abandoned for many decades when the 1942/1 dimes were struck.

"In September of each year we start engraving the numeral in the new master die for the following year," Sinnock said. "We have no punches for these numerals since they were sculptured in the first place. We follow the individual style of each sculptor. From this master die a working hub is drawn. This is retouched if necessary, then hardened. This hub is used to fabricate all the working dies for that year.

"About 1,000 dies with the new date must be ready by January 1 of each year. To attempt to 'save' one die by changing the date by hand engraving out of 15,000 dies which we have to produce would be folly. The time required to make this change and the complication of our records in such a transfer would far outweigh the value of the die.

"When a die is found imperfect it is charged off as condemned and destroyed before a commission at the beginning of each year. Each die is inspected by half a dozen skilled workmen with magnifying glasses before they are okayed for delivery. With the ever increasingly heavy demands for coins the Engraving Department has necessarily had to streamline its operations and is quite different from the methods employed a few years ago."

The Philadelphia Mint struck more than 205.4 million dimes in 1942, but the overdate specimens turned up slowly. William H. Arthur wrote in the June 1943 issue of *Numismatic Review:* "About a month ago, the writer was fortunate enough to obtain a new piece, a dime of 1942/1, struck at Philadelphia. Apparently only one die was altered, and so far only one or two specimens have been found. The original figure '1' under the final '2' is plainly visible on these pieces.

"The nonexistence of any overdated coins of the United States struck during the 25-year period between the two wars suggests that the custom may be a war measure to avoid the waste of metal for dies and other extra expenses. Of course, when the work is done neatly, as it certainly is in the present instance, only collectors are likely to notice the matter at all. But to them such a phenomenon is of great interest, and the present coin is a good example of the way in which coins do reflect and illustrate historical events."

Supporting Sinnock's explanation of the overdate dimes, Director of the Mint Nellie Tayloe Ross said that the coins were created by accident, not to save money. The fact that the last previous overdates had been struck during World War I was a coincidence. (The coins referred to by Arthur were the 1918/7-D five-cent piece and the 1918/7-S quarter.)

By the late 1950s, the 1942/1 dime was valued at $25 in Fine condition and $90 in Uncirculated condition. It was still possible to find a

The Great 1942/1 Dime Search

specimen in circulation. The March 1959 issue of *Numismatic Scrapbook Magazine* contained a letter from Dr. C. Andrew Wurst of Springfield, Missouri: "Yesterday, during my lunch time, I was going through some rolls of dimes, which incidentally I do every time I get a chance, and lo and behold there was a Mercury Head, in Very Fine condition, 1942/1. My nerves were, as they say, 'all shook up,' and for a time I could hardly believe my eyes. But now that I've settled down to reality I find it is still very much the truth."

The overdate dime story was not yet finished. Late in 1960 came news regarding the discovery of a 1942/1-D dime. In a letter published in the November 1960 issue of *Numismatic Scrapbook Magazine*, a West Baldwin, Maine collector wrote: "A friend brought in a dime and asked me to look at it. He found it in change. As I looked at the obverse I said yes, he had found a 1942/1 dime. Then he said have a look at the reverse. On the reverse there was a 'D' mintmark. Then I really looked it over and I can't find anything to say it isn't the real thing. Has anyone else ever found such a coin?"

Another report of a 1942/1-D dime was published in *Coin World's* "Collectors' Clearinghouse" in the spring of 1963. The variety was illustrated and priced in the second edition (1963) of Frank G. Spadone's *Major Variety & Oddity Guide* (error collectors were aware of the 1942/1-D dime long before it was pictured in the *Guide Book of United States Coins*). The August 30, 1963 issue of *Coin World* questioned the dime's authenticity, but a story in the August 10, 1966 issue, in which James G. Johnson illustrated 1942/1-D dimes in various states of preservation, confirmed that the overdate was genuine. James Greenwich was credited as the first person to inquire about the coin.

Why wasn't the variety discovered sooner? Probably because the overdate is not as dramatic as the Philadelphia version. Remnants of the upper and lower portion of a "1" without serif are visible beneath the "2." In addition, there are traces of micro doubling in the first "1," the "9," and the upright of the "4." Mint engravers said that such all-on-one-side-of-the-digits doubling, even when it occurs on only a small portion of the design, results from an out-of-level die adjustment or associated problems in the striking of individual pieces.

Were the 1942/1-D dimes struck from the same die as the overdate dimes minted at Philadelphia? Some numismatists thought that the Philadelphia die could have been tooled down and sent to Denver. However, a study by researcher Arthur Trogner concluded that the 1942/1-D dimes had been struck from an entirely different die than the Philadelphia coins.

The 1942/1-D dimes had a tough act to follow. "1941 Denver Dimes Already at Premium" said the headline in the February 1941 issue of *The Numismatist*. Accompanying it were a photograph and story reprinted from the January 9, 1941 issue of the *Denver Post:* "The tidy sum of $6,000, a very small part of the 26 million silver dollars in storage in the Denver Mint, is shown in this picture, which was taken at the Mint with the permission of Superintendent Mark A. Skinner. One thousand dollars are on the table and $1,000 in each of the sacks held by prominent Colorado mining men.

"The picture was taken to stimulate interest in Silver Week, which begins January 20, when 1941 Denver-coined dimes will be redeemed for $1 when presented at the registration booth of the Colorado Mining Association on January 24 or 25 at the Shirley-Savoy Hotel . . . Silver Week was proclaimed by Governor Carr in connection with the annual meeting of the Colorado Mining Association, January 24 and January 25.

"The Colorado Mining Association decided it would be a good thing to get 1941 Denver-coined coins in circulation and to pay $1 for every one of the coins presented . . .

"Arrangements for the release of the 1941 dimes at this time were made with Mrs. Nellie Tayloe Ross, Director of the Mint, through Senator Alva B. Adams."

There was no such promotion in 1942 as the Denver Mint struck more than 60 million dimes. Collectors were more interested in 1942-S dimes. Few 1942/1-D dimes survived in Uncirculated condition. By 1968 only one or two Uncirculated specimens had been reported. Today an MS-65 1942/1-D dime with Full Split Bands is worth approximately $7,000.

Not all Mercury dime varieties have enjoyed lasting popularity, though. In the November 1944 issue of *The Numismatist* R.S. Caldwell, Jr. reported the discovery of a 1944 "Leaved" dime: "An Uncirculated specimen of the Leaved dime, a variety of the 1944-P dime, was exhibited at this year's ANA Convention at Chicago," Caldwell wrote. "This coin has been so named because, on the obverse, beautiful outlines of small clusters of leaves, readily discernible to the naked eye, are formed around the head and are to be found at the forehead, at the bridge of the nose, protruding from the nostril, under the chin, and at the back of the neck. There is also the outline of a branch or limb running parallel to the near the front of the neck.

"Several members of the Chicago Coin Club, after a careful examination of the coin, concurred in the opinion that this phenomenon was caused in the following manner: When the obverse and reverse dies

The Great 1942/1 Dime Search

were placed in the coining machine for adjustment, the obverse die was forced against the reverse die, causing the leaf formations on the reverse die to become impressed into the obverse die.

"This seems to be the plausible explanation for the existence of the reverse leaf formations appearing on the obverse die of the dime.

"Presently, only 16 specimens of the coin are known to exist." Although few of today's collectors are aware of the 1944 "Leaved" dime, the 1942/1 and 1942/1-D are still going strong long after they were first reported in the numismatic press.

Early Days in Vermont

By Rev. Nathan Perkins   1988

The following is excerpted, with certain spelling corrected, from A Narrative of a Tour Through the State of Vermont from April 27 to June 12, 1789, by Rev. Nathan Perkins, of Hartford, Connecticut, as related in his diary published by The Elm Tree Press, Woodstock, Vermont, 1930.
   Rev. Perkins, born in 1749 and graduated from Princeton College in 1770, traveled through Vermont during the time Vermont was using its own copper coinage (made in Rupert circa 1785-1787). Although his narrative does not discuss Vermont coinage, it does give an interesting view of the somewhat primitive life conditions in the Green Mountain State at the time.
   The following paragraphs are but a tiny portion of the original text.

   April 27. I left Hartford and set out for Vermont. Took leave of my family, a tender companion, and five dear children, with painful reluctance and an anxious heart. I affectionately recommended them to the protection and care of a kind Providence, influenced by the call of duty and conscience. I reached Simsbury by 1:00 and dined with Rev. Stebbins; not prepared to receive company, glad to see me, and we discoursed on divinity, politics, and my journey.
   2:00 p.m. Mounted my horse—rode on as usual at a slow pace, contemplating every surrounding object—amusing myself with the works of nature and the season—the state of agriculture and rusticity of the peoples' manners. Dear traveling. No hay. No oats. My horse deeply grieved. About sunset arrived at the Rev. Clinton's of Southwick;

procured horsekeeping with a neighbor of his, two shillings per night. Mr. Clinton out, but soon comes home. I had already introduced myself to Mrs. Clinton. She was just getting up from child-bed; not very polished nor used to company; thought her boy the finest in the world, most beautiful, most spritely, most promising. I smiled and Chesterfield-like bestowed some compliments to please the vanity of parental fondness. Innocent pleasantry! She introduced me to her husband, a man of moderate abilities and moderate acquirements. The evening passed in dullness and insipidity. Poor supper. Wretched breakfast. Tea paler than water. Sugar heavier than lead. I had then began to experience that hard and course fare which wasted away my flesh in the progress of my travels and made me often, often regret my tour. How often have I remembered home—a table richly furnished and elegantly set, food dressed, in the neatness and best manner. . . .

Friday came to Bennington, capital at present of Vermont—a good town of land, people, proud—scornful—conceited and somewhat polished—small meeting house—considerably thick-settled, as many as can possibly get a living; no stone; no fencing timber; some elegant buildings; a county town; a tolerable courthouse and jail; a good grammar school. Rev. Swift, their minister, the apostle of Vermont, well esteemed among his own people and in the state, at large, put up at his house; he not at home, gone over to the college; his wife handsome, serious, weakly; lawyer Sedgwick's sister, 10 children, one at the breast, two daughters grown up, homely, unpolished, countrified in manners, and without any elegance. Visited Judge Robinson, chief justice of the state. A man of sense and religion, rich and uncommonly beautiful to an aged mother, eminent for her attainments and goodness.

Saturday, May 2nd, rode to Shaftsbury. Saw the hill where the Bennington Battle was fought, six miles from the town, a battle which will be greatly celebrated in the history of America. Called on Elder Blood of Shaftsbury, a Baptist minister of a public education, candid and supported as Presbyterian ministers are, lives low, poor; wife old, ordinary looking, serious and very dirty. . . .

The first sabbath in May, preached at Sunderland, in a barn, to considerable audience, very attentive and much affected, received much applause; a raving Armenian Methodist preached in evening. Here lived formerly the awful Deist Ethan Allen, so known in Vermont, who delighted in calling himself the old *philosopher*. In his house now lives a Quaker from Long Island, with a young girl from Seabrook whom he seduced, though a married man, a picture of beauty and elegance. . . .

Early Days in Vermont

Went on to Dorset, called on Rev. Sill, a good friendly man, extremely poor—poor looking family, poor land, got some directions of him as to my route, passed through Pawlet, through Rupert, called on Rev. Bebee, a serious man, who left honor and the prospects of wealth for the Gospel, sensible, of little reading, of narrow sentiments, a weakly wife, a poor hut, a friendly heart, a mean victuals, destitute of neatness.

Wednesday 5th May. Set out from Pawlet for Middletown, preached at one Reed's in a dark room—to a small collection of people, chiefly Connecticut Separates, very serious and attentive. Put up at Mr. Minor's, a kind man, a kind wife, wretched fare, wretched bed, eat up with fleas, no hay, my horse starving. . . .

Saturday went to Clarendon, to Elihu Smith's, a rich man, a great boaster, a fine farm on Otter Creek. Preached at his house. The people of Wallingford met with Clarendon, very attentive. I fared badly at Clarendon, and my horse worse. . . .

Lodged at Mr. Flint's in Brandon, meanest of all lodging, dirty, fleas without number.

May 10th rode to Liecester and put up at Col. Sawyer's, and Wednesday preached a lecture at his house and baptized a child for him, a rough, violent, savage man—extraordinary spot in nature for mills, and a pond by his door, where he raises fish.

Thursday rode to Middlebury, to Maj. Chipman's. . . Next day rode to Mr. Foot's, stayed all night, high tempered, boastful man, conceited, vulgar, and high inelegant in the house. Next day to New Haven [Vermont], preached at a log house—people serious and anxious to hear the word. I was greatly worried and fatigued with riding, poor living, nothing but brook water to drink. . . Slept in an open log house, where it rained on me in the night, and no keeping for my horse.

Saturday 16th of May. Rode on after preaching at Moreton, Pocock, mud belly deep to my horse and I thought I should have perished; felt warm gratitude to heaven my life was spared, my health and strength continued, through such hardships and unwholesome food, arrived just a night at Mr. Steel's, my old parishioner, was cordially welcomed. . .

My living and situation is a paradise compared to Vermont; far, far happier than any I have seen. Oh how happy I am at home! I will study to be more contented, more serene, more thankful, and to make my family so. When I go from hut to hut, from town to town, in the wilderness, the people with nothing to eat, to drink, or wear, all work, and yet the women quiet, serene, peaceable, contented, loving their husbands, their home, wanting never to return, nor any dressy clothes—I think how strange! I ask myself are these women of the same species with our fine ladies? Tough are they, brawny their limbs, their young girls unpolished, and will bear work as well as mules. Woods make people love one another and kind and obliging and good natured. They set much more by one another than in the old settlements. Leave their doors unbarred. Sleep quietly amid fleas, bedbugs, dirt and rags. Oh how vile, how guilty, how ungrateful to Providence are our women! They tell lies about one another, envy one another, go abroad, dress, and enjoy fine roads—with carriages and husbands to wait on them—and are yet uneasy and unaffectionate!. . . I can now realize what our forefathers suffered in settling America! I grieve to hear what thousands and thousands have endured, women and children in coming to this state of Vermont. . . .

Research Methods

By Robert W. Julian   1987/88

Robert W. Julian is one of the country's leading numismatic researchers. In this article, taken from a speech given before the American Numismatic Association at their convention in 1986, and also from a transcription in the Numismatic Literary Guild Newsletter, Bob Julian tells of his experiences.

Books on numismatics are the mainstay of the hobby and without the knowledge accumulated in them we would be in very poor condition, but there is no book on how to do research in numismatics—and probably never will be. Practical experience is the best guide, but how does one acquire this experience?

There is no direct answer to this question. Perhaps the best way to begin is by talking about why research is done at all. Why not just collect coins for profit and forget about why or how they were made? We all know that the mark of the true numismatist is to want to know everything possible about the coins and medals that he or she owns or wishes to own. All of us have seen exhibits that tell us nothing about the pieces displayed and we tend to ignore them in favor of those with good accompanying material that masterfully explains the contents of the case.

We have all heard the famous remark that people climb mountains because they are there, as if that were reason enough. If that were the only reason for doing numismatic research, it would be a poor one indeed. The way that I began to be interested in research, though probably not typical, illustrates one way of entering the field. In the late

1950s I was in college and trying to collect Russian coins—as well as U.S.—on a shoestring budget. I was corresponding with Dr. I.G. Spasskii, dean of Russian numismatics, and he suggested that I have certain works microfilmed at Russian libraries in order that I understand the coinage better.

Well, I contacted the Saltykov-Shchedrin in Leningrad and inquired as to their terms of microfilming. It turned out that they wanted American books in exchange on a roughly page for page basis. They then, without my ordering it done, proceeded to microfilm the books and send me a list of American books. I nearly choked when I saw the list because the books in question cost about $100, a sum somewhat beyond my grasp at that time. To make a long story short I managed to persuade them to accept a more reasonable and less costly selection, but in the meantime I wrote Lee Hewitt, then editor of the *Numismatic Scrapbook*, inquiring if he would be interested in articles on Russian numismatics. He was, and the first one was published in December 1960. From there I graduated to doing research on U.S. topics and made my first trip to the National Archives, in Washington, DC, in 1963.

There are several ways of doing research at the Archives, none of them easy.

Perhaps the best way of illustrating such research work would be to examine an instance of digging out facts long forgotten. Until recently, every numismatic reference work stated that the Gobrecht dollars of 1836 to 1839 were patterns. As so often is the case in published works—and a charge to which virtually everyone is guilty at sometime or other—the errors about these pieces had simply been copied form earlier texts written by individuals who were simply guessing or merely repeating unfounded gossip from elderly Mint officials. One should not automatically discount such information but is best to back up the oral with documentation where possible.

I first questioned the prevailing view about the Gobrecht 'patterns' when I saw the original Mint reports for the years of 1836, 1837, and 1839 and each clearly showed an official coinage of silver dollars, although a small one. Beyond the tables, in the report for 1836 the director clearly stated that a coinage of silver dollars had been executed for circulation. Since everyone assumed the pieces to be patterns, it was certainly the sole case of an official Mint report declaring patterns to be coins and also telling how many were made. One of the key points frequently made about these issues concerned 1836 where it was stated that the Mint had struck 1,000 pieces on the standard adopted in 1837;

Research Methods

in other words all the dollars struck in 1836 weighed 412.5 grains rather than the legal standard of 416 grains in force during 1836.

There were of course sources of information that tended to back up the prevailing view about the Gobrecht dollars of 1836-1839. One such instance was a conversation with a very prominent and knowledgeable dealer whose authority in matters of this sort was to be taken very seriously. He informed me that he had personally weighed a considerable number of 1836 Gobrecht dollars and all had weighed 412.5 grains and not 416 grains. It certainly was a telling point in favor of the accepted theory.

The next step was to examine the original entries in the relevant ledgers showing coinage and use of bullion for the period. For this purpose, and for the years before 1838, the so-called Waste Book (which shows every entry relating to bullion affairs) proved to be the key tool in breaking open the puzzle. It so happened that the journals showed 1,000 silver dollars being delivered in two separate batches the last day of 1836 but in the second case no other silver coins were included with the dollars. This enabled me to calculate the correct legal weight of the dollars delivered on that day and it turned out to be 416 and not 412.5 grains. What, then, had become of the 1,000 dollars delivered in late 1836?

In addition to examining the bullion entries for coinage and deposits, all of the existing incoming and outgoing letters in the Archives were read to find even the most minute of clues concerning the execution of coins, as I thought, or patterns, as most others believed.

Complicating all of this was the known fact that Mint Director James Ross Snowden had engaged in wholesale restriking of the Gobrecht dollars from original dies during the 1850s. That Snowden had used these dollars to trade collectors for prized specimens needed for the mint cabinet was interesting but of little help since no one knew how to tell the originals from the restrikes, except for some vague information concerning die rust, hardly the best indicator since dies could, and often were, replenished between usage.

One may ask, in the meantime, if I went to the Archives every single time I wished to do research; after all, I live roughly 600 miles from Washington, DC, and it is not the easiest thing in the world to drop everything just for a quick trip to the nation's capital. This sort of thing is not necessary since it is possible to order specialized microfilming from the Archives when one knows where to look.

The whole puzzle was neatly solved with the publication of Walter Breen's superb work on the Proof coinage of the United States. He had found the key to the differentiation of original Gobrechts from restrikes by noting that the Snowden strikings of the 1850s had the eagle flying flat—when the coin was properly rotated—instead of 'onward and upward' as intended by Director R.M. Patterson in the 1830s. This in turn indicated that the dealer who had weighed all of those Gobrecht dollars had not found a single original striking of 1836.

The above is discussed at some length since it shows that many different sources and ideas have to be consulted in order to arrive at the truth. It is, however, one thing to do research and publish it and then expect ready acceptance of the new factors or theories. Those who took the time to read the original material realized that the Mint entries were definitive and closed the matter for all time. Since then it has been interesting to watch to see which dealers ignored the findings—which are now in the *Red Book* for all to see and use—in their auction catalogues.

Up to now we have discussed primarily doing research on United States topics and will return to that subject in a moment, but what of the collector who specializes in a foreign nation or era and wish to do original research. Well, they are out of luck, as a general rule. It is very difficult for an American numismatist, for example to do work on Swedish coins, without going to Sweden and hiring someone to translate documents in the archives. One can, however, do secondary research in published materials.

The first step is to obtain the standard references on the series, which rarely give historical background, at least any more than is necessary to understand and price a particular coin. We next would purchase standard historical references; in the case of Anglo-Saxon England, for example, the standard history by Sir Frank Stenton comes readily to mind.

The educated collector would then join societies devoted to the same areas. In the case of British coinage the most important is the British Numismatic Society, which has published an annual volume since the early 1900s reporting on the latest research. In addition, there is also the Royal Numismatic Society annual, *The Numismatic Chronicle,* which has some material on British coinage but also has a variety of articles on ancient and world subjects.

It is also easy to subscribe to certain publications, such as Seaby's, which not only offers articles heavily weighted towards the British series, but also coins for sale. The collector may get himself placed on the mailing list of U.S. dealers specializing in British issues. One can no doubt thing of other ways for the inquiring numismatist to further his or her knowledge in the country or period chosen.

Research Methods

With respect to doing research overseas I cannot leave out one story that so typifies the English. I have been a member of the Royal Numismatic Society for more than 10 years but had never attended an actual meeting until the summer of 1983, when I happened to be staying near Cambridge. During the meeting I was called to the front of the room and formally introduced to the gathering; the introduction is really a mark of initiation.

At any rate I sought out Dr. Price, the secretary, and inquired about doing some research at the British Museum. He asked that I telephone him in advance, which I did, and a day was fixed for my visit. London is an easy trip from Cambridge and I was there at the appointed time. Upon entering I was informed that I had to fill out a card and then wait for Dr. Price to approve my presence, but that he was unavoidably absent at that time. I answered that he had informed me at the Royal Numismatic Society meeting that everything would be all right. There was a pause at this point and the person with whom I was speaking suddenly said "Oh, you are the gentleman who was introduced at the Society meeting. We can make the card out later. Now, what would you care to see?"

To return to the main topic of our discussion, American coinage and medals, there seems to be a general belief that government records are sacred and one may find all that one needs in the Archives simply by looking in the right place. Nothing could be further from the truth. For the Mint records dating before 1900 that presently exist, it is doubtful that we see more than a third of what once existed. Some Mints have lost their entire records while others, such as Philadelphia, have been heavily ravaged. Since this whole area is little known, some review is necessary in order to show what exists and what has been lost.

First of all, the records of the Dahlonega Mint, if they survived the Civil War intact, were probably thrown out within a few years by someone who did not wish to bother with them. Reports filed by the superintendents of this branch Mint to various official bodies still exist, but the working papers do not and this has caused endless confusion, especially with respect to the rare coinages of 1861. A year or two ago one researcher hit upon the novel idea of checking some of the Confederate records in the Archives and did find some hitherto unknown figures, but not quite the definitive information we have all been seeking.

The Charlotte Mint records do, on the whole, exist, but are missing many of the ordinary letters that make up history. However, the bullion and coinage ledgers are in the Archives and may be consulted by anyone having interest in this area.

The New Orleans and Carson City records are mostly lost. Both were virtually destroyed in this century, probably in 1925, though some may not have been tossed onto the trash heap until the early thirties. One miserable volume of pre-Civil War New Orleans letters exists, but it deals with building repairs and is of little direct use to anyone. Why it was kept and not the more valuable bullion and coinage records is anyone's guess.

For the 19th century the records of Philadelphia seem to have been preserved the best but the status of San Francisco is unknown to me. Some Philadelphia records were thrown out in the course of the past century (and were taken home by certain officers who considered them their personal property) but the greatest damage occurred in 1925. We have lists of what was destroyed but this does not make up for the losses.

At this point it is only fair to note that some documents ought to be thrown away as they would simply clog archival space for generations to come and would never be consulted. For example, does anyone really care that employee X was off January 23, 1900, because of a common cold? Such information has no bearing on the history of coins or medals struck at the mints and should be discarded. In a similar vein, can we keep the records showing each and every person who purchased mint or Proof sets in the past half century? Also, many categories or records simply duplicate other series.

On the other hand, I learned last summer that great quantities of very valuable 20th-century records had been ordered shredded in 1978 due to some whim from a bureaucrat not understanding or caring what was historically proper to keep. The 1978 order, with many pages of fine print listing the files to be shredded, included the great bulk of Philadelphia, Denver, and San Francisco letter files, in some ways the most important records then being kept. It is with the letter files that we flesh out the reason for a change in the coinage or the details behind a medal.

The destruct order also included many other valuable files, including the die records for the various mints. Such wanton destruction will surely be felt in the next few decades as information on die varieties is sought in order to combat increasingly sophisticated counterfeiting. We may contrast this strange behavior with that of the Royal Mint in England, which has furnished rather detailed die information on occasion to qualified individuals.

Research Methods

The curious part about the destruction of the Philadelphia Mint letter files is that the destroyed records were simply continuations of files that were already at the Archives and had been heavily used by researchers. In 1975 I had examined some of the files now destroyed—and copied 200 or 300 letters for the years prior to 1914. These copies are now the only remainder of untold thousands of letters now but a memory. This one order has virtually destroyed future research into 20th century mint history. At the risk of a very bad pun, I might say that this proves the old adage that political hacks ought to be kept out of an office involving public trust. It was certainly broken in this case.

Perhaps the saddest aspect of this sorry business is the damage that it will do to reputations in years to come. There is always that odd researcher who sees corruption in every action by a government official, no matter how innocent. The classic case is the illiterate who wrote a book claiming that George Washington had stolen money from the government when his accounts were settled at the end of the Revolutionary War; the so-called researcher did not even understand the basic monetary system of the period and it was only through the use of other records still in existence—and not destroyed by some political hack of the 1790s—that scholars could heap ridicule on this book. What is to happen, however, when the same charge is hurled against an officer of the Philadelphia Mint for some action taken in the 1920s? The records will no longer exist and an honest employee will receive an unfair verdict from history.

In the 1880s it was quite common to charge various Mint officers with improprieties, but the existence of the records for the period makes it possible to find out the truth in nearly all cases. The various charges made about the Stella and Goloid coinage are well known to students of this period and Superintendent A. Loudon Snowden, can be shown to be blameless despite dealer criticism of the era and occasionaly repeating of such information by current writers.

The Archival records are not always easy to access. During my first trip to the Archives in 1963, I became thirsty while working at night in the Central Research Room. I remembered that there was a water fountain at the other end of the building and went through two swinging doors to get there. On trying to return I discovered that these doors only opened in one direction and I was now locked in. I then remembered that one could go through the basement from one side to the other, so I used the elevator to go down to that level and cross over. When I arrived back at the Central Research Room I complained to the guard that the doors could be a little better arranged. He replied that they now knew who had set off the alarm system in the building. Every time a new guard came into the research room I was pointed out as the cause of all the trouble that evening. The next night there were notices on the doors in question warning that use was forbidden in the evening. I found another drinking fountain.

During one of my periodic trips to Philadelphia in the mid-1960s I discovered that there was an extremely valuable Mint ledger dating from 1844 which listed every die made at the Philadelphia Mint until 1924. I actually handled the volume and was allowed to look inside to verify what was there but was told that it had to be sent to the Mint Bureau in Washington. So, upon my arrival in Washington I requested a meeting with the director but was instead granted one with an assistant director. This particular meeting was not one of my better days. The assistant director first informed me that he was virtually the sole person protecting the coinage against the forces that would destroy it and it was plainly hinted that I was a front for a counterfeiting gang, or why else would I be applying to see a record of dies. The assistant director also informed me that he would personally destroy the volume should I manage to get permission to see it.

At that time the Freedom of Information Act had just been signed into law and upon my return home I made formal application to use the volume. After a year of waiting I received a curious communication, signed by the director, informing me that I could not see the record because it was an "internal memo!"

When Mrs. Brooks became director I made a formal protest about the way I had been treated and the absurd answer I had received to a legitimate request for information. She ordered a thorough search made but did not find the volume, leading to the inevitable conclusion that it had indeed been destroyed. However, in the process of searching some of the nooks and crannies that abounded in the old Bureau offices in the Treasury Building a number of valuable ledgers and documents were found which were made available to me. These proved invaluable since I had not even known of their existence; one of the books, for example, was Longacre's personal notebook recording medals and pattern coins ordered struck in the 1860s. These books were all later sent to the Archives for the use of all researchers.

I mention Mrs. Brooks by name because I would like to single her out as a friend of the collector. She did not have to go out of her way to

Research Methods

help me in my research, for I have no powerful friends in Washington, but did anyway because it was the proper thing to do. If it had not been for her, for example, the book I did for the Token and Medal Society on medals of the U.S. Mint from 1792 to 1892 would have been a far poorer effort. If awards are to be passed out, I would certainly nominate her for one. I have had no dealings with the present director and therefore it would not be fair for me to say anything in this respect.

The letter files of the Philadelphia Mint are worthy of a study unto themselves. In the earliest days the clerks made what are termed nowadays "fair copies" of all letters thought worthy of keeping for future reference. From 1792 to October 1795, however, the directors did not keep copies of their letters or at least did not leave them at the Mint for future directors to use. It is quite possible that some day we will uncover the Mint letterbooks of David Rittenhouse or Henry William DeSaussure, the first two directors.

Beginning in October 1795 Director Elias Boudinot ordered that a careful record be kept of all letters considered important and quite a few that were only marginally so. We may be thankful that he did, for without this information we would know but little about the workings of the Mint at this period. These "fair copies," which are nothing more than letters carefully copied in a bound volume, may be consulted by any researcher.

The following two directors, Robert Patterson and Samuel Moore, were very conscientious about keeping letter files and these are still in existence. Robert M. Patterson, who became director in 1835, changed the system, however, much to our detriment at this time. Fair copies were no longer made, but instead the director would write out the letter himself and the clerk would recopy it for sending through the mails. What now exists are the director's own copies, complete with erasures and crossed out sections. Patterson, however, had one of the poorer hands of the period and it is sometimes very difficult to understand precisely what he his saying.

Patterson did order that ledgers be kept showing the rough content of all important letters sent and received, but most of these small volumes were lost over the next several decades and only a few now grace the Archival shelves. It was not until 1853, when James Ross Snowden became director, that record-keeping for letters changed to a new system entirely, that of the letter-press copy. The letter was written out in ink and then a very thin tissue laid across the still-wet ink. The ink soaked into the tissue paper, forming a permanent copy. Unfortunately, in some cases the ink tended to run, leaving a blurred copy or, worse yet, the ink contained iron or other chemicals and the tissue paper disintegrated.

Until the late 1860s press copies were filed with the incoming letter—if there was one—but after that time were bound into volumes for better storage. Around 1900 the Philadelphia Mint finally began using typewriters and thus switched to carbon paper, the standard until recently. The arrival of the copier and word-processor have of course changed the routine.

Most of the record groups at the Archives have been inventoried, and the researcher can use the printed inventory to determine the type of records wanted. The archives of the various mints, except San Francisco, as well as that of the Mint Bureau, are in Record Group 104. The inventory of 1952 has been superseded by that of 1968, resulting in some changes of numbers for the various sections.

At the present time all research with original documents is done in the Central Research Room on the second floor of the Archives building in Washington. The general rule is to consult with the staff official responsible for a given section of records and present a list of documents or volumes wanted for the next day; due to the pressure under which some of the staff work, it is not always possible to have records pulled immediately.

When actually doing research there are several ways of going about the task. When copying letters, for example, I normally use a tape recorder since far more work can be done that way than by just trying to write everything. Also, one's hand gets very tired after a few hours and writer's cramp sets in. Once you get tired of writing everything down, you begin to skip more and more until you are at the point of just writing down an occasional idea; the latter is sometimes very hard to interpret when you get home.

On the other hand, with a regular tape recorder—not one of the hand-held cassette players—the researcher simply indexes each letter by the counter number when he returns and the research is good for an indefinite period. Some of the handwritten notes I made in 1963 have long since become scattered, but the tapes I made as long ago as 1967 are still perfectly useable. Now, in preparing a work for publication, I go through my index, copy off the relevant entries, and then listen to the exact letter as it appeared to me years before.

The use of a tape recorder allows a researcher to do an enormous amount of research in a very short time and thus save valuable funds in the process. It is not cheap to stay in the Washington DC area—you

Research Methods

can expect, at the least, to pay around $50 a day for your accommodations. However, I recommend eating at the Harrington Hotel, only three or four blocks from the Archives, as the food is both good and inexpensive. The only problem is that a number of Washington's seedier inhabitants are well aware of the cost so it does not pay to be too fastidious when eating there. The quality and price make up for the inconvenience, however.

Some of the government buildings do have cafeterias and it is possible to eat in them under certain conditions. At one time I used to eat in the basement of the Justice Department, directly across the street from the Archives. One of my cousins had been a special FBI agent in the influence peddling investigations of the late 1940s and he suggested that I simply act as though I belonged there when going through the halls on the way to the cafeteria. As a matter of fact, I did just this and got away with it for quite a while. The food was excellent; it was probably subsidized, like most other things in Washington. However, in 1974 I tried the same thing and was stopped at the door and asked for identification. I tried the undercover routine but they did not believe me so I went back to eating at the Harrington.

When one does work directly at the Archives it is normally possible to have xerox copies made on the spot for a fee, which is, I believe, 30 cents at the present time. This service, however, is generally restricted to single sheets of paper and one may not normally do this for bound volumes of any type.

In dealing with ledgers and other special tables that do not read well into a tape recorder, or are liable to be confused, it is best to have the material microfilmed by the Archives photoduplication service. The present fee is 25 cents per page if ordered on the spot or five cents more than that if ordered from the outside. As the rates are subject to change they should be checked before ordering, however. It normally takes a minimum of five or six weeks to get the filming done because there is a considerable backlog of other people wanting work done also.

There is a special class of microfilm that has already been filmed and is ready for use on the upper floor. For example, all of the correspondence of the Philadelphia Mint officers with Dahlonega has been microfilmed and can be used upstairs. There are three reels of film, about 4,000 pages in all. On the other hand these can be ordered directly from the archives at a cost of $22 per reel. There are several other such reels available, including Bullion Ledger A, which covers Philadelphia bullion accounts from 1794 through 1802, letters written by the directors of the mint from 1795 through 1817, and a few other specialized ledgers and documents.

In addition to the Mint documents that have been microfilmed, the upstairs microfilm reading room also has about 200,000 other reels covering all types of material, including census and diplomatic records, many of which are of value in doing work on coins and medals. One must consult some rather bulky registers to determine which reels would be of value.

I cannot speak highly enough of the Archival staff that I have worked with over the years. Mrs. Holdcamper and Mr. King are retired now but Mr. Sherman is their equal in every way and I have nothing but praise for these people. Frequently when I was stumped for a place to look for a certain item one of them would come up with just the right place to search.

It is also not a terribly bright idea to go wandering around downtown Washington at night. Being something of a greenhorn from the Midwest I did not at first understand that individuals were better off not sightseeing at night due to an overabundance of muggers and other delightful people. Each mugger is probably going to be accompanied by a member of the local ACLU, so the researcher is going to be outnumbered anyway.

Another key area of research is digging through old dealer's auction catalogues and fixed price lists in search of information on the rarity and importance of certain coins. I do very little of this, primarily because this does not usually directly concern the production of coinage. On the other hand, several individuals, such as Carl Carlson, have made an art of this work by using a computer to speed up the work of searching. The trick is to know what to feed into the computer.

For those wishing to work with actual specimens of the coins or medals they are researching, there are two major collections in this country that may be used. In both cases it is best if the researcher were to show need since frivolous requests will probably be turned down. Budget constraints at both the ANS in New York and the Smithsonian in Washington make it necessary to restrict the use of the collections to only the most serious of students. For those who think I have slighted the ANA collection, I must admit that I know little about it, but do know that strong efforts are being made to build it up to the point that it will become a strong contender with the other two main collections in this country. There are also, of course, specialized collections in various parts of the country but these are not always easy to find or use. This is a cons-

Research Methods

tantly changing area since such collections are sometimes sold or otherwise removed from public view. The Byron Reed collection in Omaha has been hidden away in a bank vault for so many years that its existence may one day become mere legend, repeated by one old collector to another.

There are two major libraries of numismatic works normally open to the scholar, and access if not nearly as restricted as it is to coins. The ANS in New York and the ANA in Colorado Springs both have very fine libraries which may be consulted by anyone with a legitimate need. ANA members may of course borrow books by mail.

While most published research is carefully done, there is a class of work that should not pass unnoticed. There is, unfortunately, a relatively small group of individuals who publish materials which should be filed under "fiction" rather than what they purport to be. In one case, a scribbler—I hesitate to use the word author, being unable or unwilling to do the proper research, simply hounded the Mint Bureau to do the work. The Mint Bureau naturally had better things to do, although some material was provided, so the aspiring author simply manufactured facts from thin air and published them as research. Those who know the writer or the subject are perfectly aware that facts were fabricated when a ready source could not be found. I once took the trouble to write this person a letter pointing out that certain data had been fabricated, but all that I received for my trouble was a returned and unopened envelope marked 'refused' on the outside.

Another common fallacy that perhaps is unavoidable is the use of the mintage figures printed in the *Guide Book*. These have been worked out over a number of years by several responsible researchers and reflect a number of coins though to have been struck of a given date but not necessarily all in that year. However, since most of these figures were changed some years ago, there are now to be found writers who assume that the figures represent annual coinage figures. Articles have actually been published which are supposed to indicate the amount of bullion flowing into the mint in a given year but which in reality show nothing of the kind. Those who do research in this manner should be well warned to understand precisely the kind of figures being dealt with before using them in a serious study. The same comment would hold true a hundred years from now if some individual would see the lack of coins bearing the 1975 date and assume that the mints were hardly doing anything in that year whereas we know perfectly well at the present time that they were busy with the Bicentennial coinage.

It is quite possible that private individuals hold records of great value in the study of American coinage and medals. Both Adam Eckfeldt and Franklin Peale took a considerable quantity of records with them when they left the Philadelphia Mint and the finding of these records might prove of immense value. Only one small volume kept by Peale, on medal dies, has ever turned up for research work. The Eckfeldt papers are known to have been kept intact within the family several decades after his death in 1852 and may well yet be owned by some descendant. They might, for example, throw light on the Proof and medal coinages prior to 1839.

In closing I would like to mention that the most important point in doing research on any period of coinage is first to understand the time period in which the coinage was made. Too many writers nowadays attempt to use modern standards to judge actions of the past and this does a disservice to those responsible for producing the numismatic treasures of our earlier days. Study the past carefully before doing the research.

Joseph J. Mickley

By Tom LaMarre   1987/88

"You will all like to know what has become of our friend Mickley," wrote W.E. DuBois of the United States Mint, in the April 1871 issue of the *American Journal of Numismatics*.

We will agree in calling him the father of American numismatics. And yet he is not to be dubbed *venerable* when he is roaming over three continents with all the life and alacrity of a young man.

Do you know what started him in the coin-collecting furor? Many years ago, when he cared no more for coins than the rest of mankind do, he heard that the cent of 1799 was very rare. That was the year he was born. A cent of that year he must have; and he got it. It was the nest-egg of an immense and rich collection, American, foreign, and antique; gold, silver, and copper; known to everybody, and too well known to a villain who carried part of it off.

Mickley was born March 24, 1799 in the Moravian settlement of Northampton in Lehigh County, Pennsylvania, about four miles from Bethlehem. He moved to Philadelphia in 1818 and learned piano-making. DuBois said:

His hospitable, old-fashioned house here was the rendezvous of all amateurs and professors of music, all lovers of antiquarian lore, all inquirers after curious coins and medals. There I had the pleasure of handling Washington's violin, a fine instrument sent to him by the French officer of his army after the war, and on which he often played. There Ole Bull took hold of the same instrument, and inspired by its history, played a delightful voluntary for an hour.

Numismatist's Lakeside Companion

At a meeting of the American Numismatic and Archaeological Society in 1886, Frederick M. Bird read a paper titled "Recollections of Mr. Mickley," in which he said:

We lived near Mr. Mickley, and I got acquainted with him somehow, and became his frequent visitor. This was easy, for he was very good natured and accessible, and his place was the resort of harmless loafers, whom he used to address as "friends and fellow-pitchers." Most of us nowadays could by no means afford to entertain the numismatic small boy, with his garrulous ignorance, his infantile enthusiasm, and his morbid desire to invest a half-dime in cents of 1799 and 1804.

But Mr. Mickley was seldom busy; he usually puttered about with some kind of light work, which could be put down at a moment's notice, and with which conversation never interfered. I have known him (not often) to go out piano-tuning, and he may have sold an instrument now and then, but he seemed to be in comfortable circumstances, and to take life very easily.

He lived in a large house on the north side of Market Street, below Tenth. The ground floor was a grocery, I think; the second story was occupied by pianos, though I never heard of anyone going there to see them. His time was spent in a shop or office in the back building, corresponding to the dining room in most Philadelphia houses, with the kitchen beneath it. Back of this was a smaller room, where he kept old almanacs, directories, local histories, and the like; these were a minor hobby with him.

I saw nothing of his family, whom he doubtless met at meal times. Morning, noon, and evening he had (or was likely to have) a stream of visitors of all ages and conditions, with whom he loved to gossip. He had a quaint humor of his own. If I had had years and sense enough, it might have "paid" to note down some of his queer expressions; e.g., he used to call a humbug a "humguffin."

I never knew his placid amiability to be ruffled but once, and then without rhyme or reason. I had found a poor Vermontensium of then unnoted type, and was very willing to exchange it for two Roman coppers which chanced to be at hand. Having been taught to love my neighbor as myself, and noticing that one of the two was very fine, I suggested that he was giving me too much: that the beautiful Nero might be needed in his collection, while an inferior one would do for a beginner like me. He growled at the delay as if it were caused by grasping selfishness instead of conscientious consideration. The incident made an impression, as such will on boys.

Joseph J. Mickley

Most of Mr. Mickley's coins were not arranged, in my time, but stored away in a desk, where they were of no use to him or anyone. I doubt if he knew what he had; those who saw them at the great sale could form a very much better idea of the collection than I ever had. The exceptions were in a large cabinet in his second floor back. Here he kept some few Romans (if I remember aright) and his splendid series of the issues of our Mint in gold and silver, for every year or near it. The large sum—in intrinsic value alone—here locked up impressed my youthful mind; on my remarking that these dollars and eagles must have cost him fabulous prices, he answered with much feeling, "No, no, they were real prices."

I have always regretted that I saw so little of Mr. Mickley in later years. Changes of residence and occupation, and even the temporary fading of numismatic zeal, seem to me now but inadequate excuses for losing sight of so original a character and so princely a collector. When the famous robbery occurred, I was living at a distance from Philadelphia. I was told that the burglars secured little or nothing, but that Mr. Mickley was so frightened by their attempt, that his coins, the pride and joy of his heart, were at once packed up and sent off to auction. Afterwards I heard that some part of the collection had in fact been stolen, and that there seemed to be a mystery about the matter. On that mystery I can cast no light.

Although W. Elliot Woodward said that the value and importance of the portion of the collection that was stolen was "greatly overrated," DuBois said:

The robbery of his numismatic cabinet, briefly mentioned in the obituary, was a prominent event, and a turning point in his life. He was always ready, too ready, in the unsuspecting openness of his heart, to show his collection to friends or strangers. Sometimes (as he told me) he would find a piece or two missing after such an opening of his drawers.

Doubtless it was at some such visit as this that the robbery was planned. It took place on an evening, about 8:00, while Mr. Mickley was at work in his shop in the back building. The cabinet was kept in the third story front room of the main building. A slight noise induced him to go up there, not in time to encounter the burglar, one or more, but in time to see the devastation. How much was taken, cannot be definitely stated; certainly as much as a man could carry away.

A large part consisted of rare British coins, gold and silver; but other countries were copiously represented, and many pieces were American dupicates. It is stated, that some time before he was offered $30,000 for the whole collection. The unstolen residue that went to auction in New York soon after brought some $15,000. It is quite likely that the booty was worth an equal sum.

I well remember when Mr. Mickley came into my office, with the painful intelligence. "Oh, I have been robbed—I have been robbed! My coins taken; I can't tell how many. But it was a mercy I did not encounter the man. No doubt he was prepared to bind and gag me, as such fellows generally are."

It was a great shock to him; probably he never fully recovered from it, even in the excitement of foreign travel. It never was certainly known what became of this treasure, but Mr. Mickley had good reasons for settling his suspicions upon a certain person. One day he said to me, "I believe I met the man that robbed me, just now in Chestnut Street."

Years after, a few very fine gold pieces of England were offered for sale at the Mint Cabinet rooms. I was so well convinced that the labels were in his handwriting that I sent for him to come and see them. He could not deny the likeness but seemed reluctant to entertain the subject at all. They came from honest hands, through the few links of ownership that could be traced, but it was impossible to go backward for eight or nine years.

Mickley's proximity to the Philadelphia Mint and his friendship with DuBois enabled him to assemble a remarkable collection. The relationship also was advantageous to the Mint, which commissioned Mickley to procure new coins and medals for the Mint Cabinet during his travels throughout the world.

Mickley was determined to see everything in Europe and the borders of Asia and Africa. He was almost stifled in the crypt of an Egyptian pyramid; needed his overcoat in Lapland, where he went in June to see the sun go all around without making a dip; fell down the ancient well of Cicero at Rome; and was knocked down by a careless driver in Constantinople and taken up for dead.

Of course, Mickley visited nearly all the mints of Europe, minutely inspected their machinery, and obtained some specimens of their work.

"Numismatic collection formed by Joseph J. Mickley, Esq., of Philadelphia; now the property of W. Elliot Woodward, of Roxbury, Massachusetts; to be sold by auction by Messrs. Leavitt, Strebeigh & Co.," said the announcement. The sale was held at Clinton Hall in New York City, October 28, 1867; Woodward and Edward Cogan served as auctioneers.

In the preparation of the catalog, Woodward wrote, "I have faithfully endeavored to give accurate and fair descriptions of the pieces under notice, but have found throughout a difficulty arising from the very superior condition of everything in the collection."

When a part of a collection is of ordinary quality, it is easy by comparison to give some idea of relative goodness; but Mr. Mickley's coins are, with scarcely an exception, Fine to perfection.

The advantages which he possessed are well known to all collectors. He commenced early, was widely and favorably known, and his residence was near to the United States Mint. With all these superior facilities, he had an accurate and critical judgment, which led him to search for, and be content with, only the best.

Before purchasing the collection, I had a high opinion of its superiority; but till I looked it over carefully at home, and made comparisons, I never realized fully the difference between it, and others; but I now unhesitatingly affirm, that notwithstanding the high character of several of the collections which have been sold, no one of them has equalled the present, either as a whole, or in any of its American departments, with the exception, be it said, of some to which Mr. Mickley never turned his attention, for instance, political and store cards.

Lot No. 1696 was an 1804 dollar, which Woodward described as ". . . the gem of Mr. Mickley's collection. It has been in circulation, but is still in the finest condition, retaining its brilliancy of surface, and being entirely uninjured. It was obtained many years ago from the Bank of Pennsylvania, and is beyond question not only genuine but original."

In the Rare Book Room of the American Numismatic Association library is a bound copy of the Mickley Collection auction catalog, donated by Mrs. Alfred Z. Reed in 1951. Next to each lot number is the successful bidder's name in red ink and the price realized in black.

According to the notes, the 1804 dollar went to Mr. Lilliendahl for $750. A 1794 dollar, "one of the finest dollars of this date in existence," realized $75. A "splendid Proof" 1794 half dime sold for $10. A 1798 dollar, "countermarked at the British Mint with the head of George III," realized $5. An Uncirculated 1792 half disme brought $7.50.

However, the heart of the collection—in scope if not in terms of dollar value—was the large cent component. The Mickley Sale featured thirteen 1793 cents, including a piece in "Uncirculated, almost Proof condition" that realized $28. A "perfectly Uncirculated" 1822 cent with "fine color and almost Proof surface" sold for $1.75. One of the most unusual coins in the collection was an 1823 cent, double struck on both sides; it realized $1.75. A brilliant Proof 1857 cent realized $5.25.

The coin that was closest to Mickley's heart was Lot No. 1975, a 1799 cent described as "very fine indeed, having been but little in circulation, one of the best ever offered for sale, the rarest of American cents." Mr. Betts purchased it for $32.

One lot consisted of "two nice little cabinets, of black walnut, each 17½" high, 15¼" long, and 13¼" deep. One contains 18 drawers, the other 17, lined with purple velvet and divided into compartments. These cabinets possess historical interest to the American numismatist. To the fact of their recent completion, and the transfer to them of Mr. Mickley's American collection, its preservation from the robbers is due."

After the sale, Mickley's interests shifted from coins to coin books. He continued to travel, journeying as far south as Thebes, as far east as Moscow, and as far north as Uppsala in Sweden.

Mickley died in 1878. A notice in the Philadelphia papers said:

Mr. Joseph J. Mickley, who died suddenly on Friday evening, February 15, at the house of Dr. J.A. Meigs on Spruce Street, above Broad, was well known both in this country and Europe for his antiquarian tastes. On the night of his death he had started out to visit Mr. Oliver Hopkinson, at 1424 Spruce Street, but feeling a sudden oppression he stopped at the house of Dr. Meigs, for many years his physician, where he expired half an hour afterward. The doctors declare fatty degeneration of the heart to have been the cause of his death.

DuBois wrote:

In fine, Mr. Mickley was an agreeable man to associate with, and an honorable man to deal with. He seemed superior to any meanness, and free from vulgar passions and habits; from pride and vanity, from envy and jealousy, from evil speaking and harsh judging. He was eminently sincere, affable, kind, and gentle; yet decided, and with a mind of his own. In the best sense of the word he was a gentleman; not with artificial elegance of manners, yet with a good address, rendering him agreeable to refined society.

Similarly, the Philadelphia papers eulogized:

Besides being extensively acquainted with European history and literature, Mr. Mickley could speak fluently French, German, and Swedish. He was very simple in his ways, and while firm in his convictions and keen in his judgment of men, he was singularly gentle and lovable. Mr. Mickley was the first president of the Numismatic Society, and a well-known member both of the Franklin Institute and the Pennsylvania Historical Society. For some time past his books have been packed away. He was, however, making alterations in a house on Wood Street,

Joseph J. Mickley

away. He was, however, making alterations in a house on Wood Street, near Franklin, where he could have his library about him, when death stepped in to cut short a life spent in quiet study and refined enjoyment.

Mickley's Cents
Selected Prices Realized

Description		Price Realized	Bidder
1793	Liberty Cap, "entirely Uncirculated, polished surface; the finest cent of this variety that I have ever seen."	$ 55.00	Smith
1793	Flowing hair; rev. UNITED STATES OF AMERI; "perfectly Uncirculated, and in splendid Proof condition, probably the finest cent of this variety in existence, of the highest rarity."	110.00	McKenzie
1794	"Perfectly Uncirculated, almost Proof, very rare indeed."	20.00	Smith
1795	Jefferson Head, "though not fine, this piece is in good condition for the variety, which is rarer than any other type of the American cent."	4.50	Sanford
1797	"Two faces on the obverse, bought in a recent sale by Mr. Mickley at a high price; in good condition, unique."	2.50	Crane
1804	Perfect die, "very fine indeed, having been but little in circulation, very rare."	10.00	Fellows
1817	"Splendid Proof, rare."	14.00	McKenzie
1837	Proof	6.50	Smith
1855	Uncirculated, straight date	.50	Crane
1857	Proof	5.25	Childs

The 1799 Cents

The cent that whetted Mickley's appetite for numismatics has long been the source of conjecture. A story published in 1860 said, "Their scarcity. . .is attributed to a shipment to the coast of Africa by a Salem, Massachusetts firm of several hundred thousand on an order from the country, where, being punched with holes, they were bartered away, probably to the chiefs. . .and subsequently used as ornaments by the natives, being suspended from the neck by a string."

A similar story was quoted in the January 1918 issue of *The Numismatist:*

The rarest cent is that of the series of 1799. It is said that the scarcity of this issue is due to the fact that a firm in Salem, Massachusetts, which was then engaged in the slave trade, procured a large quantity of them from the Mint, and after drilling holes in each one, shipped them to Africa, where they were given as ornaments to the chiefs in exchange for slaves. The veracity of this story cannot be vouched for, but, if it is true, coin collectors are much more likely to find specimens of this issue in Africa than in the United States.

According to another variation of the tale, the ship carrying the cents to Africa sank in a storm.

Design of the Buffalo Nickel

By Michael Westcott   1987/88

"The Buffalo nickel. . .was truly an 'ALL AMERICAN' coin. Although simplistic in design, James E. Fraser depicted the rugged profile of the American Indian on the obverse and a powerful buffalo or bison on the reverse, both of which played an important part in forming the western culture of this great country."–Bill Fivaz

The Buffalo nickel, which I believe is possibly the most artistic of all United States coins, was designed in 1912 by James Earle Fraser (1875-1953) and was first coined on February 21, 1913, at Philadelphia. They were first placed in circulation a day later at Ft. Wadsworth in New York City, and after that there was more in complaints about the nickel than praise. "(The Buffalo nickel is a) travesty on artistic effect. . ." "E Pluribus Unum is almost crowded out of sight. . ." "The figure on each side of the coin is so huge that it leaves no room for encircling decoration of any sort. . ." said New York Times writers. Another wrote:
"A glance at the new five-cent piece shows readily that an American Indian is portrayed on the one side, but who is the gentleman on the reverse?
"Held in one position there appears the dim outline of an aged man with a grotesque hint of a beard. Held in another there is some thing that is said to be a buffalo; a buffalo that has hunched himself in a desperate endeavor not to overflow the sides of his cage. . ."
The American Numismatic Association disliked the coin and even the Mint was not fond of it. The ANA did not like the way that the date

was placed on a mound, making it wear off rather quickly. Today a multitude of Buffalo nickels are found without dates, which, several years ago, prompted a formula to help regain the date, actually an acid that would eat around the date. The nickels treated by it—in most cases—were better off without the date.

The design caused minting difficulties in that the denomination FIVE CENTS was too high, which was corrected by replacing the mound on which the buffalo stood (above the denomination) with a line and lowering the whole area. Robert Julian once remarked that this work, done by Charles Barber (designer of the Liberty nickel), didn't help the design in many ways and that perhaps the mound should have been left and FIVE CENTS be minted intaglio, that is, sunk in.

Said James E. Fraser:

"In designing the Buffalo nickel, my first object was to produce a coin which was truly American, and that could not be confused with the currency of any other country. . .and in my search of symbols, I found no motif within the boundaries of the United States as the American buffalo or bison.

"With the Indian head on the obverse, we have a perfect unity in theme, truly American. It has a pertinent historical significance, and is in line with the best traditions of centuries of coin design where the purpose was to memorialize a country or a nation."

"No aspect of the Buffalo nickel has resulted in more interest than the identification of the Indian or Indians used by Fraser as models. . .," said Cohen and Druley in their book *The Buffalo Nickel*. It was thought for years that the model was an Indian passing through New York named Two Guns White Calf, who claimed to have been the model. He was known as the "Buffalo Nickel Indian" until his death. Because of his claims, the Bureau of Indian Affairs published a letter from Fraser dated June 10, 1931 that read:

"The Indian head on the nickel is not a direct portrait of any particular Indian, but was made from several portrait busts which I did of Indians. As a matter of fact, I used three different heads; I remember two of the men. One was Iron Tail, the best Indian head I can remember; the other was Two Moons, the third I cannot recall.

"I have never seen Two Guns White Calf nor used him in any way, although he has a magnificent head. . ."

Fraser went on to say he understood how Two Guns could have mistakenly thought that Fraser had used him, as many artists had drawn Two Guns. Still, many thought that Two Guns was the third Indian, if

The Design of the Buffalo Nickel

not the only one, because of his striking resemblance to the Indian on the nickel. The matter of the third Indian was not really resolved until April 17, 1964 when Fraser's wife, Laura Gardin Fraser, wrote to the director of the Mint:

"...I hope that I shall be able to "lay the ghost" as to the third Indian who posed (for the nickel).

"The name of Big Tree always came to my mind but I was not too sure of it as belonging to the trio who posed for the nickel until I saw his picture sent (to) me from all parts of the country in celebration of his 100th birthday. It was amazing to me that he had changed so little. I was glad to be able to make this assertion to a coin enthusiast in California who asked my opinion as to the authenticity of Big Tree's claim...(Big Tree) was the Indian I had remembered posing for Mr. Fraser."

Of the three Indians the most is known about Big Tree, an Iroquois Indian, because he died in 1967. Although he claimed to have been born in 1862—and he even celebrated a 100th birthday in 1962—some say he was really born in 1875, making him a year older than Fraser himself. He died at the Onondaga Reservation in Syracuse, New York, and the records there say he died at 92.

Iron Tail, a Sioux, died in September of 1924; Two Moons was a Cheyenne and died on April 28, 1917.

There is speculation that Big Tree was used from the nose up, the mouth was based on Iron Tail, and the hair and braids on Two Moons.

As for the reverse, there have been no direct statements on the subject by the artist or his wife, but it is accepted that the buffalo was designed after Black Diamond. The Mint seriously doubts that Black Diamond was really a model as Fraser was raised in South Dakota, bison country, and was quite familiar with the animal before coming to New York.

Black Diamond was a famous bull buffalo in the Central Park Zoo when Fraser designed the nickel. He was born in 1893 to a bull and cow given to the zoo by Barnum and Bailey. When he was 22, an old age for a bison, he was put up for sale. No bids were received when he was put up for auction on June 28, 1915. Then, for $300 in a private sale, Black Diamond was purchased by A. Sills, Inc. Some people tried to save the bull from being slaughtered in November, even offering $1,000 for him, but to no avail. The head was mounted and the skin made into a robe. For many years the location of both was unknown, but the head was recently on display at an ANA Convention.

Even if Black Diamond wasn't the model, say Cohen and Druley, he should have been.

Michael Wescott, who is 14 years of age, enjoys the five-cent series and is sponsor of an organization of nickel enthusiasts.

Re-evaluating A Famous American Token

By Q. David Bowers   1987/88

One of the most famous of all American tokens attributed to the 18th century is the 1789-dated piece issued by Motts, a New York jewelry and fine arts firm. Varieties exist on thin, thick, and extremely thick planchets, and in varying die states, indicating issuance over a period of time. Rare thin planchet specimens range in weight from 104 to 110 grains; extremely rare, extremely thick planchet specimens have been found weighing 202 and 233 grains; while the usually seen thick planchet variety ranges in weight from 164 to 171 grains.

The size of a United States large cent, the piece bears on its obverse (although some designate this as the reverse) the image of a shelf clock, of the regulator type, surrounded by an inscription in two lines: MOTTS, N.Y. IMPORTERS, DEALERS, MANUFACTURERS,/OF GOLD & SILVER WARES.

The reverse (designated by the *Guide Book* and a number of other references as the obverse) illustrates an eagle, with wings outspread, a shield on its breast, and grasping with one foot an olive branch, in the other a bundle of arrows. Above the eagle's head is the date 1789, while the following inscription is found around the border: WATCHES, JEWELRY, SILVER WARE, CHRONOMETERS, CLOCKS. The peripheral legend is continuous, separated by commas, with no apparent starting or ending point.

The *Guide Book* Listing

Most readers are familiar with the Mott token through the medium of *A Guide Book of United States Coins*. The 1988 edition describes it on page 48 as follows:

"This was one of the first tradesman's tokens issued in America. Manufactured in England, they were issued by Messrs. Mott of New York in 1789. The firm was composed of William and John Mott, located at 240 Water Street, a fashionable section of New York at the time."

Not only does the *Guide Book* unequivocally state that it was "issued in 1789," it further lists the pieces among early American coins and tokens, issues produced before the federal coinage. Thick planchet and thin planchet varieties are described, priced at $250 and $300 respectively in Very Fine preservation, with an additional variety, with the "entire edge engrailed," posted at $500 in the same grade.

Crosby's Comments

Earlier, the dean of American colonial numismatics, Sylvester S. Crosby, described the piece on page 334 of his *The Early Coins of America* as follows:

"[The Mott tokens.] A copper token, issued in the year 1789, by the Messrs. Mott, of the city of New York, dealers in watches, clocks and jewelry, is generally conceded to have been the first tradesman's token issued in America; it was manufactured in England. . . .'"

Russ Rulau Writes

Russell Rulau, who in recent years has been America's most prolific writer on the subject of tokens, in his *Early American Tokens* monograph (1981) listed five different variations of the issue:

(1) copper, 28mm (as all are). Thick planchet. Broken dies. In EF grade the piece was listed six years ago for $500.
(2) copper, thin planchet, perfect dies. EF $700.
(3) copper, thin planchet, perfect dies. Edge engrailed. EF $1,200.
(4) copper, thin planchet, perfect dies, edge lettered PAYABLE AT LIVERPOOL, LONDON OR BRISTOL. EF $1,550.
(5) pewter, apparently with plain edge. not priced; noted as "Ex Rare."

Russell Rulau gives a brief historical background of the piece as follows:

"William and John Mott were importers, dealers and manufacturers of gold and silver wares, jewelry, watches and clocks, located at 240 Water Street, then a fashionable section of New York. In 1789 they ordered the first true tradesman's tokens of America, probably from an English medallic firm which has not been traced. The thick planchet tokens normally are struck in dies heavily broken on the clock side; they usually weigh about 170 grains. The thin planchet pieces usually are struck from unbroken dies. Perfect-die thick flan and broken-die thin flan pieces do exist.

"What is not so well-known is that the firm survived well into the 19th century. William & John Mott, merchants, were still located at 240 Water Street, 1821-1822. They next appear in the directory listed as grocers for 1827-1828, at 730 Greenwich Street. Still listed as grocers, they appear in 1829-1830 at 154 15th Street, near 7th Avenue. What happened in 40 years to turn the firm from jewelry to grocery needs further study. . . ."

The preceding states Russell Rulau's opinion that the pieces were ordered in 1789 and, thus, are contemporary with the 1789 date. Of particular significance is the notation that the firm survived well into the 19th century.

Cornelius Vermuele's Evaluation

Now, let me turn to another author, who describes United States Mint coins of a later year and, in passing, discusses the 1789 Mott token. While describing John Reich's creation of a new eagle design, appearing for the first time on the federal half dollar and half eagle of 1807, Cornelius Vermeule, in *Numismatic Art in America,* stated:

"The new coin combined the Liberty in turbaned cap with a pseudo-natural heraldic eagle. The bird was later said by a perceptive government official to defy both nature and art. . . . The reverse was to remain on the silver coinage, almost without modification, until 1891.

"The form of the single 'sandwich-board' eagle that persisted for over 80 years on our coins was not a new design in 1807 nor, sadly enough, was it of American origin so far as numismatics are concerned. It graces the Mott token of 1789, manufactured in England for a fashionable firm of New York jewelers and importers of precision clocks and related instruments. The reverse of this early tradesman's token shows a fancy French tabletop clock of a type associated with the Neoclassic revival under Louis XV and XVI. The inscriptions around the obverse and reverse speak of the Motts as importers, dealers, and manufacturers of gold and silver wares, specifically watches and jewelry. . ."

Thus, this distinguished author, like others before him, implies that the Mott coinage is contemporary with date of 1789, or at least antedates the federal coinage of 1807. Vermeule was, however, among the first to note the similarity of the Reich-designed reverse eagle to that appearing on the Mott token dated 1789.

My Curiosity is Aroused

My own curiosity concerning the subject was aroused when I noticed that the eagle on the reverse of an 1838 eagle was similar in design to that found on the 1789 Mott token. In the course of handling thousands of eagles of the 1838-1907 design, the similarity had not dawned upon me until this particular moment.

I knew that the bird appearing on the reverse of the eagle of the 1838-1907 type did not represent the initial appearance of that motif, for the half eagle, believed to have been the work of John Reich, featured a somewhat similar representation. However, the treatment of the olive leaves on the left side of the Mott coin did not resemble those on the 1807 half eagle but, rather, were oriented in a direction upward to the left as *first used on the $10 piece of 1838*. An examination of the shape of the void between the eagle's lower beak and the wing and the shoulder below it reveals that either the 1789-dated Mott token was copied from the 1838 $10 issue (or the related $2½ issue which first appeared in 1840, or the 1839 $5 piece—all are the same), or else one is faced with the rather improbable conclusion that in 1838, when Christian Gobrecht revised the eagle on the reverse of the $10 piece, adjusting it slightly from that proposed by John Reich in 1807, he copied almost precisely the work of a 1789 engraver who first so drew the eagle on the Mott token dated that year. This, of course, strains credulity. The inescapable conclusion, at least to the present author, is that the Mott token was produced no earlier than 1838, and that the eagle was copied from that found on contemporary gold coins. It should be noted that the eagle on the Mott token is a composite of Reich's early design and Gobrecht's 1838 $10 design, but as it incorporates some features of the 1838 motif, the Mott eagle must have been made in or after 1838.

The significance of the weight range for the usually seen thick planchet specimen of the Mott token, 154 to 171 grains, was not overlooked by the noted numismatic researcher Don Taxay, who wrote in *Scott's Catalogue & Encyclopedia of United States Coins* (1976 edition): "It is not known whether the tokens were struck in England or America, but it is evident, from the weights of the common broken-die pieces, that *most* were made to conform with the standard for United States cents adopted in 1796." [italics ours]

Re-evaluating a Famous American Token

The earliest United States large cents, struck from 1793 through 1795, were manufactured on thick planchets weighing approximately 208 grains each. In 1795 the weight, and the thickness, of the planchet was reduced, yielding an average weight for specimens struck from 1795 through the end of the denomination in 1857 of 168 grains. Painting this with the broadest brush, if weight alone were to be considered as an indication of striking time, either the Motts anticipated the legal weight of American cents in 1789, seven years before the federal government adopted it and, indeed, several years before the government struck its own cents of any type, or else, more logically, the token was issued in or after 1796, and was made to the approximate standard weight in order to facilitate its circulation. After noting that the majority of the Mott tokens seemed to conform to the 1795/6 large cent standard, Taxay unaccountably describes the Mott token as "this piece was struck in 1789."

Anton's Significant Find

In a short article written by William T. Anton "Was the Mott Token Backdated to 1789?," which appeared in *Penny-Wise* (Vol. XX, No. 6, November 1986), the author reported a 1789-dated Mott token overstruck on a planchet which showed at the center of the reverse (noted as the obverse by Anton) the remnants of the ONE CENT reverse denomination mark found on a large cent of the coronet type 1837-39. Mr. Anton wrote:

"Though the die state for the Mott token strike is relatively late, I have seen much later—raising the question whether the '1789' Mott tokens were struck on into the early 1840s. This particular piece would suggest... that the Mott tokens were struck in the United States—and at a period much later than their date would indicate."

The weight of the piece described by Anton in his article was 196.75 grains, placing it close to the weights of the very rare, extremely heavy planchet types.

Mott History

A firm owned by William and John Mott was located at 240 Water Street in 1789, the date on the tokens, and also as late as 1821-1822. At that time their primary occupation was listed as the grocery trade. They changed locations, and at still another address they were engaged in the grocery business as late as 1829-1830.

As the tokens themselves bear no street address, it is not known at what address the Mott firm was located when the tokens were made, except that *if* they were made in 1789, the address would have been 240 Water Street. If they were made after the 1820s, the tokens might have been issued from 739 Greenwich Street or 154 15th Street. New York City directories for the period are not complete. *Representative* tradesmen are listed, but among various listings of artisans, merchants, and others in different lines of endeavors, often listings are intermittent, or primary occupations are changed to one specialty, then changed back to another. At the very least, reporting was incomplete and erratic. It seems unlikely that a firm could at once deal in clocks, gold, and silver goods and at the same time deal in groceries, especially in a metropolitan area such as New York City. It is possible that the Mott firm had a double specialty—groceries and jewelry—but, had this been the case, the token in question probably would have mentioned it.

Bushnell and the Mott Token

In 1859, Charles I. Bushnell, America's most prominent numismatic researcher of the period, published an essay, *An Historical Account of the First Three Business Tokens Issued in the City of New York*. Bushnell, who spent a good part of his life in New York, and who researched intensely subjects which interested him (and thus laid the foundation for much of the information on certain state coinages appearing in Sylvester S. Crosby's later work), wrote an essay on the subject of the Motts firm, *but did not mention their activity in the grocery business*. This is highly unusual, for had the Motts been in the grocery business *after* the jewelry business, the grocery business would be the most recent in memory. Using the 1829-1830 directory date for the grocery specialty at 154 15th Street, this was scarcely 30 years earlier than the Bushnell essay. Thus, the activity would be known to virtually anyone he consulted on the subject. After reading what Bushnell has to say, it is easy to conclude that if the Mott firm had sold groceries in the 1820s, it must have been a minor specialty, not a major one. Or, more likely, perhaps the Mott grocery firm was a different enterprise from Mott the jeweler.

You be the judge. Here is what Charles I. Bushnell wrote in 1859:

"[The first business token issued in New York City] was issued as early as the year 1789....

"Upon one of the top corners of the regulator [a generic name for a shelf clock which kept fairly accurate time] is seen what appears to be a hand. This is, however, a blur caused by the breaking of the die. On some specimens this blur is greater than upon others, while some do not show the defect at all. These coins were generally struck upon thick planchets, but occasionally a specimen will be found struck upon a thin one.

"The firm of Motts was composed of William and John Mott, and their place of business was at 240 Water Street—a location at which they continued for a number of years, and which was at the time a most fashionable business part of the city. Some of the immediate descendants of the firm were engaged in the same pursuit *until within a few years past.* [italics ours]

"The firm of Motts was well-known in its day and generation. Their store was the resort of the rich and the great, of the gay belles and beaux of the time. The learned judge who wished a pair of spectacles to aid his failing sight, the lovely maid who craved a splendid ring to deck her tapering hand, their wants supplied with hearts' content from Motts' extensive stock. More than one venerable dame now living can produce, in the shape of a watch of somewhat antique style, but still faithful to its early mission, her bridal gift, purchased in her days of youth and beauty from their well-furnished establishment. Many a venerable timepiece, solid and substantial as the maker, and bearing upon the face the name of "Motts," has out-lived a host of modern abortions, and still graces the dining rooms of some of our oldest and most respectable, though not, perhaps, our most fashionable citizens, and still chronicles the days of man, and re-echoes still, the steps of passing time."

It seems to the present writer that Charles I. Bushnell, who observed the descendants of the firm were engaged in the same pursuits "until within a few years past," would have remarked had the firm's main emphasis shifted from fine objects to groceries. It seems probable that the token-issuing Mott firm was different from the grocery firm, but the token issuer, engaged in the jewelry business, used the 1789 founding date of a common ancestor's trade. Bushnell does hedge somewhat concerning the year of issue of the token, for he says that the Mott token was issued "as early as the year 1789." This implies that it could have been issued later, although there is no other evidence to suggest that Bushnell believed this.

Putting It All Together

Bushnell's statement that "some of the immediate descendants of the firm were engaged in the same pursuit until within a few years past," indicates that they may have been in the jewelry business as recently as the early 1850s, but almost certainly since 1838 (the date the design first appeared on the $10 piece). It is important to note that the name on the token appears as "MOTTS" with no first name given for any of the principals. Thus, although numismatic writers for many generations have assumed that the Motts referred to was that establishment located at 240 Water Street and operated by William and John Mott circa 1789, as neither the first names of the Mott principals nor the street address was given, there is no evidence to support the claim that the tokens were issued in 1789 from the Water Street address. Further, the fact that many specimens seen approximate the weight of federally issued cents of 1796 and later years, suggests that the pieces were not issued in 1789. Still further, the regulator clock of the type shown on the token was a common product of the 1830s and 1840s, at which time dozens of different firms were making them. An additional clue appears in Russell Rulau's *Early American Tokens* monograph, indicating that William and John Mott, merchants, were still located at 240 Water Street in the directory for 1821-1822. In addition to the earlier quoted description of the firm of William and John Mott, Russell Rulau went on to note:

"A possible related firm which did not issue tokens in its own name was W. W. & R. Mott, Hardware Store, 241 Pearl Street. William W. Mott was the senior partner, and this firm appears at this address 1821-1827. Then it became William W. Mott & Co., merchants at 241 Pearl Street, 1829-1830. William W. Mott died about 1832 and was succeeded in his business by his widow, Susan F. Mott.

"The firm of William H. Mott, Hardware, issued tokens with the address 'corner Old Slip & Water St.'

"On some of his tokens the address is given as 'Old Ship' rather than 'Old Slip.' The firm has not been traced at this Old Slip and Water Street corner back to the 1822 New York City directories, however. The firm does appear in 1829-1830 as hardware merchants at 396 Hudson Street. His home at the time was at 442 Greenwich Street. In 1832-1833 his business address was 109 King Street."

Inasmuch as the "MOTTS" inscription on the 1789-dated token does not refer to any specific individuals with that name, it seems to the present writer than it is entirely possible that the 1789-tokens were issued by some later Mott, not William and John, and that the 1789 date simply refers to the date that an earlier, related Mott family enterprise was *founded,* not to the date that the token was issued. In addition, apparently there were *multiple* Mott businesses and tradesmen in New York City in the early days, and the directory record of them is incomplete.

The evidence of the weights of the usually seen thick planchet Mott tokens; the type of regulator clock pictured on the token; the almost exact similarity in design of the eagle on the Mott token with the eagle appearing on the $10 piece of 1838, the $5 piece of 1839, and the $2½ piece of 1840; and the uncertainty inherent in the listings found in New York City directories of the early 19th century; all lead the present writer to suggest that the Mott token was produced around 1838 or later, probably before 1850, for Bushnell certainly did not view it as a contemporary issue when he wrote of it in 1859. If issued from 1838 through the early 1840s, it probably properly belongs in the Hard Times token series. This view is supported by William Anton's observation of a Mott token struck over a large cent of the 1837-1839 type.

Unfortunately, the place of striking of the Mott tokens may never be known with certainty. On the evidence of the fourth variety enumerated by Russell Rulau (see above), it has been suggested that the entire issue was struck in England. It is interesting to note that the heyday of token manufacture in England was the period of 1790-1805, much earlier than the newly suggested dating for the Mott token. Additionally, the specimen described by William Anton in the article referenced above was clearly struck on an American made planchet. In fact, there is nothing about the fabric, style, or method of manufacture of the Mott token which suggests a British origin. It is possible that the piece with the "LIVERPOOL" edge represents the use of an earlier British-made token as a planchet for a token struck in America. The use of previously-struck coins for planchets is evidenced by the cent overstrike described by Anton. The use of British-made tokens for planchets in America had ample precedent, including the Philadelphia Mint's utilization in 1795 of thousands of Talbot, Allum and Lee tokens, made in England, for planchets for cents and half cents.

The idea of confounding the date appearing on a later token with the issue date of the token is not at all new in the field of numismatics and has ample precedents. For example, Lyman H. Low, in his *Hard Times Tokens* book (1900) devoted two paragraphs to an 1837-dated card issued by C.D. Peacock, a Chicago jeweler, noting:

"The issue of this card, bearing the date of 1837, seems to warrant special notice, in order that it may not be improperly placed with a series of Hard Times tokens. Elija Peacock (who died in 1889), grandfather of the present Charles Daniel Peacock, who issued the card, found the business in 1837, and to this event the date refers. It has no other connection with the "hard times". . . The first issue was made about 1900, of which there were 10,000 struck in copper and four in silver. . . "

Why did many numismatic authors over the years, including the present writer, unswervingly attribute Mott tokens to a 1789 origin? The answer is painfully obvious: The date was examined, and contemporary trade references revealed that indeed in New York City in 1789 a firm comprised of individuals named Mott was doing business. Apparently, few other questions were ever asked.

In mid-May of the present year I glanced through my copy of *The Numismatist*, the journal of the American Numismatic Association. In it was an article, "The Eagle Motif on Early American Coinage," by William Justin DeLeonardis. That writer presented a general discussion of eagles as found on various and sundry early American pieces, and illustrated the feature with pictures ranging from the 1787 Massachusetts copper cent to the Morgan silver dollar introduced in 1878. Pictured in juxtaposition were the reverses of a 1789 Mott token and quarter eagle of the 1840-1870 type, accompanied by the following caption: "The eagle depicted on the 1789 Mott token is strikingly similar to one on the reverse of the 1863 Coronet Head quarter eagle."

Mr. DeLeonardis found this a bit unusual and noted separately in the text:

"Curiously, the Mott token of 1789, one of the earliest tradesman's tokens issued in America, bears an eagle very similar in design to that depicted on the Classic Head and Coronet Head gold coinage of the 19th century." A footnote referred the reader to Sylvester S. Crosby's 1875 volume, the excerpt mentioned above.

Conclusion

Although several writers—Taxay, Anton, and DeLeonardis among them—have alluded to the inconsistency of the date vis a vis the design or weight of the 1789 Mott token, so far as the present writer knows, the present essay is the first time the status of this curious piece has been evaluated in detail. Behold the 1789-dated Mott piece—a *Hard Times token*.

The 1873-CC No Arrows Quarter and Dime

By P. Scott Rubin												1987

Recently *Coin World* carried a front-page story about the Norweb Collection and the fact that Auctions by Bowers and Merena, Inc. is the company which will soon be offering this collection for sale. The story went on to describe in words and pictures some of the fabulous rarities included in the collection. The one item that caught my attention, if I can be allowed to lie and say only one item did, was the fact that an 1873-CC No Arrows quarter was included in the Norweb holdings. I have always found this particular coin interesting and was very much surprised that such a rare coin could be in such a famous collection without word of its existence leaking.

So, with the discovery that the Norweb Collection contains a specimen of the 1873-CC No Arrows quarter, an examination of just how many of these coins exist and their known background seems appropriate.

The 1873-CC No Arrows quarter is one of the rarest coins in the United States coinage series. Just how rare this coin is has never been completely identified. The main reason seems to stem from the fact that early collectors and writers of the quarter series have never given the general collecting public all the known information.

The first appearance of an 1873-CC No Arrows quarter seems to have been ignored by most numismatic writers for over 100 years. Edward Cogan in his sale of the John Swan Randall Collection (large cent collectors know the Randall Hoard gets its name from this collector) catalogued under the quarter heading, as Lot 795, a coin described as "1873-CC Mint. Old style. Nearly Uncirculated."

If there was a question as to what was meant by "old style" the next lot was described as "1873 New Style With Arrows. Uncirculated." So it appears the No Arrows variety was the old style coin. If this were the only surprise in the sale it would be enough, but Lot 902 was described "1873 Old Style. C.C. Mint. Fine impression," and this was under the dime heading. (Carl Carlson supplied me with the information that the quarter realized 35 cents and the dime 17 cents, he also believes that the term "Fine impression," could refer to a coin in Uncirculated condition, when it was used in the 1870s.) So this sale not only contained the quarter but the dime of this issue. The amazing thing about the dime is that to the present time only one is known and that coin has been reported to have been in the Mint's hands until the early 20th century when it finally became the property of Mr. W.H. Woodin. So it appears that a possibility exists that a second dime exists and that it may turn up again, just as the quarters have come from unknown sources.

In 1893 when Mr. A.G. Heaton wrote his landmark monograph *Mint Marks, A Treatise on the Coinage of the United States Branch Mints,* he stated that the 1873-CC No Arrows quarter along with the relatively more common 1873-CC With Arrows quarter were both exceedingly rare. From this statement I would guess that Mr. Heaton had seen or heard of at least one specimen of each coin.

It should be noted that the 1873-CC No Arrows dime is mentioned in this pamphlet, but the 1873-CC With Arrows is not. It is also stated that the 1874-CC is the rarest of the 1871 to 1874 Carson City dimes. In trying to understand this I checked my notes of auction appearances of the With Arrows dime and quarter and found that before 1893, the date of Mr. Heaton's monograph, I had only one appearance record of each. A With Arrows quarter was sold in the Chapmans' 1890 sale of the Cleneay Collection as Lot 1454 and a With Arrows dime was sold in 1880 as part of Woodward's 32nd Sale, the collection of Ferguson Haines, as Lot 899 (it realized 17 cents). The question is did Mr. Heaton know of these sales? It is possible he did and that the reason he did not know if the dime was a With or Without Arrows coin might be because the lot did not describe it as either. However, the preceding two lots in order were, a No Arrows P mint coin and a With Arrows S mint coin, leading me to believe that the CC mint coin which followed would have been a With Arrows coin or it would have been noted. Mr. Heaton may have come to another conclusion, if he indeed knew of this sale listing.

After mentioning the above publications it is still a fact that general knowledge of the 1873-CC No Arrows dime would wait until the

The 1873-CC No Arrows Quarter and Dime

1914 American Numismatic Society Exhibition when Mr. H.O. Granberg displayed his 1873-CC No Arrows dime, the coin having come to Mr. Granberg from Mr. Woodin. A year later Mr. Granberg offered this dime for sale in a U.S. Coin Company auction. He did not display the quarter, which he offered for sale at a B. Max Mehl auction in 1919. If he had believed the quarter as important as the dime he most probably would have loaned it to ANS for exhibit. So even after the notoriety given the dime in 1914 the quarter remained obscure as a extreme rarity.

The next time an 1873-CC No Arrows quarter was to appear at auction, after 1919, was 1945 when F.C.C. Boyd's collection was sold at a sale titled the "World's Greatest Collection," by the Numismatic Gallery (Abe Kosoff and Abner Kreisberg). No information about the ownership, past or present, (Mr. Boyd's name was not mentioned in the catalog or at the time of the sale) was mentioned by the cataloguers. The coin was just said to be an extreme rarity. Since this 1945 sale the coin has remained in the collection of the late Louis Eliasberg.

This variety was not offered at auction again until 1975 when the James A. Stack Collection of quarters was sold at auction by Stack's. The coin was reported to have come from the Browning Collection, Mr. Browning was the author of a die variety book of early date quarters. At the time of this sale it was reported that Mr. Stack had obtained this coin in the 1940s. This coin, like the Boyd coin, is Uncirculated. The price realized at the auction was $80,000. The Stack coin was then offered at auction and fixed prices, without changing ownership until a 1980 New England Rare Coin Company auction at which it was reported to have changed hands for $205,000.

The existence of the Norweb 1873-CC No Arrows quarter has been unknown to most of the numismatic world until the recent *Coin World* story of the upcoming sale of the Norweb holdings by Bowers and Merena. Michael Hodder supplied me with the following information from the Norweb inventory. The coin was purchased from Imperial Coin Co. (Ben Stack), on July 29, 1954, and was also credited with being ex. Numismatic Gallery. It is interesting to note that Numismatic Gallery had closed its doors July 1, 1954. The two partners, Abe Kosoff and Abner Kreisberg, continued business separately after this date. It was stated in publications at the time that any business under the name Numismatic Gallery would be handled from a post office box number. Was this coin an item owned jointly by these two individuals at the time of their breakup? The other person involved with this coin, Ben Stack, was operating his own company at this time. He would in the next couple of years rejoin the family coin business, Stack's. No other information about this coin's pedigree is known at the present time.

Comparing photographs of the Boyd and Stack coins with the Norweb coin shows that they are all different specimens. (I used the photographs from the "World's Greatest Collection" auction catalogue, New England Rare Coin Company's 1980 Sale, and one kindly supplied by Michael Hodder of Bowers and Merena.) They all appear to be Uncirculated and all have the same characteristics. All three are of the Closed 3 variety which according to Harry X Boosel, (Mr. Boosel has done extensive research on the die varieties of all United States coinage of 1873) the no arrows coins should have; all the With Arrows quarters with the Carson City mintmark have the open 3. All have the placement of the "CC" in the same place as the 1870 to 1872 quarters; the placement changes say for 1878 which would be a prime candidate for people wishing to modify a coin to appear to be the rare No Arrow 1873 issue.

The existence of one or two other 1873-CC No Arrows quarters has been rumored for a number of years. Walter Breen in his upcoming book, *Walter Breen's Complete Encyclopedia of United States Coins,* states that Abner Kreisberg once had a coin of this issue in Very Fine condition.

There was also a California collector named H.M. Budd, who wrote a letter to the editor of *The Numismatist* that appeared in the January 1949 issue, who reported owning an 1873-CC No Arrows quarter. He also stated that no 1873-CC No Arrows dimes were struck (over 12,000 of these dimes were struck and 4,000 of the quarters). He did not mention the condition of the coin he owned nor where he obtained it. He did state that he had only observed this coin at auction once in the last 25 years. This I would guess would be the 1945 W.G.C. Sale coin that went to Mr. Eliasberg. It seems possible that the Budd coin, if it was real, could be either the J.A. Stack coin, which was obtained sometime in the 1940s, or more likely the Norweb coin, for which information only dates back to 1954, thus accounting for all the three known pieces.

At the present time it would appear that the 1873-CC No Arrows quarter is one of the rarest of all United States coin issues. Only the above mentioned three Uncirculated coins are known to exist with certainty. This coin has to be considered the rarest of the quarter series.

I for one will be waiting for this coin to take its place in the history of numismatics when Auctions by Bowers and Merena, Inc. include it in one of their upcoming auction catalogues of the Norweb Collection. At which time the general collecting public will have the opportunity to vie for ownership of this great American coinage classic, in a

The 1873-CC No Arrows Quarter and Dime

format I expect will be as spectacular in scope and presentation as their past Garrett and Eliasberg sales.

The following is a list of pedigree information of both the 1873-CC No Arrows quarter and 1873-CC No Arrows dime.

1873-CC No Arrows Quarter
1. Uncirculated
   A. U.S. Mint
   B. A.L. Snowden
   C. J.W. Haseltine
   D. J.K. Nagy
   E. W.H. Woodin
   F. H.O. Granberg
   G. 1919 B. Max Mehl's 54th Sale, Lot 358
   H. F.C.C. Boyd
   I. 1945 World's Greatest Collection Sale, Lot 378 (realized $725)
   J. Louis Eliasberg
   K. Louis Eliasberg family
2. Uncirculated
   A. John Swan Randall
   B. 1878 Cogan's 5/6 Sale, Lot 795 (realized 35 cents)
   C. Browning Collection
   D. James A. Stack
   E. 1975 James A. Stack Collection Sale, Lot 136 (realized $80,000)
   F. William Grayson (B & B Coins)
   G. 1979 NASCA's London Sale, the coin had a reserve bid that was not met and did not sell
   H. 1980 Metropolitan New York Sale, Lot 519 (was said to have realized $205,000)
   I. Bob Riethe and Greg Holloway
3. Uncirculated
   A. H.M. Budd
   B. Numismatic Gallery
   C. Imperial Coins, 1954
   D. Norweb Collection
4. Very Fine
   A. May exist.

1873-CC No Arrows Dime
1. Uncirculated
    A. John Swan Randall
    B. 1878 Cogan's 5/6 Sale, Lot 902 (realized 17 cents)
    C. Whereabouts unknown
2. Uncirculated
    A. U.S. Mint
    B. A.L. Snowden
    C. J.W. Haseltine
    D. J.K. Nagy
    E. W.H. Woodin
    F. H.O. Granberg
    G. 1915 U.S. Coin Company's 5/19 Sale, Lot 580 (realized $170)
    H. Rudolph Kohler
    I. 1950 Numismatic Gallery's Menjou Collection Sale, Lot 399 (realized $3,650)
    J. James Kelly
    K. Louis Eliasberg
    L. Louis Eliasberg family

The Early Silver Coins of the United States

By J.G. Macallister   1987

This article, which was called to our attention by reader Carl Herkowitz, is by James G. Macallister, a well-known Philadelphia dealer, and appeared in the August 1935 issue of The Coin Collector's Journal. The text is interesting from two aspects. First, it gives a view from the standpoint of 50 years ago concerning the rarity and availability of certain issues. Note, for example, that Uncirculated 1796 quarters were considered to be fairly plentiful! It is a curious comment on market cycles that the author notes examples of 1796 and 1804 sold for higher prices 50 to 75 years earlier than they did in 1935! By way of comparison, a prooflike Uncirculated 1796 quarter would bring the best part of $50,000 today—in 1987! Second, the text dramatically illustrates the rise in coin values in the 55 years since 1935. All one has to do is compare the prices in this article with those in the current issue of the Guide Book to note the difference. (Reprinted courtesy of John J. Ford, Jr., copyright owner.)

The series of quarter dollars is perhaps the least popular of all the denominations among American collectors. One reason for this is that in the early years it was a sort of disjointed series, there being numerous gaps in the sequence of years of issue. It is perhaps just as well that the series is not a popular one, because with few exceptions, all the early quarters are very scarce, particularly when in Fine to Uncirculated condition. If we had as many collectors of quarters as we have of half dollars, the prices at which they now sell would be multiplied several times.

This denomination was first issued in 1796, and the quarter of this year is one of the most beautiful of all modern coins. That the Mint authorities thought well of their product is indicated by the considerable number of Proofs which were evidently made, and that collectors of the time thought well of it is indicated by the number of specimens which have been preserved in Mint State. Notwithstanding the fact that the coinage amounted to only a little over 6,000 coins, nearly every collection of any importance contains a specimen in Uncirculated or Proof condition, while the next year of issue, 1804, with a coinage about 10% greater, is almost unknown in Mint State, we doubt if there are half a dozen coins of this year known in that condition. Because it is the first year of issue, and also because of its beauty, the 1796 brings a relatively higher price than the 1804. Proof specimens of 1796, if well struck on the reverse, which is rarely the case, bring up to $75 to $100 while Uncirculated specimens bring $40 to $50. 1804, which in choice condition is many times rarer than 1796, brings little if any higher prices; we don't recall one selling for more than $100. Singularly, both of these dates sold for higher prices 50 to 75 years ago than they do today. Specimens of both dates in ordinary condition sell for from $7.50 to about $15, depending on how badly worn they happen to be. There were two dies used for the obverses of each of these years, but the differences were merely in the spacing of the figures of the date.

 1805 offers nothing new in the way of variety from the previous year. The coinage was considerably greater: a total of over 120,000 coins being struck, but even with this large coinage the coin is very rare in Uncirculated condition. Four varieties of obverse dies were used, but the differences were slight and are only important to the variety collector. The value of coins of this year ranges from about $1 for a considerably worn specimen up to $100 for an absolutely perfect one, though there are very few known that would warrant the last named figure.

 1806 and 1807 were both prolific years, with over 200,000 coins being struck in each. There are nine varieties of 1806, but only one of them is worthy of special mention; the 1806 over 1805. This variety is very scarce in any condition and very rare in choice condition, with an auction record of $150 or more for a perfect specimen. The other varieties of 1806 are obtainable in Fine condition, but none of them is common in Mint state, with values ranging from $1 for a worn one to $25 for a perfect one.

 1807, with a Mint report of a coinage about 10% greater than 1806, is a much scarcer coin, and it seems reasonably safe to assume that many of the quarters struck in 1807 bore the date of the previous year, as we note all through the early years the practice of the Mint of using the dies as long as they held up, regardless of the date they bore. The quarters of this year rarely are found well struck, particularly on the obverse. Only two dies were used bearing this date, which fact tends to confirm the assumption that most of the quarters struck in this year bore the date of the year before. The value of 1807 quarters ranges from about $1 for a Poor specimen, to $50 for a choice one, and a considerably higher figure would be warranted for a specimen in perfect condition if it had a complete border on both obverse and reverse and was sharply struck.

No quarters were struck after 1807 until 1815, when about 90,000 were made. This year is scarce in all degrees of preservation, though it never commands a very high price. Another lapse of two years occurred before the next date of issue, but in 1818 the issue was the largest of any of the early years, the Mint reporting a coinage of over 360,000 coins. Ten varieties are known of 1818, only one of them offering an important distinction; the 1818 over 1815. This variety is very scarce in any condition and rare in Mint State. The value of coins of this date runs from about 75 cents for a Poor specimen, to $10 for a perfect one, and up to $25 for a perfect specimen of the overdate.

1819, 1820, and 1821 offer nothing outstanding in the way of variety. All are obtainable in all states of preservation, though perfect specimens of 1819 are a lot scarcer than is generally known. The values of these three years run from about $1 to $10 or $12.

1822 offers one of the rarest and most interesting varieties of the whole series, the variety with 25 over 50 on the reverse. The die engraver, accustomed no doubt to making dies for half dollars, first cut in a 50 on the reverse, then corrected it by recutting a 25 over it. Evidently not many were struck bearing this reverse as the coin is one of the rarest of the whole United States series. Only one obverse die was used in 1822, though at least three other obverse dies were made, and were subsequently used in 1823, 1824, and 1825. The coinage of this year amounted to 64,000 coins and specimens are scarce today in all states and very rare when sharp and brilliant. Values run from $1 to $25.

1823 offers a knotty problem to account for its rarity. The Mint reports a coinage of 117,800 coins for this year, and of that number, certainly not two dozen are known today. One possible solution, though not a satisfactory one, is that the considerable number of coins bearing the date of 1824 were struck, or at least reported in the year 1823. The fact the Mint does not report a coinage of 1824 quarters lends some weight to this theory, but it is a little hard to believe that coins were ever issued bearing a future date. However, if the Mint reports cover the fiscal year which is July 1 to June 30, rather than the calendar year, this theory is entirely probable. At any rate the coin ranks next to the 1827 quarter as the rarest date of United States silver coinage, and its value runs from $50 for a very Poor specimen to $1,000 for a Gem. All the known specimens are struck from a die altered from 1822.

1824 is another year struck from one of the left-over dies of 1822 altered to 1824. That only one set of dies was used, and that a considerable number of coins were struck is indicated by the fact that the date is not particularly rare in ordinary condition, its rarity being about on a par with 1822. In strictly Uncirculated ccondition however, this year is extremely rare, with records at private sale in excess of $100.

1825 offers three varieties, one of which was made by altering a die of 1822. The coinage for the year was 168,00 coins, and they are fairly common in ordinary preservation and only scarce in Mint State. The overdate variety is the rarest of the three. Values run from about 75 cents to $10 with the overdate variety worth considerably more in the finest state of preservation.

No quarters were coined in 1826.

1827 is the rarest of the whole series and is, we believe, the rarest United States coin with possible exception of the 1822 half eagle. The Mint reports a coinage of 4,000 coins, but it is very doubtful if many of them ever got out, as at the present time there are probably not half a dozen specimens known. The obverse of this coin was combined with a reverse used in 1819 to make the well-known restrikes. Just when these were made is not definitely known, but it is likely they were made about the same time as the 1804 dollars, sometime between 1836 and 1843. As to the value of 1827 quarters, your guess is as good as mine, no fine specimen having come on the market for many years, in fact we don't recall a specimen in any condition. A specimen of the restrike brought $425 in the last Morgenthau sale.

1828 offers two obverse dies combined with four reverse dies, one of them being the very rare die used in 1822 on which the 25 was recut over 50 on the reverse. When combined with the 1828 obverse, this die is also rare, but not nearly so rare as the combination with 1822. The Mint reports a coinage of 102,000 coins, and the date is scarce in all conditions though not particularly rare in any, with the exception of the variety noted above. The value of 1828 quarters runs from $1 for a Poor specimen to about $15 for a Gem, the rare variety being worth considerably more than either of these figures.

Random Notes from United States Mint Reports

By Franklin Perry 1987

The following article is reprinted from the August 1935 issue of The Coin Collector's Journal and is presented through the courtesy of John J. Ford, Jr. (present copyright owner). Although written more than 50 years ago, the article has lost none of its relevance. The notations concerning the specie payments refer to the withholding by the government of gold and silver coins from circulation from the mid-1860s until the mid-1870s. During this period of over a decade, silver coins were rarely seen. In their place appeared a flood of paper fractional currency notes as well as the new format nickel three-cent and nickel five-cent coins.

In the Mint Report for 1873 there is mention that at various times applications have been made by some of the South American governments that our mints make for them some of their coins. These requests have been declined on the ground that according to law only United States coins can be issued from our mints. This law was changed by Act of January 29, 1874 and accordingly we, today, make coins for various countries. The director of the Mint was in favor of doing such work, not only as a friendly act but also that it might do away with the exportation of our subsidiary silver coins as considerable amounts of these have been sent out of the country for several years and are in circulation in Central America and parts of South America.

It may be of interest to know that prior to the coinage act of 1873 our subsidiary silver coin on the Pacific Coast passed at from 2% to 3% discount in relation to gold coin, causing at times much inconvenience.

At this time specie payments had not been resumed, and except for the Pacific Coast and parts of the Southwest, paper money and scrip were the chief circulation media. It was estimated that in gold coin there was $135 million and in subsidiary silver about $5 million in circulation, the silver being principally in use in California, Oregon, Nevada, Idaho, Arizona, and Texas.

The new coinage act of February 12, 1873 omitted any mention of the standard silver dollar and consequently none was coined after the passage of this act for the space of four years, when the Act of 1878 again brought forth a new issue of these dollars. The Act of 1873 also discontinued the striking of the silver half dime and three-cent piece, as well as the bronze two-cent piece. This is the reason so few of these coins were struck in 1873. The law also called for a trade dollar.

I think few collectors realize why the halves, quarters, and dimes of 1873 come both with and without arrow points at sides of the date. This is because the new law changed very slightly the weight of these three pieces, and the precedent started in 1853, when the weights of the silver pieces were changed, to differentiate the two weights by a distinguishing mark, caused the arrow points to be again put on the coins. The interesting part of the 1873 law was that it legalized the metric system. Heretofore the weights of our coins were enacted in grains, but in the case of the three subsidiary silver coins, the new law stated that the weight of the half dollar should be 12.5 grams and the quarter and the dime in proportion; the purpose being to bring our silver coins into harmony with that of the Latin Monetary Union. The weight since 1853 of the half dollar was 192 grains. The new half dollar was .9 grains heavier and in the case of the dime would be less than one-fifth of a grain. The rest of the coinage remained the same, i.e. on the regular troy weight.

The law also provided that the obverse working dies at each mint shall, at the end of each calendar year, be defaced and destroyed. This was the die bearing the date. This clause was evidently put into the bill to prevent restrikes and other abuses.

The mint reports of this period were evidently not written for the benefit of collectors as the tables of pieces struck are wholly by fiscal years, i.e., from July to July, and the report for 1873 carefully refrains from stating the number of pieces struck with and without arrow points. It was drawn up of the coinage by calendar years.

The trade dollar, decreed under the law of 1873, the striking of which did not begin until after July 1 of that year, proved at the outset very popular. The demand for these during the first year was more than the mints could supply, especially the San Francisco Mint. Most of these pieces were bought by merchants for use in China. Apparently they at first proved popular there, but within five years their popularity was gone and the demand for these was over by 1878. While the boom lasted, over 36 million were made, or four and a half times as many as there were standard silver dollars struck from the beginning in 1794 until the resumption of the coinage of these in 1878.

An explanation for the reason of the new 20-cent piece is given in the report for 1874. This was chiefly for use on the Pacific coast and Texas. The smallest coin in use in those places was the dime which passed for a "bit," following the old Spanish system of recoining. The old silver five-cent piece had about gone out and was seldom used anyway, and the nickel five-cent piece did not circulate. If a payment for one "bit" was to be made, and a quarter tendered, the purchaser got back one dime instead of 15 cents. The issuing of the 20-cent piece was hoped to remedy this.

The following reasoning on the discontinuance of the silver half dime is rather amusing, especially as the nickel five-cent piece was issued as a more convenient coin than the old silver five-cent and was much in demand except on the Pacific coast and Texas.

The account is as follows: "Inquiry is occasionally made as to why the coinage of the silver five-cent was discontinued. The reason appears to have been that it would, on the resumption of specie payments, be likely to expel from circulation and drive into the Treasury for redemption the five-cent copper-nickel coins. At first glance this may seem improbable, but when it is considered that the original law authorizing the issue of the copper-nickel five-cent coin provided for its redemption in lawful money of the United States, it will be seen that there must come a time when it will be superior to the five-cent silver coin and for the reason that it will be exchangeable for notes redeemable in gold coin. The silver coin, which would have a greater nominal than intrinsic value and not redeemable in lawful money, or gold coin, would become the inferior currency."

The mint during the fiscal year ending in 1874 made 215 gold medals, 2,629 in silver and 1,237 in bronze at a selling value of $6,802.82; 34 gold Proof sets, 905 in silver, 600 in base, as well as 42 silver pattern pieces for $3,772.60. The profits on medals and Proof sets amounted to $4,018.80.

The 1964 Peace Dollar Episode

By Tom LaMarre   1987

"If Congress acts favorably on the request for the necessary appropriation, silver dollars may be struck in 1964," said the January 1964 issue of *The Numismatist*. Silver dollars—316,076 of them—were struck, but none of the coins made it into circulation.

At the time the coins were under consideration there was rapid growth in world consumption of silver while production remained stagnant. With rising silver prices came increased demand for silver coins, and a request by the Johnson administration for $1,250,000 to mint 100 million silver dollars in fiscal 1965.

A congressional committee turned down the request. However, the Olsen amendment, supported primarily by representatives of the western states, sought to restore the appropriation. Backers of the amendment claimed that the committee's rejection of silver dollar coinage would have a "disastrous" effect. Why resume production of silver dollars, last minted in 1935? One reason given was that silver dollars were traditional coins in the West. Furthermore, some representatives believed that Congress should suppress the numismatic value of silver dollars by authorizing the minting of additional dollars. Note that they didn't say "bullion" value, but numismatic importance of dates, mintmarks, or quantities produced. In their view a silver dollar was a silver dollar.

Backers of the Olsen amendment, including Compton I. White, Jr. of Idaho and Walter S. Barring of Nevada, failed to mention that silver dollar production would benefit the mines in their home states.

Opposition to the amendment was led by the bill's floor manager, J.

Vaughan Gary of Virginia, and Silvio O. Conte of Massachusetts. It was an "inappropriate" time for dollar coinage, they said, because the Mint was unable to keep up with the demand for cents, nickels, dimes, quarters, and half dollars. A resumption of dollar coinage would result in even greater demand for silver and therefore lead to price increases. Silver dollars would be melted for profit.

On March 24, 1964, the House of Representatives rejected the Olsen amendment by a 68 to 75 vote. However, the Senate then reversed the House decision by approving the use of $600,000 for the minting of 45 million silver dollars. Several reasons were cited for the Senate's action. Because coins last longer than paper money, silver dollars would be more economical to produce than dollar bills. In addition, silver dollars were needed for the redemption of silver certificates. The supply of Morgan and Peace dollars was exhausted, forcing the Treasury to redeem silver certificates with envelopes of silver crystals. Responding to the charge that silver dollar production would prolong the coin shortage, the Treasury said that it could mint silver dollars without reducing the output of other denominations.

The Senate gave its approval of silver dollar coinage by a voice vote, setting the stage for one of numismatics' biggest stories in decades.

"The Senate appropriations committee on June 17 approved the minting of 45 million silver dollars," said the August 1964 issue of *The Numismatist*. "If the Senate accepts the committee's recommendation, a Senate-House conference must determine if they will be minted, as the House has previously rejected the Treasury's request for the coins. The Secretary of the Treasury says it is now too late to issue silver dollars this year even if approved by Congress but that minting could be done in 1965."

On August 3, 1964, President Johnson signed legislation providing for the production of the first silver dollars since 1935. Plans called for all of the coins to be struck at the Denver Mint and shipped directly to Federal Reserve banks in the western region of the country. "The Mint cannot sell these dollars to anyone, nor can the Mint arrange for persons to receive them," said the October 1964 issue of *The Numismatist*. "Distribution will be made from commercial banks only." In other words, collectors in the east would have to pay a premium for the coins, buying them from dealers, or wait for some of the silver dollars to stray from the West.

No Proof dollars were to be struck. As of late 1964, the Mint had not decided whether it would offer Uncirculated sets of coins in 1965,

The 1964 Peace Dollar Episode

but said that if such sets were made they would not include the new silver dollar.

Perhaps the biggest surprise was that the Peace design would be continued. *The Numismatist* explained:

First issued by the United States Mint in 1921, it commemorates the declaration of peace between the United States, Germany, and Austria, exchanges of peace treaty ratifications having been made in Berlin on November 11, 1921, and in Vienna on November 8, 1921, and peace having been proclaimed by the President of the United States on November 14 and 17, respectively....

The design, selected by the Commission of Fine Arts from models submitted by nine prominent sculptors, is the work of Anthony de Francisci. A female head emblematic of Liberty, and wearing a tiara of light rays, appears on the obverse, together with the word "Liberty," the motto "In God We Trust," and the date. The artist's initials, AF, in stylized form, are below the neck and above the last date figure.

On the other side is an eagle perched on a mountain top, witnessing the dawn of a new day, and holding in its talons an olive branch; the word "Peace"; the denomination—"One Dollar"; "E Pluribus Unum," and the words "United States of America."

Anthony de Francisci died on October 24, 1964, believing that his design would be used again.

Why weren't the coins struck immediately? Legislation was pending to permit the freezing of the 1964 date on coins during the shortage. Instead of striking some dollars dated 1964 and some dated 1965, the Mint awaited Congressional action on the legislation. If the act did not pass, the dollars were to be struck beginning in January with the 1965 date and none would be minted in 1964.

But the legislation did pass. Public Law 88-580, effective September 3, 1964, specified, "...all coins minted from the date of enactment of this Act until July 1 or January 1, whichever date first occurs after the date on which the Secretary of the Treasury determines that adequate supplies of coins are available, shall be inscribed with the figure '1964' in lieu of the year of coinage." Section 2 of the law stated, "The requirement...that the obverse working dies at each mint shall be destroyed at the end of each calendar year shall not be applicable during the period provided for in section 1 of this Act." Production of 1964 Peace dollars was ready to begin.

On May 15, 1965 the White House said that coinage of 1964 Peace dollars could commence. A total of 316,076 silver dollars was struck.

Then, on May 25, the Treasury announced it had decided against the minting of any new silver dollars. Why the about-face? A Treasury Department press release stated:

Last year, in response to a Treasury request, Congress appropriated $600,000 to manufacture 45 million silver dollars. To carry out the expressed intent of the Congress, the Treasury recommended to the White House that the United States Mint be authorized to begin production. It was on this recommendation that the White House announced May 15th that production could begin.

Since that time, however, members of the Congress who by reason of their committee assignments have a direct and responsible interest in United States coinage, have strongly urged the Treasury not to proceed with the production of these dollars. After conferring with the White House, the Treasury has therefore determined that the Mint will not make any of these dollars at this time.

The Mint later reported that all of the 1964 Peace dollars were melted. However, rumors persisted that some had been saved. In *Adventures With Rare Coins,* Q. David Bowers quotes a letter from Denver dealer Dan Brown:

I was talking with Fern Miller a few years back when she was director of the United States Mint here in Denver. She was telling me that when the order came in stating that the Denver Mint was to make the new Peace dollar everyone at the mint was elated. They set up the machinery for it, and at the proper time struck a large quantity. As has been the custom throughout the years, mint employees were each allowed to buy two of these new dollars. Quite a number of the mint employees took advantage of and bought two pieces each. Soon afterwards, word came in from Washington that they were not to strike any more dollars, and that if any had been given out they were to be taken back and held until further orders, which probably would be that the coins would be melted down at a future date.

Mrs. Miller did mention the fact that she thought that everyone who had purchased the dollars in the morning they were first coined turned them in, but as no record was kept of purchasers, there was really no way of knowing for sure. So, as a result, there possibly are some of the dollars still in existence. These may show up in future years. Of course they would be great rarities. I don't think that the mint could declare them illegal under the circumstances and confiscate them, although this is a legal point.

The 1964 Peace Dollar Episode

Chicago Daily News columnist John M. Johnson, commenting on "The Cartwheel Fiasco," wrote, "The President's willingness to issue this bizarre order (May 15 to strike 45 million dollars) helps to explain how he achieves his celebrated legislative victories. His retreat proves his acumen, without erasing the demonstration of propensity to go a long way to please his political supporters."

Instead of resuming the production of silver dollars, the Mint was soon making the switch to clad coinage, authorized by the Coinage Act of 1965. The law stipulated that, "No standard silver dollars may be minted during the five-year period which begins on the date of enactment of this Act."

The signing ceremony was held in the Rose Garden of the White House on July 23, 1965. President Johnson said, "Now, all of you know these changes are necessary for a very simple reason—silver is a scarce material. Our uses of silver are growing as our population and our economy grows. The hard fact is that silver consumption is more than double new silver production each year. So, in the face of this worldwide shortage of silver, and our rapidly growing need for coins, the only really prudent course was to reduce our dependence upon silver for making our coins."

Nevertheless, Johnson made no apologies for authorizing the coinage of 1964 silver dollars, and his remarks still left room for a return of cartwheels in the future. "There is no change in the penny and the nickel," he said. "There is no change in the silver dollar, although we have no present plans for silver dollar production."

The President also declared, "Our present silver coins won't disappear and they won't even become rarities.... If anybody has any idea of hoarding our silver coins, let me say this. Treasury has a lot of silver on hand, and it can be, and it will be used to keep the price of silver in line with its value in our present silver coin. There will be no profit in holding them out of circulation for the value of their silver content."

However, the provision for the Coinage Act established a Joint Commission on the coinage, to be composed of the secretary of the Treasury, the secretary of Commerce, the director of the Bureau of the Budget, the director of the Mint, the chairman and ranking minority member of the Senate Banking and Currency Committee, four members of the Senate, and four members of the House of Representatives. One of its duties was to study the time when and circumstances under which the United States should cease to maintain the price of silver, and such matters as renewed minting of silver dollars.

The here today-gone tomorrow 1964 Peace dollars joined some pretty elite company. They can be compared to the 1873-S silver dollar; 700 were minted, but the coin is unknown in any collection. Similarly, 50 1841-O half eagles may have been struck, but according to the *Guide Book of United States Coins* it is "unconfirmed in any collection." Perhaps the best analogy can be made with the 1933 double eagle. Nearly a half million $20 gold pieces were struck that year. As a result of Franklin Roosevelt's gold order, though, none of them was placed in circulation.

"Now I will sign this bill to make the first change in our coinage system since the 18th century," Johnson said in 1965. "To those members of Congress, who are here on this very historic occasion, I want to assure you that in making this change from the 18th century we have no idea of returning to it. We are going to keep our eyes on the stars and our feet on the ground."

He should have added "and the Peace dollar dies in mothballs."

Frank Gasparro Reminisces

By Frank Gasparro   1987

We are honored to present an original article by Frank Gasparro, who for many years served as the chief engraver of the United States Mint, in the process designing countless medals and other numismatic items, including the Lincoln Memorial cent reverse (first used in 1959), the reverse of the Kennedy half dollar (first used in 1964), and the Susan B. Anthony dollar.

Frank Gasparro is, of course, well known to our readers as the designer and engraver of our illustrious series of silver "art" medals which we have been issuing since 1983. Certainly he is one of the most prominent figures numismatics has ever known.

I would like to relate my experiences leading up to my employment at the United States Mint and also some of the events that occurred in my earlier years as a sculptor-engraver.

During my studies at the Pennsylvania Academy of Fine Arts I was keenly interested in sculpture relief. I was receiving instructions under Walker Hancock and Albert Laessle, both renown in the medallic field. I made numerous sculpture reliefs in class. It was then that I felt the urge to enter the employ of the United States Mint. I was then to embark on the first trials of my career. This is a story of perseverance.

I planned to visit the Mint. I requested an appointment with the superintendent. Going to the Mint, I entered the building, and after a short period of time I was escorted by a guard into the main office. There I met Edwin H. Dressel, superintendent, and Mrs. Helen C. Moore, assistant. I stated that I desired a position of sculptor-engraver if available.

At that time I did not understand such procedures as having available positions posted through the Civil Service Commission and registering for positions and then filling out applications. I was informed that no position was available at that time in the Engraving Department. However, I was invited to see the Engraving Department and to meet John R. Sinnock and Adam Pietz, his assistant. They treated me cordially and showed me around. They, too, informed me that there was no vacancy, and they were sorry for this. There was work for only the two of them. The time was 1942, and the country was just emerging from the Depression. Meanwhile, I liked what I saw, admiring the coin and medal patterns.

Walking home I said to myself that I must get work at the Mint! So, within a few months I made plans. I would work with a few plaster medal patterns along the style of coinage to better understand the techniques of coin relief. I waited for a convenient day to apply again. The day came and I was ready to go back to the Mint with my plaster medallions under my arms. I "banged" so to speak on the iron gate of the Mint. The Mint guard opened the door. By this time he was used to seeing me. I asked to see Mr. Dressel. I was cordially received, he saw my plaster medallions, and he liked them. In the meantime he must have sized me up. He had a keen sense for human evaluation. He saw a young man of ambition and perseverance. The good part was that he and Mrs. Moore, who came into the office at that moment, were impressed by me. They requested that I fill out an application. Conditions may change, and the war may require more coinage and medals, I was told.

Mr. Dressel suggested that I go to see Mr. Sinnock. I showed Sinnock my reliefs, and he liked them and suggested that it would be worthwhile if I continued my sculpture studies.

I went home and told my wife that there was nothing at the Mint, that it was of no use, and that perhaps I should study sculpture more, for a job elsewhere. I should have stopped there, for I really had no hope of gaining employment with the government.

Six months passed, and then I received a letter from Mrs. Helen C. Moore asking me to come to the Mint. I ignored the request. I thought it was just a procedure for me to fill out more applications or more questionnaires. I told myself again that it was a useless pursuit. Then I received a second letter, angry in tone, demanding that I come to the Mint for a new interview. It looked like a position was opening!

At the designated time I went to the Mint. I met with Mr. Dressel, Mrs. Moore, and a dignified lady whom I did not know. She was introduced as Mrs. Nellie Tayloe Ross, the director of the Mint, a lady who formerly had served as governor of Wyoming. I must have made a good impression. Mr. Dressel informed me that a position was now open for junior engraver and that I had been selected for the position. My background had passed the test.

I pondered the situation. It was 1942. I had a three-month-old daughter, and I was listed as 3-A in the war draft. What was I to lose? I accepted. Mrs. Ross stated that I was to work on a temporary war basis.

My job was to learn how to engrave in steel, lettering with hand engraving tools. I also was to clean working dies used for coinage.

My first opportunity to design coinage came in 1943. I was given the job of designing and modeling the Guatemala 25-centavo reverse. (The obverse working die and master hub pattern was already in existence and had been done by someone else.) Mr. Sinnock assisted me and pointed out the proper dimensions and coinage height of relief. The day came for the coinage reduction to come off the transfer engraving machine from the six-inch model pattern, to the 25-centavo-size master hub and master die.

When the reduction was completed, I was pleased. The motif, a building, was beautiful to begin with, and my work showed it to excellent advantage. Now came the test. After machining, the new reverse die was matched with the obverse die. Blanks were then fed into the coining press. That day there was success. The coins fell into the press bucket, sparkling and beautiful. On observation, all of the design detail was there. Everyone on hand cheered! Mr. Sinnock complimented me on a job well done.

From that point I went back to my daily duty of cleaning working dies, cutting lettering and steel by hand, and constant drawing. I was also called upon to retouch plaster models.

One of the interesting periods in my early years was when I was closely associated with Adam Pietz, who served as assistant engraver at the Mint. Mr. Sinnock directed him to have me learn how to engrave in steel. This is an important function of every engraver at the Mint, for it is necessary to learn all of the skills required to execute a workable coinage master hub and working die. I started by having Mr. Pietz show me how to engrave good lettering in steel. It was hard work for a novice.

Then I went on to engrave a good "date" steel punch from a flat-surfaced blank bar. When completed, this date punch was used to date gold bars. I watched Mr. Pietz engrave soft steel like butter with his powerful hands. In his early youth he was a top single scull oarsman in Germany. He looked very strong and commanded respect when he approached you. I watched him engrave, hammer, and push a steel punch (which had a one-inch by two-inch surface), which was dated 1942, changing it to read 1943. He told me that you can push steel around with a hammer and your hands if you have confidence in yourself. That knowledge was very useful to me in later years. Then he showed me how to engrave a portrait in soft steel.

I was very happy with my newfound knowledge. After six months, I had engraved and completed a likeness of John Paul Jones suitable to fit a two-inch diameter medal surface. To me, that was like the day I graduated from high school. There are very few engravers living today who can match the talents possessed by Adam Pietz. He was truly a great craftsman.

In the meantime, I was not drafted. Once the war was over I passed the test to be made a permanent employee of the Mint. Then in 1959 my second big test came: designing a new reverse for the Lincoln cent. At the time I was assistant engraver. The old wreath-style had been in use since 1909, and it was desired that beginning with the 1959 coinage, 50 years later, a change would be made to celebrate the anniversary. My design featuring the Lincoln Memorial was selected from 17 designs submitted by Mint artists.

I proceeded with the plaster model. That was on November 20, 1958. The one-cent 1959 trial must take place on January 1, 1959, I was told. I had very little time. The reverse die I designed had to conform and match properly with the Lincoln cent obverse already on hand. There was no room for error. The design could not be done over if it didn't work, at least not without causing great complications.

The manufactured blanks already on hand for use with the "wreath" Lincoln cents had to be used for the Lincoln Memorial cent coinage trial on January 1, 1959. Should the Lincoln Memorial design fail in striking, all trials would have to be set aside for the time being. There would be no time for retooling and no time for new reductions. Those processes require many months. Then, the Mint would have to go back to the "wreath" design. Therefore, it was essential that the new reverse be successful.

I studied the relief of the wreath on the reverse of the cent. It measured 3 one-thousandths of an inch from the flat background to the highest point of the wreath, which was about the thickness of a human hair. I made my Lincoln Memorial reverse to measure the same 3 one-thousandths of an inch in relief height. By the way, the Lincoln portrait on the one cent measures 13 one-thousandths of an inch in height of relief.

The day came when a trial test committee consisting of Rae V. Biester, superintendent, Sidney Engel, coiner, a Bureau of the Mint representative, and myself watched the 1959 one-cent trial. It was a success! Everyone there gave me tremendous support that eventful day. Through the years my association with the Mint family was very important to me, and now that I am retired from the Mint, I still value my many supporting, kind friends.

Index

A

Abe Kosoff: Dean of Numismatics, 45
Act of 1878, 204
Act of February 12, 1873, 91; 92; 203; 204
Act of January 29, 1894, 203
Adams, Edgar H., 144
Adams, President John, 123
Adams, John W., 12; 13; 112; 139; 140; 143
Adams, Harkness & Hill, 12
Adams, Senator Alva B., 150
Adams-Woodin, 144
Adventures With Rare Coins, 118; 210
Akers, David W., 46; 47; 117
Alexander Classical School, 21
American Journal of Numismatics, 141; 142; 171
American Numismatic Association, 11; 27-29; 45; 46; 52; 57; 61-63; 105; 140; 142; 150; 157; 168; 169; 175; 179; 181; 192
American Numismatic Authentication Certification Service (ANACS), 27; 29; 49
American Numismatic Society, 139; 140; 144; 168; 169; 172; 176; 195
Amherst Sale, 17
Anton, William T., 187; 191; 192
Appleton, William Sumner, 130
Arlin, Liz, 61
Arnold, G.C., 143
Art Institute of Chicago, 140
Arthur, William H., 148
Attinelli, Emmanuel Joseph, 129; 130; 131
Atwater Sale, 45; 138

B

Bagg, Richard A., 109
Bank Holiday of 1933, 32
Bank of Pennsylvania, 175
Barber, Charles, 14; 92; 95; 180
Barber, William, 14
Barber coins, 95-99; 117
Barker, Ralph, collection, 144
Barnum & Bailey, 181
Barnum, P.T., 34-35
Barrett, Mary Lou, 61
Barring, Walter S., 207
Baruch, Bernard, 106-107
Bass, Harry, collection, 139; 140
Battle of San Jacinto, 33
B & B Coins, 197
Becker, Tom, 55-56
Beckett, William D., 19
Bell Sale, 45
"Bell, Jake" (a.k.a. Jake Shapiro), collection, 111
Berenstein Collection, 45
Betts, Mr. 131; 176
Bettman, Otto, 116
Bicentennial coinage, 169
Biester, Rae V., 217
Big Tree (Indian), 181
Bingham, Inglis & Gilmor, 121
Bird, Frederick M., 172
Black Diamond (buffalo), 181
Black List of Men Reported Bad, 143
Bland-Allison Act, 14
Bland, Del, collection, 139
Bluestone, Barney, 137
"Bogard, Mr.", 123
Bogert, John (see "Bogard, Mr.")
Bolender, catalogues, 137
Boone, Daniel, 23
Boosel, Harry X, 196
Boudinot, Elias, 165
Bourne, 111
"Bowditch, Dr.", 128
Bowers, Q. David, 11; 27-29; 31; 41; 45; 51; 65; 66; 101; 113; 138; 142; 183; 210
Bowers and Merena Galleries, 61; 66; 75; 82; 95; 106; 107; 138;
193; 195; 196
Bowers and Ruddy Galleries, 137; 138
Boyd, F.C.C., 111; 144; 195-197
Brackin, John H., 22
Brand, Virgil, 128; 129
Brasher doubloon, 66; 79; 121; 128; 129; 131; 139
brass tokens, 118
Breen, Walter, 68; 97; 111; 159; 196
Walter Breen's Complete Encyclopedia of United States Coins, 196
Bressett, Ken, 58; 63
Brettell, Ruthann, 58
British coins and tokens, 117; 160; 173; 174; 191
British Mint, 175
British Museum, 161
British Numismatic Society, 160
bronze medals, 205
Brooks, Mrs. Mary, 164
Brown, Dan, 210
Browning, Mr., 144; 195
collection, 195; 197
Budd, H.M., 196; 198
Buffalo Nickel, The, (by Cohen & Druley), 180
Bureau of Indian Affairs, 180
Burns, Thomas P., 89
Bushnell, Charles I., 188; 189; 191
Byrne, Ray, 95; 140

C

Caldwell, R.S., Jr., 150
Carlson, Carl W.A., 128; 130; 168; 194
Carr, Colorado Governor, 150
Carson City Mint, 14; 15; 17; 162; 194; 196
"Cartwheel Fiasco, The", 211
Cashin, Thomas A., 90
Central Park Zoo, 181

— 219 —

cents, 90; 92; 123; 141; 208
 Indian: 48; 49; 51; 114; 115
 Large: 12; 13; 59; 60; 62; 104; 105; 112; 118; 126; 139; 171; 172; 175; 176; 178; 183; 186; 187; 190; 191; 193
 Lincoln: 49; 55; 70; 77; 80; 113-115; 213; 216
Champa, Armand, 137
Chapman, Henry & S. Hudson, 110; 112; 116; 143; 144; 194
Charlotte Mint, 161
Chicago Coin Club, 150
Chicago Daily News, 211
Christie's, 67
Civil Service Commission, 214
Civil War, 92; 130; 131; 161
Clapp, (Mr.), 12
Cleneay Collection, 194
Clisbee, Eugene, 89
Cogan, Edward, 110; 129; 174; 193; 197; 198
Cohen and Druley, 180, 181
Cohen, David H., 19
Cohen, Mendes I., 129; 142
Cohen, Milton G., collection, 67; 76
Cohn, Arnold, 147
Coinage Act of 1965, 211
Coin Collectors' Guide, 118
Coin Collector's Journal, The, 199; 203
Coin Dealer Newsletter, The, 59
Coin Galleries, 75
Coinhunter, 66
Coin World, 27; 59; 65; 73; 74; 116; 141; 149; 193; 195
Cole, (Thomas, painter), 121
Colliers, 37; 38
colonial coins, 58-60
Colorado Mining Association, 150
Colorado Springs Coin Club, 28
Colorado-Wyoming Numismatic Association, 28
Commemorative Coins of the United States, The, (by B. Max Mehl), 31; 37
commemoratives, 13; 31-36; 61; 76; 77; 104
 Albany, 35-36
 Arkansas, 34
 Bridgeport, 34-35
 Cincinnati, 35
 Cleveland, 35
 Columbian Exposition, 11; 114
 Boone, 34
 Elgin, 35
 Fort Vancouver, 33
 Grant Memorial, 32

 Hudson, 34
 Isabella quarter dollar, 11; 36
 Lexington-Concord, 32
 Lincoln-Illinois, 32
 Long Island, 35
 Lynchburg, 35
 Maine Centennial, 17; 32
 Maryland, 33
 McKinley Memorial gold dollars, 36
 Monroe, 32
 New Rochelle, 17; 36
 Oregon Trail, 33
 Panama-Pacific, 31
 Pilgrim, 32
 Rhode Island, 34
 Sesquicentennial, 33
 Texas Centennial, 33-34
 Washington-Carver, 70
 York County, 35
Commission of Fine Arts, 209
Comprehensive Catalogue and Encyclopedia of U.S. Morgan and Peace Dollars," (by Van Allen & Mallis), 14
Comstock Lode, 14; 18; 52
Conant, Charles F., 144
Confederate currency, 138
Continental Currency, 58; 60; 127
copper coins and tokens, 58; 59; 118; 125; 131; 153; 184; 191
Coolidge, President Calvin, 33
Conover Sale, 138
Conte, Silvio O., 208
Cowell Sale, 38
Cripple Creek, Colorado (gold mine), 28; 60-62
Cromwell, Oliver, 23
Crosby, Sylvester S., 184; 188; 192
Currency of the Confederate States of America, The, (by Dr. Wm. Lee), 139
Cuyp (Aalbert, Dutch painter), 121

D

Dahlonega Mint, 161; 167
Dates of United States Coins and Their Degree of Rarity, (by Mickley), 141
Davis, Col, collection, 144
Davis, Robert Coulton, 128
Declaration of Independence, 123; 124
de Francisci, Anthony, 209
DeLeonardis, William Justin, 192
DeLorey, Thomas, 49
Denver Mint, 34; 64; 92; 149; 150; 162; 208; 210

Denver Post, 150
Denville, Mr., 51
DeSaussure, Henry William, 165
Devonshire, 66
dimes, 41; 42; 92; 114; 147-151; 194-198; 204; 205; 208
 Barber: 95-98
 "Leaved": 150; 151
 Mercury: 149; 150
Disney, Walt, 41; 43
dollars,
 Gobrecht (patterns): 158-160
 Susan B. Anthony: 213
 trade: 204
 silver, 14; 48; 58; 63; 104; 150; 158; 159; 175; 204; 205; 207-212
 1804 silver dollar: 141; 142; 175
 Liberty Seated: 14; 48; 78
 Morgan Type (Liberty Head): 13-17; 48; 51; 59; 76-78; 104; 105; 117; 192; 208
 Peace type: 78; 104; 207-212
Donald Duck, 41-43
double eagles ($20 gold), 17; 45-48; 117; 212
Dow-Jones & Company, 119
Drake, Raymond L., 61
Dressel, Edwin H., 213-215
Dreyfuss, David, collection, 56
Dubois, William E., 126-128; 141; 171; 173; 174; 176
Duke of Northumberland, 124
Dunham, William Forrester, 16; 84; 111; 138
Durst, 111

E

eagle design, 15; 35; 183; 185; 186; 191; 192
eagles ($10 gold), 90, 125, 126, 173, 186, 189, 191
Earl, Robert, 140
Early American Cents, (by Wm. Sheldon), 13; 62
Early American Tokens, by Russell Rulau, 184; 190
Early Coins of America, The, by Crosby, 184
Eckfeldt, Adam (chief coiner), 121; 124; 126-128; 170
Eckfeldt, George, 140
Edward I pattern groat, 131
Elder, Thomas, 143
Eliasberg, Louis E., Sr., 47; 84; 111; 195-198
Elm Tree Press, The, 153
Empire Coin Company, 115; 142
Encyclopedia of U.S. and Colonial Proof Coins, 97

Index

Encyclopedia of United States Half Cents, 68
Engel, Sidney, 217
Englehardt, Herman, 138

F
Fairfield Sale, 110
Fantastic 1804 Dollar, The, 58
Farouk Sale, 138
Farrell, J.J., 89
Federal Reserve Bank, 147; 208
Feinberg, Charles, 138
Feldman, Aaron R., 109; 142
Fivaz, Bill, 179
five-cent coins, 92; 140; 141
  nickels: 87; 89-92; 114; 148; 182; 203; 205; 208; 211
  "Balonian": 42
  Buffalo type: 49; 179-181
  Jefferson type: 80; 105; 107
  Liberty Head: 55; 60; 66; 73; 180
  silver: 205 (see also half dime)
Flanagan Collection, 111
Forbes, 102
Ford, John J. Jr., 111; 139; 140; 144; 199; 203
Forest Lawn Cemetery Association, 22
Forman, Harry, 105
Fort McHenry, 122
Fort Wadsworth, 179
Forty Fort State Bank, 113; 114
Fractional currency, 203
Franklin, Benjamin, 58
Franklin Institute, 176
Fraser, James Earle, 179; 180
Fraser, Laura Gardin, 181
Freedom of Information Act, 164
French, Dr. George P., 38; 143
Frossard, Ed., 143; 144
Fugio cents, 58; 60
Fuld Library, 139
Fulrodt, Owen, 62

G
Garrett Collection, 70; 79; 84; 109; 110; 116; 197
Garrett, T. Harrison, 110
Garrett, Chester A., 115
Gary, J. Vaughan, 208
Gasparro, Frank, 213
Gehring Collection, 144
Geiss Sale, 138
George III, 175
George II, 130; 131
General Services Administration, 17
Gilmor, Robert Jr., 121-132
Harry, 131

Louisa, 123; 124
Robert & Sons, 122; 126; 128
Robert Sr., 121-124
William, 122
Glass, Senator Carter, 35
Gobrecht, Christian, 117; 186
Gold Coin Mine, The, 60-62
Gold Coin Club, 61; 62
gold coins, 13; 46; 47; 80; 96; 98; 117; 125; 126; 131; 173; 174; 186; 203-205
gold medals, 122; 123; 205
Golden Leaves (bookstore), 61
goloid coinage, 163
Gould, Maurice M., 115
Granberg, H.O., 138; 144; 195; 197; 198
Grant, General, 32
Grayson, William, 197
Greek coins, 121; 125; 129; 130; 131
Greely's "American Conflict", 22
Green, Dr., 45
Green sale, 138
Green (dealer), 143
Green, Nancy, 62
Greenough, Horatio, 122
Greenwich, James, 149
Griffin sale, 138
Griffith sale, 38
Guatemala 25-centavo, 215
Guide Book of United States Coins, A, 16; 17; 47-49; 52; 59; 60; 77; 97; 98; 149; 160; 169; 183; 184; 199; 212
Guttag, Julius, 140

H
Haines, Ferguson, collection, 194
half cents, 13; 59; 60; 191
half dimes, 52; 77; 78; 126; 172; 175; 204; 205
half dismes, 52; 175
half dollars, 12; 114; 123; 126; 138; 185; 199; 201; 204; 208
  Barber: 95; 96; 98
  Kennedy: 213
  Liberty Seated: 115
  Liberty Walking: 77; 114
half eagles ($5 gold), 126; 130; 185; 186; 191; 202; 212
Hallenbeck, June, 27
Hallenbeck, Kenneth L., 27-29; 61
Hancock, Walter, 213
Hard Times tokens, 110; 144; 191; 192
Hard Times Tokens, (by Lyman Low), 191

Harrison, President Benjamin, 23
Haseltine, John W., 112; 141; 197; 198
Harvard University Library, 139
Hays, (Mr.), 12
Healy, Timothy E., 90
Heath, George F., 11-13; 139
Heath, Laban, 143
Heaton, Augustus G., 126; 194
Henderson, Bill, 60; 61
Henderson, J.M., sale, 144
Heritage, 66
Herkowitz, Carl, 199
Hesslein, (Mr.), 143
Hetrich-Guttag, 144
Hewitt, Lee F., 63; 143; 158
High Profits from Rare Coin Investment, 102; 103
Hines (Mr.), 12
Hirtzinger, Karl, 75
Historical Account of the First Three Business Tokens Issued in the City of New York, (by Ch. Bushnell), 188
History of Nevada, 52
History of United States Coinage, (by Q. David Bowers), 52; 142
Hodder, Michael, 55; 195; 196
Holdcamper, Mrs., 168
Holloway, Greg, 197
Hopkinson, Oliver, 176
Huey, Dewey, and Louie, 41; 42
Hunter, W.H., collection, 110

I
Iacovo, Jim, 65; 66
Idler, William, 141
Illinois Trader, 143
Imperial Cabinet of Natural History (Vienna), 122
Imperial Coin Company, 195; 198
Indian Peace medals, 56; 130; 131
Indiana State Numismatic Association, 28
Ingle, Dr. Charles, collection, 64
International Association of Professional Numismatists, 105
Investing for Pleasure and Profit, 119
Iron Tail (Indian), 180; 181

J
Jefferson, President Thomas, 121; 123
Jenks Collection, 84
Johns Hopkins University, The, 70
Johnson, Byron, 140
Johnson, James G., 149

— 221 —

Johnson, John M., 211
Johnson, President Andrew, 55; 56
Johnson, President Lyndon B., 207; 208; 211; 212
Jones, John Paul, 216
Journal of the Pacific Coast Numismatic Society, The, 93
Joy, Fred, collection, 38
Julian, Robert W., 157; 180
Jungle, The, (by Upton Sinclair), 87
Justice Department, 167

K
Kagin's, 66
Katen, Frank, 111
Kelly, James, 198
Kendrick, J.R., 143
King, Colin, collection, 144
King, Mr. (of National Archives), 168
Kingswood Galleries, 17
Kohler, Rudolph, 198
Kolbe, George, 111; 139-141
Kosoff, Abe, 47; 74; 111; 195
Kreisberg, Abner, 111; 195; 196
Krueger, Kurt, 66

L
Ladner, Foster, collection, 144
Laessle, Albert, 213
Lafayette, Marquis de, 122; 123
LaMarre, Tom, 147; 171; 207
Lange, David W., 87
Last Gold Rush, The, (by Drake), 61
Latin Monetary Union, 204
Leavitt, Strebeigh, & Co., 174
"Lee" Collection (see Eliasberg), 111
Lee, Dr. William, 139
Lepczyk, Joe, 66
Lesher Referendum dollars, 60
Lesher, Joseph, 60, 62
Levine, Joseph, 56
Liberty Seated silver coins, 96; 99; 117
Library of Congress, The, 139
Lillienthal, Mr., 141; 175
Lincoln Memorial, 216
Littleton Rare Coins, 71
Long Hungry Trading Company, 61
Longacre, James B., 117; 164
Louis XIV, 121
Louis XV, 185
Louis XVI, 185
Louis Philippe, 122

Low, Lyman H., 128; 131; 139; 143; 191

M
Macallister, J.G., 199
MacDougald, John E., 89
Maine Antique Digest, 70
Major Variety and Oddity Guide, by Spadone, 149
Mallis, A. George, 14
Mann, H.O., collection, 38
Manning Sale, 38; 138
Maris, Dr. Edward, 12; 139; 144
Marvin, 144
Massachusetts Bay silver coins, 59
Massachusetts copper cent, 192
May, William L., 22
McIntire, 66
McKinley, President William, 36
Mehl, B. Max, 16; 31; 36-39; 110; 111; 116; 128; 137; 138; 140; 144; 195; 197
Mehl, Ethel Rosen, 37
Meigs, Dr. J.A., 176
Melnick, Herbert, 140
"Memorable Collection" (Jake Shapiro), 111
Menjou, Adolphe, collection, 45-47; 111; 198
Mercer, Ray, 65
Merena, Raymond N., 106
Merkin, Lester, 111; 112; 139
Metropolitan New York Sale, 197
Mickley, Joseph, 126; 130-132; 140-142; 171-178
Mid-American, 66
Miller, Fern (Director of Denver Mint), 210 Mint Marks, A Treatise on the Coinage of the United States Branch Mints, by Heaton, 194
Monroe, President James, 122
Moore, Mrs. Helen C., 213; 214
Moore, Samuel, 165
Morey, (Mr.), 143
Morgan, George T., 14
Morgenthau Sale, 202
Mott, William and John, 184-185; 187-190
William W., 190
W.W. & R., 190
William H., 190
Susan F., 190
Mott token, 183-192

N
Nagy, J.K., 197; 198
Narrative of a Tour Through the State of Vermont, A, 153

NASCA, 66; 197
National Archives, 158; 159; 161-164; 166; 167
National Cabinet of Curiosities, 124
National Institute for the Promotion of Science, 124-125; 127; 129
National Numismatic Collection (see also U.S. Mint Cabinet), 126; 127
Neil Sale, 138
Nebraska State Historical Society, 19
Neptune, 34
New Hampshire copper coins, 58
New Netherlands Coin Company, 70; 111
New Orleans Mint, 14-16; 92; 162
New York Coin & Stamp Company, 144
New York Customs House, 123
New York Times, 70; 179
Newcomb, Howard R., 12
Newcomer Collection, 38
New England Rare Coin Company, 195; 196
Newman, Eric P., 57-58; 140
Nichols, C.P., 142
Norweb Collection, 193; 195; 196; 198
Numisgraphics, 129
Numisma, 144
Numismatic Art in America, 185
Numismatic Chronicle, The, 160
Numismatic Gallery, 111; 195; 198
Numismatic Investment Journal, The, 65; 66
Numismatic Literary Guild Newsletter, 157
Numismatic News, 59; 65; 73; 104; 116
Numismatic Review, 148
Numismatic Scrapbook Magazine, 63; 115; 143; 147; 149; 158
Numismatist, The, 11; 12; 115; 139; 140; 150; 192; 196; 207-209

O
Old Cars (newspaper), 69
Old Fort Coin Club, 28
Old Homestead (museum), 61
Olsen Amendment, 207; 208
Olson Collection, 138
Ormsby's Bank-Note Engraving, 140
Orosz, Joel U., 121

Index

P

Pacific Coast Numismatic Society, 93
paper money (see also fractional currency), 46; 92; 127; 204; 208
Paramount International Coin Corp., 66; 112; 142
pattern groat of Edward I, 130; 131
Patterson, Robert (Mint Director), 124; 160; 165
Paxman, Dr. Curtis, collection, 137
Peacock, Charles Daniel, 191
Peacock, Elija, 191
Peale, Franklin, 170
Pennington, Sam, 70
Pennsylvania Academy of Fine Arts, 213
Pennsylvania Historical Society, 176
"penny" (see also cents), 211
Penny-Wise, 187
Perkins, Reverand Nathan, 153
Perlmutter, M., 140
Perry, Franklin, 203
Peters, Jess, 140
Peterson, John, 119
pewter tokens, 184
Pharmacist Mine, 60
Philadelphia Mint, 12-16; 23; 33; 35; 51; 59; 70; 91; 92; 142; 148; 149; 161-165; 166; 167; 170; 174; 191
Phillips, 21
Philpot Collection, 140
Picker, Richard, 139
Pierce, C. David, collection, 45; 46
Pietz, Adam, 214-216
Pine Tree shilling, 12
Pittman Act, 15; 16
Pittman, John Jay, 140
plastic credit cards, 28
Poinsett, Joel Robert, 124; 125; 127; 128; 131
Pollock, Andrew W. III, 95
Poussin, (Nicholas, French painter), 121
Pratt, J.J., 88
Price, Dr., (Secretary of Royal Numismatic Society), 161
Princeton Collection, 64
private medals struck by U.S. Mint, 124
Proceedings, 125
Professional Numismatists Guild, 80; 103

Public Law 88-580, 209
Public Ownership Association, 88

Q

quarter dollar, 42; 114; 148; 193-202; 204; 208
  Barber: 95-98
  Liberty Seated: 48
  Washington Head: 55
quarter eagles ($2.50), 186; 191; 192

R

Rahn, Nathan, 89
Randall, John Swan, 193; 197; 198
RARCOA, 66; 97; 112
Rare Coin Review, 59; 61; 105; 107; 119; 137
Raymond, John T., collection, 131
Raymond, Wayte, 144
Red Book, (see Guide Book of U.S. Coins, A,) 160
Reed, Byron, 19-25; 169
Byron Reed Company, 22
Reed, Mrs. Alfred Z., 175
Rees Collection, 38
Register of the Confederate States Treasury Notes, 138; 139
Reich, John, 185; 186
Revolutionary War, 163
Riethe, Bob, 197
Risk, James, 75
Rittenhouse, David, 165
Roach Sale, 138
Roe Sale, 138
Rolph, Mayor James S. "Sunny Jim", 87-91
Roman coins, 121; 125; 129-131; 172; 173
Rooke, Harmer, 66
Rooks, Professor, sale, 38
Roosevelt, Franklin, 212
Roosevelt, Theodore, 60; 87
Rosa Americana coins, 59
Ross, Nellie Tayloe (Director of the Mint), 148; 150; 215
Royal Mint (England), 162
Royal Numismatic Society (England), 160; 161
Rubin, P. Scott, 193
Ruddy, Jim, 115
Rulau, Russell, 184; 185; 190; 191
Rusbar, Robert, 113-115
Rush, Dr. Benjamin, 124
Ruskin, John, 83
Russian coins, 158
Rywell, Martin, 118; 119

S

Saint-Gaudens, Augustus, 117
Saltykov-Shchedrin, 158
San Francisco Mint, 14; 15; 33; 34; 89; 92; 162; 166; 204
San Francisco Municipal Railway, 87-91
Santayana, (George), 63
Saunders, Ebenezer Milton, collection, 56
Schleicher, William, collection, 144
Schook, Florence, 58
Scott, J.W., 112
Scott's Catalogue & Encyclopedia of United States Coins, 186
Scrooge McDuck, 41-43
Seaby's, 160
Sears, Deane, 118; 119
Senate, 208; 211
Senate Banking and Currency Committee, 211
Sewall, Judge, 12
Shapiro, Jake (a.k.a. "Bell"), 111
Sheldon, Dr. William H., 12; 13; 62; 63
Sheldon System of Numerical Grading, 62-63; 97
Sherman, Mr., 168
Sieber, Arlyn, 104
Siegel, Joe, 66
Sills, A., Inc., 181
silver certificates, 208
silver coins, 90; 95; 98; 125; 126; 131; 144; 159; 173; 185; 191; 199; 202; 203; 204; 205; 207
silver crystals, 208
silver medals, 55; 213
silver week, 150
Simon Petition Crown, 117
Simpson, F.D., collection, 144
Sinnock, John R. (Chief Engraver), 147; 148
Sinclair, Upton, 87
Sinnock, John R., 214; 215
Skinner, Mark A., Denver Mint Supt., 150
Skulan, Tom, 41
Slack, Judge, collection, 38
Smith, Elliott, 140
Smith, H.P., 144
Smith, John, 23
Smithson, James, 124
Smithson, James, bequest, 124-125; 127
Smithsonian Institution, 117; 124; 126; 127; 168
Snow, E.J., 130
Snow Collection catalogue, 131

— 223 —

Snowden, A. Loudon, 163; 197; 198
Snowden, James Ross, 159; 160; 165
Sotheby's, 67; 138
Spadone, Frank G., 149
Spangenberger, Hank, 142
Spasskii, Dr. I.G., 158
Stack, Ben, 195
Stack, James A., collection, 195; 196; 197
Stack's, 66; 111; 195; 196
Stearns, William G., 128
stella ($4 gold), 163
Stenton, Sir Frank, 160
Stenz, George, collection, 130
Stevens, 36
Stickney, Matthew, 126; 132
Stoddard Collection, 38
Stone, William, 140
Strobridge, William Harvey, 112; 130; 131
Sundman, Rick, 71
Superior Galleries, 66; 73

T
Talbot, Allum & Lee tokens, 191
Tarbell, Ida, 87
Taxay, Don, 186; 187; 192
Ten Eyck, James, 38; 128; 129; 138
Tennett, William B., 143
Texas Division of the American Legion, 33
Thian, Raphael P., 138
Thomas, Lowell, 62
Thompson, "Big Bill", 91
three-cent pieces, nickel, 52; 203
three-cent pieces, silver, 204
Token and Medal Society, 165
tokens, early American, 184
tokens, private, after Confederation, 183; 184; 192
Treasury Department, 15; 17; 48; 60; 92; 144; 164; 205; 208; 210; 211
Tribune, (New York), 21
Trogner, Arthur, 149
twenty-cent pieces, 52; 205
two-cent pieces, bronze, 204
Two Guns White Calf (Indian), 180
Two Moons (Indian), 180; 181

U
Union News Company, 111
United States Bureau of the Budget, 211
United States Coin Company, 144; 195; 198

United States Congress, 14; 21; 35; 36; 91; 92; 124; 125; 207; 208; 210; 212
United States Exploring Expedition to the Southern Pacific, 124
United States Gold Coin Collection, The, (a.k.a. Eliasberg Collection), 47; 110
United States Gold Coins, An Analysis of Auction Records, Double Eagles, (by Akers), 46
United States House of Representatives, 208; 211
United States Mint (see also Philadelphia Mint), 18; 36; 131; 123-129; 132; 140; 141; 147; 158; 160; 175; 179; 181; 185; 194; 197; 198; 200; 201; 208-211; 213-217
United States Mint Bureau, 164; 166; 169
United States Mint Cabinet (Nat'l. Numismatic Collection), 126; 127; 159; 174
United States Mint Engraving Department, 15; 148; 214
United States Mint Reports, Records, Files, 158; 161-166; 200-204
United States Numismatic Literature, by John W. Adams, 112
United States Pattern, Experimental and Trial Pieces, 52

V
Valentine, Daniel, 144
Van Allen, Leroy C., 14
Vermuele, Cornelius, 185
Victor, Colorado (gold mine), 28; 60-62

W
Walker, Jimmy, 91
Wall Street Journal, The, 102; 119
Washington, George, 12; 33; 60; 123; 163; 171
Waste Book, 159
Webster's New Collegiate Dictionary, 101
Westcott, Michael, 179; 182
Western Publishing Co., 59
White, Compton I., Jr., 207
White House, 209-211
Whitman folders, 114
Wilde, Adna, 60; 61
Wilharm, Dr., collection, 38
Wilkes-Barre Coin Club, 114
Williams Gallery, 66
Williams, Anna, 14

Williams, George, 114
Wilson, 111
Wilson, W.W.C., 139
Woodin, William H., 144; 194; 195; 197; 198
Woods Brothers, 60
Woodside, George, collection, 144
Woodward, W. Elliot, 112; 130; 141; 142; 144; 173-175; 194
Wordsworth, William, 121
World's Fair, 33
"World's Greatest Collection, The" 47; 111; 195-197
World War I, 148
Wright, B.P., 143
Wurst, Dr. C. Andrew, 149

Y
Young Numismatists Group, 59

Z
Zabriski Sale, 140
Zerbe, Farran, 139; 140
Zug, Charles, collection, 144